D1577271

John Gregory
THE BOSS

John Gregory
THE BOSS

John Gregory with Martin Swain

André Deutsch

First published in Great Britain in 2000
by André Deutsch Ltd
76 Dean Street
London
W1V 5HA
www.vci.co.uk

ISBN 0 233 99885 3

Jacket photograph taken by Jason Tilley
Jacket design by Button Design
Plate section design by
Design 23

Typeset in Liverpool by Derek Doyle & Associates.
Printed and bound by
Mackays of Chatham

5 7 9 10 8 6 4

DEDICATION

I could dedicate this book to so many people. Most obviously my wife Michele, and our children Luisa, Stewart and little Bella for all their love and support. And many times I have found myself wishing so much that my dad, John, had lived long enough to share with me the events of the last couple of years, not least because I imagine his counsel would have been both uncompromising and invaluable.

And then there are my staff at Villa, too: Steve Harrison, Paul Barron, Kevin Mac, Jim Walker and so many more. Cheers, lads. Plus, of course, all the players who have pulled on the claret and blue and I hope, like their manager, have felt the same quickening of the pulse as each battle has neared.

I am equally grateful to those who have rejected me. Like Ken Furphy, the old Watford manager, who reduced the 14-year-old John Gregory to tears by telling him he would never be good enough as a player. Or Jim Gregory, my old chairman at Portsmouth, who kicked me out of the big chair after 50 weeks. They never knew how much their decisions inspired me.

Neither should I forget Steve Stride whose clearly brilliant mind(!) summoned the name John Gregory as Aston Villa still shook from the departure of Brian Little. His help and advice have been pillars ever since.

All have been in my thoughts as these words have been compiled. But most of all, I wish to dedicate this book to my old gaffer, Brian Little.

When the game treated me like something it had just scraped off the bottom of its shoe, Brian had the faith to take me back into the fold as a coach at Leicester. And when he left Aston Villa for reasons I guess only he will truly ever know, the quality of his work meant I hit the ground running with a fantastic group of players. As you will read, without Brian, there would have been no phone call to join the glorious asylum that is Premiership football.

Cheers, mate. I will forever be in your debt.

John Gregory   March 2000

CONTENTS

FOREWORD

'Marion? Who's Marion?'

'Hello, John?'

'Yeah?'

'It's Marion.'

Marion? Marion who? I could not find a face or a voice to match the name. Is it that new girl who works part-time in the wages office? No, her name's not Marion. Who's Marion?

'Where are you?' asked the voice I still could not identify. Increasing puzzlement.

'You know where I am; you just phoned me at this hotel.' Who is this? Who on earth is Marion? Who is bothering to track me down here in Bristol a few hours before a match?

'Yes, I know you're in Bristol, but whereabouts is the hotel? Stephen is trying to find you.'

Stephen! The name was accompanied by a great 'clunking' sound; a huge penny had dropped out of the clouds and into my head. Stephen. Of course. Why hadn't she said so earlier? That had to be Steve Stride, the only Stephen I know. And the only person who calls him Stephen is Marion at… Villa. *Villa?* Christ, it's Marion; as in Doug Ellis's Marion; his secretary. It's the Old Man's secretary. It's Villa for God's sake!

What the hell is this all about? Why is 'Stridey' looking for me? Brian wants me back and he's asked Stevie to have a word? Maybe.

'Have you heard the news?' Marion continued.

'No. But whatever it is, I don't want to know – I'll wait to hear it from Stevie.' I didn't want it to be dull. I didn't want Marion to

1

say, 'Well, he's got some old pictures he wants signing' or 'He's after some tickets for a gig' or whatever. I wanted it to be exciting and if it wasn't, I could at least keep the thrill of the unknown going until I met him.

'Well, he's in Bristol, here's his mobile phone number. Ring him now.'

I rang Stevie's mobile.

'Where are you?' I asked.

'I'm sitting in my car outside your hotel.'

So he had found it after all. What on earth is this all about?

'Stay there Stevie, I'll come and see you.'

Please don't let this be dull...

Sure enough, Steve Stride, good friend, a fellow wannabe-guitarist and Beatle-freak and – even more importantly as it turned out at this moment in my life – the secretary-director of Aston Villa Football Club, was sitting in his car 100 yards from the entrance to my hotel. A short walk, especially when feet are racing to keep up with a pounding heart. Still, time enough to skim over a million and one possibilities.

OK, I tell myself, best case scenario: Brian wants me to come back to the coaching staff and Villa are going to make it worth my while. Worst case scenario... well, try not to look too disappointed.

Ah well, here goes. I quickly got in the passenger seat.

'Have you heard the news?'

'Stevie, I haven't got a clue what this is about.'

But that must be it. Brian wants me back. They know how happy I am at Wycombe; I made the break and went out on my own. Showed them I was a big boy. I wasn't content to just bum a ride on someone else's shoulders. They know they have to come up with a big incentive to make me leave. Brian doesn't want to ask me himself. He's sent Steve. That's got to be it.

'Brian's resigned. This afternoon. We want you to come back.'

'What as?'

'What do you think? As *manager*.'

And that was it. The start of it all. Tuesday 24 February 1998. The day a phone call changed my life. One simple phone call, a call I never expected, and suddenly nothing is ever going to be the same again. Welcome to showbiz. Welcome to insanity.

Welcome to the Premiership. Welcome to Fergie, Wenger, Vialli, Graham. The big boys. You fancy your chances Johnny boy? You're about to find out.

I had had a little appetizer, of course. Sixteen months earlier, I had been a coach alongside Brian Little at Villa. Good times. Good players. Team of the Season in 1996. Yeah, we did well. But I was now thoroughly immersed in life as manager of Wycombe Wanderers. The world of Aston Villa was a couple of galaxies distant. That was why the name Marion did not register at first. The Premiership was a distant sun.

We were in Bristol to play Rovers at the Memorial Ground, a trip I was not particularly thrilled about even though the previous year we had come back from 3–1 down to win 4–3 at that same venue. But the disgrace of a pitch, barely fit for rugby, never mind football, and Portakabin changing rooms made it a fixture I did not relish.

As usual, I had spent the coach journey locked in a card school with our press officer Alan Hutchinson, my assistant Richard Hill and physio Dave Jones, a video or music tapes providing the entertainment behind the banter. Significantly, neither the TV nor the radio were on.

I had absolutely no idea of the events that were unfolding at Villa Park where Brian was telling Doug Ellis, venerable chairman and Mr Villa himself, that he had had enough. He was resigning.

Since leaving Villa, my contact with the club had been scarce for very good reasons. When the team started to struggle, I knew there were whispers about my going back. But that's all they were. Whispers. I did not want to embarrass Brian, a man for whom I hold the highest regard, by ringing him for a chat that might be misconstrued as a job enquiry; neither did I want to ring friends on the staff for fear of it being misrepresented in the same way. I think, in fact, my contact had been restricted to one lengthy conversation on the phone with Stevie – during which he painstakingly described the chords of 'Wonderwall'!

It's like that in football. I get old mates ringing me up first thing Monday to tell me about a great goal they had scored on Saturday. But you don't call when things are not going well. It's not the done thing. And the press reports told me that things were not going well at Villa, at least not in the Premiership.

3

But I still never imagined Brian would resign, especially as he had taken Villa through to the UEFA Cup quarter-finals. They had beaten some very credible European teams on the way – Bordeaux, Athletic Bilbao and Steaua Bucharest – and now, in a week's time, they had a fantastic tie against an exciting Atletico Madrid team. Whatever problems the Villa boys might be having in the bread-and-butter stuff, they had not surfaced in the European games. And who would want to walk away from that?

So when Steve told me Villa were offering me the job, I was speechless – and people who know me will realize that's no mean achievement. But I couldn't act dumb for long. When I had gathered my senses, I realized it was time to start looking at all the angles. Villa, after all, were in a mess in the Premiership where the dreaded R word – relegation – had been uttered.

'I'm not coming to keep it warm for someone else,' I told him.

Steve assured me the post was mine. There would be a contract.

'How long?' I asked.

'Well, if you're any good, mate – for life.'

Wycombe fans will probably always suspect otherwise but I can honestly say that my focus on the match that night never wavered. We lost 3–1 but it was a defeat that had nothing to do with the head-spinning events that had unfolded just a few hours before kick-off.

I had shared the news with only one other living soul. Before the game, I had phoned home and my wife, Michele, could not wait to tell me what was now filling the news bulletins.

'Have you heard about Brian?' she asked.

When I told her not only had I heard about it but that Villa wanted her old man to be the new manager, she thought I was winding her up. But, she later told me, she had also detected a tremor in my voice; the enormity of what was about to happen to her, to her husband, her family and our lives together started to sink in during that telephone conversation.

Normally I am a great sleeper. I can honestly say that never before had I spent a night lying awake, fretting and worrying over one thing or another. But when I finally got back to our home in Windsor about 1.30 in the morning, I knew this was going to be different. Insomniac City, here I come.

My mind would not switch off. Villa were playing Liverpool in less than three days and I, me, Jesus – *me*; I would be their manager. Christ. What team do I pick? What team will Liverpool pick? Liverpool. THE team of my playing days; Graeme Souness strolling past me and saying: 'You've been living in London too long, son.' as I tried to wind him up. Liverpool. Steady on, you're not manager yet. But what if I am? Can I do it? Of course I can. It's what I've wanted; it's what I'm all about.

No, sleep was pointless.

I have never understood folk who get up and make a cup of tea when they can't sleep. I've always imagined that must make things worse. But I joined them that night. And my suspicions were confirmed – yep, the cuppa only made things worse.

All that was left to try to help me think straight was a walk at about 4.15 a.m. It was late February but I couldn't tell you to this day how cold a night it was. I could have gone out in a pair of shorts and flippers and it would not have made the slightest difference. Physically I was numb; mentally, I was plugged into the National Grid at tea-time. Liverpool. Bloody Liverpool. Villa Park will be heaving. This can't be happening.

What I can remember is suddenly recalling that there had been a spate of burglaries in the area recently and that I might come across three or four lads turning a house over.

What if they saw me and kicked the living daylights out of me? I would never get the chance to manage Villa. I'd be lying in hospital and some other lucky sod would get it. Jeez, I'm getting paranoid already. My walk lasted about three minutes.

I gave up. This would have to be one night without sleep. Anyway, it was time to snap out of it. In a few hours I had two meetings, one I was not looking forward to, the other I was. At 10.30 a.m., I was due to meet Steve, Doug Ellis and Villa's financial director Mark Ansell in Birmingham to try to secure the job of a lifetime. Fantastic.

Before that, I had to tell my Wycombe chairman Ivor Beeks that I wanted to leave.

Lovely chap, Ivor, with a lovely family. We might not have socialized but we had a terrific working relationship. He was the perfect chairman. One of those bosses who lets you get on with all the football and concentrates on employing his considerable financial acumen to the benefit of the club.

But at 8 a.m. on the Wednesday morning, he put his business head on and I struggled to handle it. Yes, I could go to Villa, he said – providing they coughed up £250,000.

WHAT?!?

I wasn't daft. I had soon worked out that one of the attractions for Villa coming in for me was that I could be easily and cheaply recruited. Or so they thought. Certainly cheaper than the figure Ivor had in mind.

I told Ivor he was being excessive. He disagreed. Villa were a big Premiership club who deal in millions and they were not going to take little Wycombe for a ride. That was his attitude and you couldn't blame him.

I argued and pleaded and begged and cursed... but he would not budge. For the first time, our relationship was souring. You can go and speak to them, he told me, but unless they pay £250,000, you're staying as my manager.

By the time I got to the Birmingham hotel where I was due to meet the Villa contingent, I was a nervous wreck. Not only was the news I had to impart from Ivor not good but now I was about to meet the three men who would decide my fate.

OK, think positive. Stevie, you know. He is batting for you. So that's one vote you can bank on. But the chairman? I just didn't know him. I had never had any real dealings with him at Villa.

Calm down, this is different now. I mean, the chairman is legend at Villa. The big cheese. You're not a cheeky young coach any more; he's going to be looking at you to see if you can manage the team. And what about this other guy, Mark? I don't know him at all.

But I must be half-way there at least or else I would not be here. So stop panicking, stay calm. The 'good mornings' begin, followed by the chit-chat. Before I tell them about Ivor's demands they get down to the terms of the contract they would offer. Despite that, Mark is looking at me and his look is not giving anything away. That's not a good sign, I thought. But I was wrong.

My contract was quickly agreed. Villa were to pay me a hand-some salary with a £50,000 bonus to keep them up. All in all it was the biggest pay day of my life so I was not going to argue. But if we went down, I had one year to bring them back otherwise that was it. Contract terminated; sorry, it hasn't worked out, now toddle off will you while we get in a proper manager.

OK, they are taking a gamble with me; I could live with that.

But what happened next was, in hindsight, quite comical. Following the meeting it was decided I would barter for my own release. I would leave the hotel room to call Ivor down in Wycombe with details of Villa's compensation offer, before returning to listen to the response from the chairman, Mark and Stevie. Then it was back outside to ring Ivor with the counter-offer.

And this went on for hours – or so it seemed. I would tell Ivor of Villa's offer but then advise him as to what I thought they might go to – and then tell my prospective employers what Ivor was after and what I thought he would accept.

I kept thinking, this can't be right. This can't be how these sort of things are done. But I was aching for this job and ready to try anything.

Still, it was not going well. No one was budging enough to find the compromise that would conclude the deal. I even tried tugging at Ivor's heart-strings. His family would often look after Bella on match days and, knowing he had a soft spot for her, I was pleading down the phone: 'You could be denying Bella's father the chance to manage one of the biggest clubs in the country! Do you really want me to tell her that?'

It was a low blow. But then I was practically on the carpet, begging him to say OK. But all to no avail.

Now I was in trouble. I was seeing the job I craved denied me by this dispute and so I did what a lot of folk do when they are desperate.

I closed my eyes and gambled.

Villa's opening offer was £75,000. Ivor wouldn't take less than £200,000. Eventually, we got it down to £100,000 plus a pre-season friendly at Wycombe. Nearly there. But Ivor wanted all the gate money – approximated at about £50,000 – and Villa wanted it shared, 50-50.

When I phoned Ivor back with instructions from Mr Ellis to demand 50 per cent of the gate for Villa, I knew he would not go for it. So I told him Villa had, indeed, agreed that Wycombe could have all the receipts. To hell with it, I thought, I'll worry about the discrepancy when the time comes. Bloody hell, with the money Villa are offering, I'll pay it myself if I have to. Just give me that flamin' job.

And at that moment, I heard Ivor's voice change. That was it, the deal was done, agreement had been reached. The cold-eyed businessman departed. The Ivor I knew returned. The words that followed I will never forget.

'Go on then, John,' he said, 'Go and be the new manager of Aston Villa Football Club.'

CHAPTER 1

'That's not a corner shop son. It's a bloody megastore.'

They're going to hate me, I thought. The fans I mean. Well, maybe not hate me but be... indifferent. Yeah, even worse, that. Indifferent.

This was three days later and I approached the players' tunnel, sucked in my breath and braced myself for that first run down the touchline. The players had gone ahead of me. There was no avoiding those next few minutes; my run to the Villa Park dug-out.

I was telling myself to stick to the pitch. That way I won't be able to hear what they were saying.

I was convinced that it was not going to be a pleasant experience, that the most I could expect was indifference. A polite round of applause, maybe. But mainly murmuring and grumbling. They wanted Gullit or Robson or Venables; instead they got John Whatsisname, fresh from the rump of the Second Division.

What happened next has never left me; in fact I doubt it ever will. That step from the subdued light of the tunnel into the brilliant afternoon sunshine and the explosion of noise and colour and excitement and tension... it just swamps your senses.

Even the sheer size of the place – breathtaking. I had been there and felt something of it as a player.

But this?

This was an even more intoxicating refresher course. And

anyway, I was older now, less blasé about this kind of experience. Different perspectives, I guess. Just thinking about it now still makes the hair on the back of my neck stand on end.

This is Villa. Villa for goodness' sake. You are manager of this place. I repeated the words in my head to help convince myself this was happening and I wasn't back in Windsor having a kip before Wycombe versus Bristol Rovers. Yep, there's my lot in front of the Holte. A glance to the left. That's Liverpool all right.

Damn, they've turned up then.

I could not control the shivers and tingles, as if every nerve in my body was on the edge of its seat. By the time I had reached the rest of the staff and substitutes in the dug-out, I had a very real grasp of how Brian must have felt when he first made that journey as gaffer. And Ron Atkinson. And Graham Taylor, even the stern-faced Ron Saunders, all former managers.

It doesn't matter how long you have been in the game or how well-practised you are in keeping your emotions under control, shut down and concealed from public view.

I knew this feeling bouncing around my system right now 103must have got to them at times. Christ, surely that's why we're in it; to feel this *alive*.

The ovation from the Villa fans also felt like a bonding and eased my anxieties over my reception. Oh, I knew there were questions and doubts. I knew the best part of 40,000 were still looking at this bloke running up the touchline wondering if I had what it took, whether I was up to the task now confronting me.

But there was warmth there too. I was sure of it. It was as if they were saying, OK mate, you may not have been who we were expecting but you're the Villa's manager and that's good enough for us. We're with you. And it was as if everything in my career had been preparing me for this moment.

This is what I want, I thought; this is what I need to feel.

Of course, I wished my old man could have been there. Like he had been many, many times before when I played for Villa. He used to sit up in that big old Trinity Road stand and scrutinize my game and the matches. I still felt his presence. If you had filmed that excited jog down the touchline you would have caught me glancing up at the seats, still searching for him.

But I had lost him to heart trouble in 1996. So I had to imagine him up there, whispering to himself: 'Go on son, you'll be all right, you show the bastards.'

Would I be all right?

You'll soon find out, son, you'll soon find out.

Hang on. I'm getting ahead of myself here. Before I take you any further forward, let me take you back for a moment; that way, you will know how much all of this meant to me.

You see, I have known nothing else but football for all of my 45 years and that all starts with John, my father.

He was an ex-pro, who had started at West Ham but failed to make an impact and transferred on to Scunthorpe – my birthplace – before finishing at Aldershot. The most he probably ever earned from the game was £8 a week.

So it was what we could call an undistinguished career – but it was a treasure trove for me. We were a big family of seven children. After 'warming up' with a couple of girls, my sisters Jeanette and Janice, I was the first of his five sons. My younger brothers Joe, Jason, Jerry and Jimmy – yes, I know, the 'J' thing; I think it became a bit of a joke with Mum and Dad – could all play a bit too but it would be me who would actually follow the old man's trade.

I was christened John Charles, which was a bit of a giveaway as to what hopes Dad held for me. And after the vicar had cupped the water over my forehead, Dad set about drenching me in the magic of football.

He became the first full-time manager of St Neots, a Metropolitan league club then, in Cambridgeshire. And there I was, aged four or five, acting as a ball boy and collecting the signatures of the teenage Bobby Moore, Martin Peters and Geoff Hurst when they came with the West Ham 'A' team for friendlies. You're never really going to get over an experience like that, are you?

Dad was a little bloke but he was a hard so-and-so, as many of his contemporaries still write to remind me. He was shaped by his tough upbringing in London's East End streets around Shoreditch, Hoxton and Dalston, and he brought into our house their simple code of conduct.

The biggest fear of my childhood was facing the old man if I had stepped out of line. I remember his taking the belt to me when I was 10 or maybe 11 after a stone fight in the street had finished with my cutting another lad's lip – and when that belt came off, boy, you knew you were in trouble. 'If you're going to fight,' said Dad as he dealt out the punishment, 'stand up and fight like a man.'

He did not take any prisoners. I can also recall his chinning one of my sister's boyfriends one night because he had made what my dad considered a facetious remark. And Lord help them if they didn't walk the girls home all the way to the door.

Yes, simple, working-class stuff, that most of us remember.

Anyone who gave him trouble which he deemed outside of that code... well, Dad would have chinned them and worried about the consequences later. I can't think who that reminds me of.

But he filled me with a passion for the game – matched only by his passion for the Sinatra songs that filled our house – and a determination never to let the inevitable setbacks defeat me; by the time he had finished with me, I wasn't going to be an accountant or a ballet dancer.

The moments that really terrified me, however, came when he turned up to watch me as a kid. He'd be there on the touchline, shouting and hollering; I would be embarrassed by his comments because he was my fiercest critic as well as my greatest advocate. And after the game I would get my performance dissected, piece by piece, usually with the conclusion: 'Ah, you'll never make it son. You'll never make it.'

I'm not sure whether that was a deliberate spur but it definitely drove me on. And there was an emotional side to him, too. Crying and whingeing he regarded as 'ponce behaviour'; but I saw the tears of pride in his eyes when I played for Villa or when I showed him my first England cap. I guess all any son can ever ask is that one day he knows he has made his father that proud.

So it was Dad that got me started and filled me with awe for the game and the fortitude to stretch every last drop of potential from whatever talent I possessed. Maybe I surprised him. But one by one I set the targets. And one by one I hit them. That is how it has always been for me. Set yourself goals and then do everything you can to reach them.

The first was to get accepted at a pro club – Northampton obliged. The next to get a professional contract and that came two years later. Then I wanted a bigger stage, I wanted to advance – a dream move to Villa. And so it went on. Via Brighton and QPR and all the way to the England squad.

And coaching and management? Well, that's where the voices of other figures were whispering in my ear.

Bob Paisley. Sir Alex Ferguson. Brian Clough. The three best managers the English game has ever seen. I haven't really got a pecking order for them. Maybe Paisley first because I played against his Liverpool and it was always a pretty chastening experience; his record is incredible and stands the test of time. Fergie's treble is astonishing and Cloughy has to be there because of his European and domestic successes with comparatively smaller clubs.

But if it were possible to merge my two greatest mentors into one, the hybrid might give all three a run for their money. Terry Venables is the greatest coach and tactician with whom I have ever come into contact, and Arthur Cox is the best, the canniest, man-manager I know. The two of them have had a profound impact on my life. They didn't do too badly individually. But if there were some way to join them together, I guarantee you would have a truly awesome managerial force.

Terry – 'TV' as I have always known him – signed me from Brighton to play for QPR. One of my biggest regrets is that by then I was already in my late 20s; he improved me so much as a player I always wondered how much better I might have become had I worked with him from the age of 18. I won my England caps under Bobby Robson while I was at QPR. I doubt I would have anywhere else or under any other coach.

But it was also 'TV' who got me thinking about what came after playing. I geared myself up for management from the day Venables sat me down at QPR and asked me what I was going to do when I hung up my boots.

As I was only 27 at the time, I wondered what on earth he was trying to tell me. I'm not that bad am I? But Terry's point was that too many players reach 34 or 35 and then think, oh, I'll be a manager now.

The time to start was *now,* he said; 'Go on coaching courses, start making notes of sessions, start watching matches, see how teams play, don't rely on the press but build up your own knowledge of players throughout the divisions and if anything catches your eye, jot it down. On the back of a bus ticket if needs be.'

I was focussed on management from that conversation onwards. 'TV's sessions were the best I had ever known as a player and so I began. I would log a whole week's training, write down the team, giving players marks out of 10 (frequently giving myself star marks, naturally). I'd dream up set-pieces and free kicks. After all, I had finished work by 1 p.m. and it was 20 hours to the next training session. There was plenty of free time. And I've still got all the notes and books to this day.

I also made another key decision. We all love playing and most of us want to go on and on until no one will have us. But I resolved to finish my playing career early. Not for me the steady drop down the divisions. By the time I was 38, I wanted at least a couple of years' experience in coaching or management behind me. There I went, setting those targets again.

My playing career at the top level closed at Derby. I had helped them come up from the old Second Division but, back in the top flight, I began to struggle the following season. The signs that I feared were now before me – I couldn't get near opponents and two games a week were proving too much for me.

So, in July 1988, I got the chance to make my first move towards the Big Chair. Jim Gregory, my old chairman at QPR, was now in charge at Portsmouth. I knew he liked me; he had even put me in his all-time QPR XI and that was some compliment. But was that the invisible hand of 'TV' I saw pushing this opportunity my way? Jim offered me the coach-cum-assistant manager's position under Alan Ball.

Not that Bally had much of a say in it. I believe I was presented to him by Jim as a *fait accompli* really. 'Here's your new coach Alan – and if you don't like it, you know what you can do,' was essentially the message. Bally must have suspected a conspiracy theory but he had been relegated the season before and… well, he couldn't really argue, could he?

He must have thought I wanted his job and I could tell by the way the coaches' room went quiet the moment I walked in. The staff were deeply suspicious of me. But so what? I have never been bothered by what people say about me and you could understand their perception of this new arrangement.

We've had some frosty conversations in the years that have followed but Ball has since had plenty of opportunities to prove what a good manager he is.

And the truth was that when Jim took me in I was happy to sit back and learn as much as I could from Bally. So I did. Sadly, in my opinion, I don't think I learned that much.

I had walked into a club which as far as I was concerned had a different attitude to drinking to me.

As a player, I had quit drinking at 30, four years earlier, and wasn't much of a drinker anyway. It became a big thing with me. I knew alcohol was a fitness killer. 'TV' filled me with stories of how the Continental players spurned drink; he told me how at Barcelona, the players would take one glass and one glass only from all the complimentary bottles of red wine at team dinners. Their English counterparts would have drained every last drop.

At Portsmouth we'd all have a drink on the bus coming back from away games. It became a tradition – a classic case of, 'We may have lost on the pitch boys, but we won in the boardroom. We drank them senseless!' Great fun of course. We started off brilliantly that season but by the turn of the year we had fallen to 13th.

Anyway, there I was, keeping my head down and getting on with it when in January of 1989 I was invited to dinner at the chairman's house. The table was set for three and I assumed Jim's wife would be joining us. A bit of small talk, me still wondering what this is all about. And then a knock at the door – and who should stroll in but Terry, by then manager of Spurs.

'So have you asked him then, Jim?' he said as we settled down for dinner.

Asked me what? I wondered.

'Well, are you ready son?' the chairman began.

'Ready for what?'

'Do you think you can do the job?'

It all began to dawn on me, of course and, again, the influence of Terry was unmistakable. Jim idolized him, I knew, and 'TV' had clearly given me a strong recommendation.

'Are you giving him the job then?' Terry asked. Jim nodded and my old gaffer came round to give me a big hug.

'Dead proud of you son,' he said.

The rest of the night was a bit of a blur really, although I recall Terry again looking after me with some pertinent questions about contract and salary. But he thought I was ready. Jim thought I was ready. I thought I was ready.

Was I heck.

Lesson number one. There is no comparison, none whatsoever, between coaching and management. You might as well ask a dentist to be a fireman. You might be the greatest coach in the country but when you sit in that chair it means nothing. Especially if you have not learned how to handle people.

I tried to change the world at Portsmouth and I tried to do it overnight. I did not stand a chance. For a start I was under the impression that every pro loved the game as I did. Sure, I liked a laugh and an occasional drink with the best of them; but always at the right times.

Unfortunately, I found at Portsmouth the most ill-disciplined collection of players it has ever been my experience to work with. They could pass the ball all right; it was just a pity they were not equally proficient at passing the pub. For them, the football would get in the way of their social lives.

I tried to get them in shirts and ties and to perhaps re-acquaint themselves with a razor; forget it. I would ask them to start turning up at club-related functions. No, it wasn't compulsory, I would say, just a show of support from the club. I'd still be waiting for one of them to appear long after it had finished.

Before the start of the following season, I arranged for a blessing service at a nearby church, an idea I picked up from another of my previous managers, Arthur Cox. It was intended as a kind of bonding, very much a family occasion.

Alan Knight, the goalkeeper, checked with me whether the service was compulsory. It could not be, of course.

And two out of 25 of the staff turned up. I should have organized a day at the races and then everyone would have been there.

Oh, I knew what I was taking on, but I thought I could change it. Quickly. Feet first. That was my problem. I wasn't one of the lads anymore. Instead the dressing-room would now go quiet when I walked in. Now I was the enemy – and I had made the biggest career mistake imaginable. I was so cocky, so sure of myself, that I honestly thought the sack was not something that would ever happen to Johnny Gregory.

I lasted a year.

In that time, I lost the players' attention and I lost the fans. Jim didn't desert me quite so quickly. One Saturday, they were chanting 'Gregory Out' and I told the chairman they were referring to him!

But he was totally supportive. It was difficult for him because he was not from the Portsmouth area; he still lived in Wimbledon. He hated publicity, hated talking publicly and didn't even have a column in the programme. We were the 'outside team' who had got rid of Bally, the World Cup hero and popular local.

But Jim threw his arms around me and tried to fight them off. When some fans called for a boycott, he told me: 'Sod 'em. We'll lock the ground and we'll watch the match on our own.'

But New Year's Day 1990, third from bottom, pissing down with rain, and a 2–0 half-time lead overturned by Leicester. Kevin Campbell scored two as they won 3–2. 'Gregory Out' was heard again and this time I couldn't pretend it was the chairman they were talking about.

'I think it's time to say goodbye, son,' he told me at our next meeting.

'What do you mean?' I was still hoping what was about to happen was not about to happen.

He explained. He had not slept a wink knowing he was going to tell me this but it was not working out.

I wanted to put him up against a wall.

Do you realize what you're doing to me? You're making a big mistake. Defiance was all I could offer.

'I'll have the last laugh because I'm going to be the best manager in the country. I won't rest until I come back and haunt you. You mark my words,' I said.

I had time to thank the lads who I had signed or who I felt had not let me down – good pros like John Beresford, Steve Wigley, Kenny Black, Kevin Ball and Guy Whittingham, whose £450 release from the army I had paid myself – before throwing my desk contents into a bin-liner, ringing home and telling Michele it was time to pack the china.

I got home and wouldn't talk to anybody. I didn't want to whinge in the media even though the local press were camped outside the door. The TV that night had pictures of my house and the commentary saying: 'The Gregory household was silent today.' God, it was awful.

It was also a professional and personal disaster. When we moved to Portsmouth, we took a huge mortgage to buy a house in the area but the sack came just as the bottom fell out of the property market.

A house we had bought for £250,000 we eventually sold for £130,000. It wiped us out. We had never indulged in an extravagant lifestyle but 14 years of savings had gone up in smoke. And now me, a failure at 35.

I had settled up with Jim after about a month of haggling. I was owed £60,000. He offered £11,352.27! In the end I received £25,000 but had to hand back the car. He had bought me a Mercedes when I took the job and offered to give me a letter as proof of ownership. I said it wasn't necessary – which proves how naïve we all can be at times. Jim was a car dealer, they were his favourite currency and he naturally took the Merc back off me when he gave me my marching orders.

'But it's mine, you gave it to me when you gave me the job,' I squealed.

'Check the papers, son,' Jim replied.

What a lesson that turned out to be.

Michele never forgave Jim. Nothing to do with our financial disaster. But he had once promised our then teenage children Stewart and Luisa that he would never sack their dad. 'I love him, you know, and he's going to be the best,' he had promised them one summer when we shared a holiday in the south of France. She could not believe he would break that promise to our children.

As for me? Well, it was a massive learning experience. There is nothing like the fear of the sack to drive you on; I have used it as a spur ever since. And once the anger subsided, there were no grudges.

Jim died a couple of years ago and I remember his funeral was held on a day when Villa were top of the Premiership. I still think he would have had a chuckle to himself from upstairs and thought: 'See, told you I had a good 'un there.'

But in the weeks that followed, it became graphically clear that the sack had inflicted nuclear damage to my career and ambitions. Football was all that I knew and the game had now passed sentence – that's it, he's messed it up, he's not up to the job. Portsmouth left the scars of failure that even now have not gone away. They never will.

I was desperate. I took any job that would toss some money into the household budget. I covered the 1990 World Cup for Greater London Radio. That was great fun, especially when my visits coincided with the fledgling Chris Evans' radio show. I loved Chris's spontaneity, his determination to break new ground if it felt right. Those were qualities that struck a chord with me in terms of what I wanted to do.

Not until I took the Wycombe job seven years later would I get another chance. I've got the replies from the letters that went out in the desperate months that followed. And they are the same – thanks, but no thanks.

I've even got one from someone called Doug Ellis – I bet he's forgotten that – when I thought there might be a vacancy on Villa's coaching staff. And when Birmingham City made one of their many managerial changes, I tracked down their chairman Samesh Kumar's offices in London, barged through reception and went knocking on his door. All to no avail. As a player I had fought my way up from Northampton to the top division; I had played for England. I had got what I wanted. But I had never known failure like this before.

Fortunately, there was a way back.

Brian Little and I had always kept in touch and it was this relationship which would eventually give me my path back when he took me on to his coaching team at Leicester. I had a lot of time for Brian and admired his management achievements – still do – and now I was ready to sit back, watch and learn. Time to start taking notes again.

It was a good relationship and, when he paid me the ultimate compliment of demanding I join him at Villa as well, life was sweet. But this was now 1994 and I warned Brian that I would give him another couple of years but would then be looking to give management another go.

Still it was a good time. We were successful and I had a cushy little number. I went home on Friday nights not knowing what the team was unless Brian wanted to tell me. No burdens; no worries. I was well-paid, with a nice car, nice house and none of the pressures; they were all Brian's. And yet as coach, I could bask in the reflected glory.

I could have sat there and picked up the cheques and the kudos. But the disaster of Portsmouth nagged away at me. I had to do it; I had to get back in the saddle and, fortunately, along came a horse called Wycombe Wanderers, bang on schedule. Not a thoroughbred I know, but still the chance I was looking for.

I have never really had the chance to record my appreciation of those 16 months at Wycombe. I do now. I learned from my errors and rebuilt my managerial confidence. We were in an awful mess when I got there but survived a desperate relegation fight and, I felt, made some progress. In all, another major learning experience. On top of the task of winning a few points, there was the challenge of trying to shave pounds off the bills. I knew every corner of that ground and every member of staff; I wasn't sure where the job would lead but I was blissfully happy.

On the day that I was appointed Villa manager, I was not surprised by the identity of my first telephone caller. Or by what he had to say.

'You're in the shit now son. That's not a corner shop they've given you y'know? It's a bloody megastore.'

It was Arthur Cox, 'Coxy', a manager who signed me for Derby when I was already 31 but, like Terry before him, a guy who proved I still had much to learn, even then, as a player.

It is difficult to imagine two more contrasting men. Where 'TV' would turn up for work driving a Mercedes and wearing an Armani suit, Arthur came in a Ford Granada and a track suit. As I have suggested, Terry was the superior coach and a wonderful, master tactician; Arthur's man-management was his greatest strength. They were from different backgrounds and occupied different worlds but in their love and knowledge of the game they were united. And I could never put one above the other.

Terry signed me for QPR as a 27-year-old and left me wishing I had worked with him 10 years earlier. It was much the same when Arthur took me on.

Those days at Derby are a cherished memory.

'I want you to come and do for us what Dave Mackay did before you,' said Arthur when he was selling the move from QPR to me.

Derby were in the old Second Division and wanted promotion within a couple of seasons. In fact, we went straight through with a decent team, packed with honest journeymen, but with enough quality to take us up.

And watching Arthur at work was another important experience for me. He was a one-off who never missed a trick and knew the game inside-out, backwards, frontwards, every which way.

I especially remember our long-distance Monday morning run around the nearby Allestree golf course, designed to rid our bodies of the weekend's excesses. I'll never forget the day we thought Arthur had not turned up and, as we disappeared into the woods out of the vision of coach Roy McFarland, slowed to a gentle trot in the belief we could take it easy.

'What do you think you lot are doing?' screamed a voice seemingly out of nowhere. 'Get a bloody move on.'

We all looked at each other in astonishment. It sounded like Arthur but he was nowhere to be seen. We kept trotting for a few more seconds until the voice boomed out again: 'Oi, Gregory you lazy sod. Didn't you hear me?'

And there he was – hiding up a tree with his binoculars! It was his way of letting us know that even when we didn't think he was around we couldn't take anything for granted.

And he toughened us up. He would not stand for track suit bottoms – 'You can't wear them in matches so why do you expect to wear them in training?' – no matter what the weather. And we were always made very, very aware of how lucky we were to be professional footballers.

There was no place for whingeing with Arthur even when, on those Monday morning sessions, he would deliberately lead Derby's finest through knee-high brambles, muck and nettles which would rip our legs to shreds. We would have to lift our arms above our heads like soldiers on exercise carrying their rifles. It was uncomfortable stuff at times, but then it would have been worse if we had started moaning.

No, it was no surprise that he was the first to call me that day. Gregory's great fortune could barely have hit the radio news bulletins and evening newspaper headlines but Arthur knew everything that was going on in the game and still does. And generally three or four days before anyone else.

He is fanatical about his profession and always superbly informed. An average day would be, say, a trip to watch Brentford's reserves in the afternoon followed by Kingstonian at night while leaving specific instructions with his wife as to what matches she should tape from the satellite TV for him to watch when he came in.

A workaholic and, without doubt, the number one football fan in the world.

I thought he was brilliant – still do – and regard it as a criminal waste that he is no longer a manager. He would still have a lot to offer any club and it has to be significant that Kevin Keegan has drafted him into the England camp since taking over the national job.

Most of all, Arthur has this wonderful way of testing you, making you confront issues that you might be ignoring. He would bombard you with questions that left you thinking and wondering. It was no surprise to hear that familiar voice starting to grill me.

'Are you sure you can run a megastore?' 'Do you know how to run one?' 'Are you ready for this?' 'Do you know what to do next?'

His last question I clearly remember.

'Do you know what you're doing?'

My first game sped at me like a train and all of these experiences, layer upon layer, made up the John Gregory that drove to his first training session as Villa manager wondering what on earth had gone wrong with this team.

I had spent the previous night at the chairman's house with a sore throat from so many media interviews and a head full of thoughts for company. Those thoughts were obvious. I had not yet made contact with the men who really mattered in all this. The players. The players who had, it seemed, become so difficult, so frustrating to handle that Brian had invoked this crisis by walking out.

What was I taking on? What could have happened to make such a good manager as Brian quit like that? I had left a happy dressing-room at Wycombe. What was I going to find at Villa?

I had a big advantage. I knew all but one of the players from my previous time there. Sure, 'Stan' Staunton was a strong personality who wanted everything right. But treat him straight and you got a straight response. So was Mark Bosnich, Gareth Southgate. They were a good bunch. OK, Savo Milosevic could be a bit moody, a loner and he didn't mix particularly well but... no, these were largely good pros, bloody good players too, no trouble at all. Plenty of talent still there. What the hell had been going on?

As I turned into the Bodymoor Heath training ground, it was inevitable I would think the answer had to be connected to the one name who had come to dominate the headlines as far as Villa were concerned. He was also the one player I did not know. Stan. Stan Collymore. Not so much the man but his performances within the team. I read the papers, after all. Maybe the stories were right.

No, don't pre-judge anything or anyone, I reminded myself as I parked the car. You'll find out for yourself soon enough.

As coach at Villa, I always used to say: 'Come on, let's go, don't be late' as we went out for training, and those were the first words they heard from me that Thursday afternoon. No formal meeting. No heavy-duty session. I was keen to make the point that while I was now the gaffer, I had not changed. I wanted to keep the sessions bright and lively. The last thing they needed was to stand around in that February wind doing set pieces and throw-ins; they had always enjoyed finishing practice. Fine. Let's do that.

It seemed to go well but, again, there was a little hint of the brooding atmosphere that had obviously penetrated the dressing room. When Stan Collymore scored with a diving header one of the coaches told me: 'Bloody hell, if you can get him to do that, you've cracked it.' Had things really got that bad?

But the boys seemed fine. And one player I liked immediately. Lee Hendrie. I had left him as a right-footed, wide left midfield player; I could not believe how easily he had made the transition into the centre of midfield. And he could give us things in midfield that no one else on the staff could provide. Save for maybe Dwight Yorke. But he could not get around the pitch so well.

No, Hendrie would play against Liverpool. Let's go for it. Let's be bold. Push the wing backs in, play Collymore, Yorke and Joachim. 3–4–3. That's how I want to play. This is the one chance the players will have this season to make a fresh start, to blow away all the doubts that had clearly infected their game. This was an occasion to squeeze firmly in the hand and shake until every last drop of benefit had fallen at our feet. I just wished it wasn't Liverpool. I mean Liverpool. Their team used to give me the shudders when I was a player. They were also a bogey team for Brian and I when I was last here. Fowler would only have to look at the ball and it seemed to end up in our net.

And not only that, but this was a Liverpool who were on a bit of a roll. I surveyed our position once more. We had 29 points and looking at the fixtures, I was confident we could get the four wins we needed to stay up; but we had to make a positive start. If we lost this game, I would lose some of the natural momentum of a new appointment. The clouds would be hanging over us again. First, we had to get past Liverpool. Why did it have to be Liverpool?

So where was I? Ah yes, the touchline, the dug-out, Liverpool to my left, Villa warming up in front of the Holte. It was packed. It was electric. This is what I had come for.

If that reception from the supporters was a delightful surprise, the next 10 minutes were awesome. Seriously.

Don't forget, I had been away from the Premiership for 16 months. I had been coaching Second Division players and looking at even lower levels for possible bargains.

That was no preparation for what was before me now. I could not catch my breath when that first match started. The pace was frightening. And the ability of the players was from another world.

I had watched Michael Owen's emergence on TV; now here

was the real thing, right in front of me, and he was unbelievable. I took my eye off him for a split second and when I glanced back he was 30 yards up the pitch. Hell, no one is that quick, surely?

And all my worst fears were beginning to materialize. Liverpool were determined to spoil my day; they wouldn't give us a kick to begin with and when Bosnich brought down Oyvind Leonhardsen after six minutes I was convinced this dream job would begin with a nightmare.

The referee was Graham Poll and as the two players clashed my mind flew back instantly to a confrontation we had had some years before while I was working at Leicester. Nothing too serious, mind; I just accused him of the usual stuff. You know – incompetence.

He's not going to miss the chance to make me pay for that, I thought. It had to be a penalty and Poll surely would send off Bozzy for bringing down a player in a goalscoring position. 'Oh God,' I muttered under my breath, 'this could be six.'

Owen scored from the spot but Bozzy stayed on – thank you, Lord – and somehow we got back in the game. I like to think it was partly due to the team selection. It was adventurous and designed to have a crack at the least convincing part of Liverpool's team – their defence. And when the boys found their feet, that's exactly what they did.

But every Villa fan who was there will also know we were treated that afternoon to two goals and an epic, inspirational 75 minutes from Collymore; the kind of performance that had eluded him until then and had maybe contributed to the events that had brought me back. I couldn't understand what the problems had been because Stan was magnificent, an inspiration for the rest of the team and the supporters. Such a player in that mood. Well, that can't be the problem, I thought.

And we got our win. We hung on, Stan coming off near the end to a standing ovation. 2–1. What a dream start.

I knew there had been quite a few 'verbals' with the Liverpool lads that day, as Stan's well-publicized allegations against Liverpool's Steve Harkness would later confirm. So, when I saw the man-of-the-moment relaxing in the bath later, I wanted to make contact. Get rid of the bullshit. Make sure he knew just what had happened.

I told him: 'You realize what you've just done out there, don't you? You've won. You've done it.'

No reaction. Try again.

'OK, you went up to Liverpool and you did not have a great time. But you've beaten them. You've done Liverpool. You've scored twice and beaten them. You're the King of the Hill tonight.'

Still no reaction; just a glazed look on his face. If I had performed like Stan that afternoon, it would have set me up in the game for the next six months. But I would later discover that by the time he got home, so deep was his depression he could barely get out of his chair.

Ignorant of any such problems, however, there were no difficulties for me. If you wanted to freeze frame a shot of pure elation or contentment in a man's life, then the Gregory household that Saturday night would be as good a choice as any.

Michele, Stewart and Luisa, and little Bella, all sat watching the game's highlights on *Match of the Day*, sharing a Chinese takeaway. Wonderful. I had taken Bella with me into the TV interview room afterwards and the last frame of the programme was a picture of her, beaming from ear to ear. A perfect end to a perfect day.

Come on then world, give me your best shot. I'm ready for you now...

CHAPTER 2

'He's bloody useless!'

I can be a soppy sod at times and three months after that bliss-
ful February night at Villa Park, I was to wander down the back-
streets of a Majorcan village and cry like a baby for the first time
in three years.

In 1995, I had twice been reduced to tears. I wept at the birth
of Bella in May and then five months later, at Dad's funeral.
When Sinatra's 'My Way' started up and then, my choice, Bruce
Springsteen's 'Walk Like A Man' echoed around the church I
could not hold back the tears.

Both Dad and Bella and many more besides would be in my
thoughts in that anonymous Palma street while, a few hundred
yards away, the Villa coaching staff were locked in heavy celebration.

But that was ahead of me. For now, there was simply no time
for such emotional indulgence – or 'ponce behaviour' as my dad
would have labelled it.

As any manager will tell you, Saturday's victory all too quickly
becomes Sunday's newspaper headlines and, by Monday, history;
for me there was no time to wallow in the satisfaction of our
defeat of Liverpool. When I awoke after that all-too-brief
moment of domestic contentment, it was to another daunting
realization. We had a flight to Spain on Monday for the opening
leg of our UEFA Cup quarter-final against Atletico Madrid. Just
72 hours separated the games and there was too much to be done
to waste any more time slapping myself on the back.

One uncomfortable matter had already been dealt with. Way
back in May 1977 on my first day at Villa as an eager trialist

from Northampton, a young lad from Dunfermline turned up on the same day. His name was Allan Evans, and I have never forgotten how we were shown to our 'quarters' at the club hostel run by long-time Villa staff man, Jim Paul.

He took us down to the basement, pointed to a couple of mattresses on the floor and said, 'There you are lads, make yourselves at home!' We got our bread and water rations for the week and, the following night, caught the bus to St Andrew's to watch the 'Second City derby' with all the Villa fans crammed in behind one goal.

Ah, happy days. Not as much fun for Jim, though. He is our kit manager these days and, don't you worry, always gets the worst rooms on our trips abroad!

And Allan? He went on to win championship and European Cup winners' medals before teaming up with Brian and myself in the management structure first at Leicester and then Villa.

When I left for Wycombe, Allan had stayed on at Villa.

And now I had to sack him.

I never really had a problem with Allan but, for some reason, I think he had a problem with me. There was never a chance we would work together.

I felt Allan had never liked me. I couldn't care less about whether he liked me or not, but I knew it was going to wreck any chance of our working side by side now.

Especially as he had applied for the job himself and lost out to me. No, Allan could not stay and I had to get my hands dirty on arriving by telling him. But the echoes from Portsmouth were still clear. I could not be everyone's mate now but I would need someone to lean on, to spark off, to trust.

I am a great believer in fate, destiny... call it what you will. During my days at Wycombe, I had received a letter from Steve Harrison, a coach closely associated with the Graham Taylor regime at Villa and with England, complimenting me on our successful fight against relegation in my first season there and the manner in which we had gone about it. That impressed me. There was no obvious advantage for Steve, who at that time was coaching at Preston, in jotting down those few lines; it was a nice touch of no foreseeable gain to him. And I liked the guy, too. Whenever our paths crossed during our Second Division sojourn we got on well. I had taken a mental note; yep, he's someone I would not mind working with in the future. There was already a good staff at Villa but I definitely wanted my own man with a fresh approach.

I imagine all of football knows about Steve's reputation for clowning. Within the game, the stories are the stuff of legend. But he had calmed down a little without, I suspected, losing the precious ability to shatter tension with a giggle. And most importantly of all, I knew him to be a darned good coach, a man capable of keeping players bright, lively and smiling during the long hours on the training pitch.

The day I was introduced to the media as Villa's new manager there was an immediate opportunity to check out the youngsters in a reserves match that same evening when our opponents would be Preston. And who should be in charge of them but Steve.

That was it as far as I was concerned; the coincidence was too much to ignore. Steve was a guy I would have been interested in taking on anyway, especially with his experience and previous connections at the club, but this collision of circumstance seemed too obvious a case of 'destinies calling' to be ignored.

So when we boarded the plane to Spain on the Monday morning, it was with Steve – or 'Harry' as he is known to us – as my new first team coach. Bright-eyed and bushy-tailed we were, like two kids setting off on a great adventure on one of those endless summer days from childhood. Unfortunately there was an obvious drawback to this fledgling partnership – what we knew about Atletico Madrid could be covered in perhaps one sentence.

They were bloody good.

Even with the brilliant Brazilian Juninho injured, they still had Italy's Christian Vieri at the head of their attack and I was a big admirer of his abilities.

Again I had to rely on the coaching staff, and I was particularly indebted to Kevin MacDonald, to fill me in on their capabilities and their set-pieces. It wasn't much to go on but at least it was something. And anyway, it has always been a big thing of mine to be positive.

If we're right, we'll give them problems; let them worry about us, I thought. Sure I was anxious about what I was stepping into, but I certainly did not want my anxieties transmitted to the players.

I spent most of the trip out there reading up on as much information as we had gleaned about Atletico. No doubt about it, this is top-drawer European opposition.

The adventure, though, was just beginning. That night, we trained at Atletico's stadium and after a bit of light work I turned to Harry and said, 'What do you think?' He felt we should rein them in but I opted for another 20 minutes' shooting practice.

The pair of us, coach and manager, then stood back and feasted our eyes on the players we had been given. Volleys and shots and crosses were flying in from all angles; sharp, crisp and sure. It was bloody fantastic for the two of us, fresh out of the Second Division. We had been used to players whose first touch was generally to hump it; we had both been away and forgotten about the sheer quality of the guys we were now dealing with. Harry and I glanced at each other as if to say, 'Bloody hell, can you believe this lot?'

And that night, it really dawned on me for the first time as to what – or perhaps who – I had inherited. After 16 months feeding off the pauper's table at Wycombe, I could now eat like a king. I looked around the Atletico dressing room at Yorke, Bosnich, Staunton, Collymore, Southgate and their mates and felt such immense pride at being *their* manager.

This is *my* team, I kept thinking, once again half-wondering if someone was going to wake me from all this. 'This ain't half bad at all.'

At the same time, there were those nagging doubts. This was too good to be true. Just how terrible had it become for Brian to have walked away from this lot? I thought about my old boss. I knew he could be impulsive. And I sensed that now, shut away from the electricity and tension already surrounding a tie he had done so much to bring about, he would already be regretting it...

Now a more sombre mood came over me. As we drove back to our hotel from that training session, I was struck with a sense of responsibility to Brian. I felt a bit of a cheat. I had effectively been given a bye to the quarter-finals of the UEFA Cup and was convinced that these players were good enough to win the tournament that year. I mustn't let him down. In the end, I felt that's exactly what I did.

The two legs against Atletico proved to be classic matches and I think we were a little unlucky to go out to them. We were good enough to have taken them but I think we only realized that when it was too late.

But we left the UEFA Cup with our heads held high, having given them a huge fright. In Spain, I was again struck by that 'Liverpool feeling'; Atletico were so good, we could not get out of our half for the opening 20 minutes. But we did get better and should have brought a goal back with us instead of a 1–0 defeat.

The missed chances were one factor but the hammer blow was conceding another in the home game. We won 2–1 but went out on away goals, although not before Stan, troubled by a groin injury and unable to start, had come off the bench and again given us a glimpse of the Collymore we would all love him to be. He scored a spectacular second goal and the response from the fans was incredible. I thought the noise inside the stadium would lift the roof off the stand. Once again, so much for my fears about Stan being the catalyst for whatever problems had shunted Brian towards resignation. If we can get this guy fit and charged up like this, he is a match-winner. He will have Villa Park rammed full.

Hendrie came close to popping in a third goal that would have taken us through but it wasn't to be. A glorious failure. Sorry Brian, I thought. Throughout all the troubles of that season, he had still done brilliantly to take Villa so deep into a very tough competition only for me to muck it up. Those players really could have won it that year.

Still, I was up and running and determined to learn from my mistakes of the past. Instead of £20,000 a year footballers, these guys could earn £20,000 a week. But as you go through the game, you realize that the more things change around you, the more they stay the same.

Take the dressing-room, for example. I've been in and around them for 30 years and all the players come from similar backgrounds and are of similar intelligence. There is what I call my *Only Fools and Horses* cross-section – always a gang of Del Boys, a Trigger or two, two or three Rodneys, a Boycey here or there.

And it's no different at Villa. The challenge is to try to make sure no one falls through the bar hatch.

Only the noughts at the end of their pay cheques had changed; the rules would be those I followed at Wycombe and had learned to my cost at Portsmouth. You can't be their mate but you can get on with them.

And I had the natural dynamics of my appointment on my side. I was new, fresh and, essentially, on a hiding to nothing. I was able to experiment; I was able to be bold and positive, which is my natural inclination; I could try things.

Brian had come under fire for being too cautious, although I could see what he had been trying to do. However, that mood around Villa Park gave me a blank cheque to 'go for it'. I looked at our position – 15th with 30 points – and felt we needed a dozen more for guaranteed safety. And we had already pocketed three against Liverpool. I also looked at the fixture list and the bulk of the remaining games was against teams from the bottom half of the Premiership. I surveyed the talent at my disposal and backed them to get us out of trouble at a canter.

But there was an extra edge to my boldness. Despite Stridey's assurances, I was convinced that I was an emergency, perhaps even a panic, appointment and I felt that just avoiding the drop might not be good enough to keep me at Villa. Football is ruthless and had we survived by the skin of our teeth, it would not have surprised me if the chairman and directors had come along and said, 'Thanks a lot, John, here's your bonus and well done. Now bugger off so we can make a proper appointment.'

Maybe I was being paranoid or reflecting an inevitable insecurity about the whole scenario. But that was there, at the back of my mind. I had to make an impact or at least show them I had something going for me. As I saw it, I might as well be hung for a sheep as a lamb.

All of these things were running for me and so I went for it. And, boy, did it work.

Spectacularly.

We were to win eight of the 10 league games that remained; it was as if everything I touched turned to gold. The reality, of course, was that I was doing what every other gaffer in the country would have been trying. But it just kept working. Everything just kept working.

I remember on one occasion, we were struggling to get past West Ham and I sent Milosevic on as a substitute. Within a minute we had scored and then he popped in a second. Suddenly, I was reading about 'Gregory's stroke of genius' in the papers. But every other manager would have been trying the same things.

What no one could deny, though, was the increasing quality of the performances over the remaining weeks of the season. Everywhere we went we were positive. It was 'Come on, we can win here as well.' And we got better... and better... and better.

This was very much me in my element in terms of how I like to operate – instinctively, quickly, positively. If I didn't like something I said so. Perhaps Brian had got into situations whereby if he did not like certain things the players never got to hear about it. Maybe he avoided those confrontations and I would imagine he felt he had good reasons for doing so. But we were winning and I was having none of that. I called it as I saw it and then moved on. I am very much a guy who believes you can have a right 'up and downer' with someone one day and shake hands and get on with it again the next. That is the nature of professional football to me.

There was no secret to any of this. I was reacting every day to problems or otherwise, thinking on my feet and just doing what came naturally. I would wake up in the morning thinking, right, what's going to happen today? and off I would go. Or at least that's how it felt.

As I say, I trust my instincts and they were not letting me down. I like to think I can judge people very quickly – I might not always be spot-on but I don't think I am ever too far off – just by the way they react to others in a room. The way they talk, the way they respond to different situations. I get strong gut feelings about things and I was dipping into this source a good deal for my team selections. Often, one plan I had in mind all week would be torn up by something I saw at a Friday morning training session.

And I love getting my coaches to react the same way. Nothing intrigues me more than to hold a very thorough, pre-session

briefing with them in which everything is set out for that morning's training, only to stop them as we are walking out and say:
'No, change of plan – you do this, you do that.' I like to see how they
react; if they are sharp enough to adapt; if they can be flexible.

It was exhilarating and sure enough, in between the two
games against Atletico, we beat Chelsea at Stamford Bridge and
at one stage rattled off five wins in a row against Crystal Palace,
Everton, West Ham, Coventry and Southampton.

Either side of those games came defeats that infuriated me.
Barnsley and Bolton would be relegated that year but both won
at Villa Park. They were stupid results, especially the Barnsley
match which I believe we should have won comfortably.

But I could not complain too much. At Everton and
Southampton, the players were sensational and we finished the
season off with probably the best two performances of the entire
sequence – a 3–1 win at Sheffield Wednesday and our defeat of
the champions, Arsenal, with 10 men, at Villa Park on the last
day of the programme.

By then, it was all getting very interesting and even more serious. All the time we were winning, I never really imagined that
anything other than a mid-to-upper table finishing position
could be on the cards. But above us, Blackburn Rovers, one of the
favourites for a European qualifying place, were sinking like a
stone; they could not win a game for love nor money and
suddenly, there we were at the gates of the UEFA Cup on the
final Sunday of the season. Victory for my lot, and anything less
for Blackburn at home to Newcastle, and we would finish sixth
and qualify.

Life so far had been a breeze. Premiership management? It's
easy, I would joke to myself. What's all the fuss about? This is
bloody great fun. But the truth was by the time that final weekend of the season arrived, I was beginning to get a handle on
some of the problems that had undermined my predecessor.

Collymore had been out of the side since his near match-turn-
ing cameo against Atletico two months earlier but was fit again
in the build-up to the Hillsborough trip. By then, however, Julian
Joachim had come through and struck up a profitable partnership with Dwight Yorke and when I stuck by the pair for this

penultimate match of the season, Stan seemed to me to have got the 'hump'.

I am a big believer in doing things together. Train together. Work together. Play together. And even walk out together for the warm-ups. But that day, Collymore and Savo Milosevic didn't feel the need to join the main group as they went through the warm-up routines and instead, knocked a ball back and forth between each other. They couldn't stand each other normally and yet here they were having a combined sulk. I thought it was pretty pathetic.

I also recall another big signal from the smallest of gestures before that game. Held up by autograph hunters, one of the lads was late getting into the dressing-room and missed my reading out the team to the rest of the boys. It meant he was the last to get changed and, as the other players left, he pulled me to one side to apologize.

'Sorry Gaff,' he said, 'I missed the team – who's up front?' I knew what he was really asking. Speculation locally about whether or not Collymore would be recalled for Julian Joachim had been intense during the week.

'JJ,' I replied.

'Yeeessss,' he muttered under his breath in triumphant tones before, realizing that I had heard him, adding: 'Sorry Gaff.'

'That's all right, son,' I replied. 'I understand.'

Or at least I was beginning to.

We were outstanding that day, probably my favourite performance as Villa manager. We kept the ball so well and when I think back to the performances of Yorke and Steve Staunton – genuine world-class talent – it only underlines the scale of their loss that very same summer. We also lost our always-dependable Ian Taylor through injury in the first half and I guess the 'safe' thing to do would have been to bring on Collymore and drop Yorkey into mid-field. Avoid another confrontation, John, put him on. But that's not me.

Sod you Stan, I thought. If you want to give me the hump you can have some back. Instead, I sent on a 17-year-old kid who had not yet kicked a first-team ball. I'm glad I did. What I saw from Gareth Barry that afternoon was logged away for future reference.

It didn't stop our carnival display. It was bordering on taking the mickey at various stages and it meant an awful lot to me to have Big Ron – Atkinson, of course – shake my hand after our victory and congratulate me on the team's performance. I'm a big fan of Ron's and, although he was then Wednesday's manager, he still knew a darned sight more than me about managing Villa. And a few of the players who had just tortured his team had either been signed or groomed by him.

Milosevic's attitude that day, meanwhile, did not surprise or perturb me. In my first face-to-face meeting with him a couple of months earlier, he had told me point blank that he wanted to go that summer.

I knew that his career at Villa had taken a bad turn. His relationship with the supporters had plummeted when he spat at them after missing a chance during a horrible 5–0 defeat at Blackburn before I got there. It was one of the factors I was sure had soured Brian's last weeks in charge. But I knew Savo had talent; he could be of use to me and I was not in a hurry to show him the door.

'Why?' I kept asking. 'Make a fresh start. You can see where we're heading. Why do you want to leave?'

'Because I do,' was essentially his response. I think he had developed a taste for foreign climes – especially Spain – and the money-earning potential.

'Ah well, please yourself,' I said. I was not going to beg. 'You're going to miss something special, though, and don't come crying to me when you regret it later'.

That was my attitude. As much as I liked Savo as a player it was not going to be a major loss to me in terms of trying to make the dressing-room a happier, more unified, place.

I'll never forget during my days as a coach seeing Savo speed away from training as quickly as possible while, over on one of the pitches at Bodymoor Heath, our defender Ugo Ehiogu was putting in some extra finishing practice with Yorkey. Funny, I remember thinking at the time, that's the wrong way round, isn't it? Ultimately, Savo had reinforced my view that, as for so many other foreigners, Aston Villa FC were just his current employers. And that was as far as it went.

But Stan was with us for at least three more years and I

needed to sort out the previous Saturday's problems. That week, with the Arsenal match approaching, every ticket sold and that European place suddenly dangling before us, we sat down together to address the discord at Hillsborough. It was yet another one of those occasions when, after we had both had our say, I thought I had got through to Stan.

When Manchester United started to build that massive squad at Old Trafford, I remember reading Sir Alex Ferguson's response to a question about how he was going to keep all his players happy. 'I'm not here to please the players,' he said. 'They're here to please me.'

I thought that was brilliant. He summed it up and, with the team playing so well and the results following on accordingly, it was up to Stan to show me he should be in the starting XI. He seemed to accept the point.

When Sunday came, and we were leading Arsenal 1–0, I again had Stan on the bench. We had lost big Ugo to a red card in the first half but the players were fighting like tigers to keep Bergkamp and co. at bay and book that UEFA Cup place. As the last third of the game arrived, I turned to Stan. God, he looked magnificent; a beast of a player. He also looked mean and hungry. Our chat had worked, I thought; when I sent him on, I was convinced Stan was going to tear off a few heads and give us another glimpse of the awesome player we had seen against Liverpool. His appearance again lifted the roof off and I sat back to watch the fireworks.

And do you know what? He was crap. He barely raised a trot. And I was dumbstruck.

How could he not be inspired by what the players were doing that afternoon? How could he not get into that? They were fighting tooth and claw against the best team in the country and he just didn't show for them.

That afternoon would finish with a lap of honour in which he refused to participate. We had enjoyed an astonishing climax to the season and a Villa Park full house wanted to salute it. But Stan would not make the effort. Not for the first or last time, I was left totally perplexed as to what it was that made him tick.

Still, we clung valiantly to our 1–0 win only to discover that Chris Sutton had kicked us in the nether regions and scored a winning goal for Blackburn just two minutes from the end of their match. All that effort, from 15th to seventh place, and still no UEFA Cup place. Shit.

But there was one last chance. The following Wednesday, fourth-placed Chelsea would be playing Stuttgart in the European Cup Winners' Cup final; victory would send them back into that competition as defending champions and throw open another UEFA Cup spot.

To us.

And so there we were, three nights later on the club's end-of-season trip to Majorca. The lads all out on the town – minus a back-at-home Collymore – and letting their hair down. They had earned it. And I gave them the space to party. I joined the chairman, Stridey – the man who had started this incredible adventure with that question from his car outside a Bristol hotel three months earlier – Steve Harrison, our physio Jim Walker, fitness and goalkeeping coach Paul Barron and the ever-faithful kit man Jim Paul for what we knew would be a night of unbearable tension. Chelsea v Stuttgart, live on TV.

But what to do? I couldn't stand watching the game from start to finish. After all, it's those bloody Germans. They're bound to equalize in the last minute and then win it on penalties. But not knowing was as bad as knowing.

In the end, we settled for a meal at a restaurant with a TV inside. We sat outside to eat and feigned a kind of casual interest in what was happening in Stockholm, where the final was being played.

At least that's what we tried to do. Unfortunately, the chairman couldn't contain himself. He was inside watching the game and putting us through agonies.

Every so often we'd hear 'Oh my God, they're going to score,' or 'They've got a corner' and then 'Oh that's it now, the Germans are on top.' He kept painting the blackest picture. I kept thinking, please, Mr Chairman just shut up and calm down. But you can't say that to the boss, can you?

Then he shouted out to us: 'Chelsea are bringing a sub on'.

A few moments pause.

'It's Zola'.

'Zola?' said Jim Paul. 'He's bloody useless. Why not Hughesy?' (Mark Hughes)

Well, within 30 seconds Gianfranco Zola had scored an absolutely stunning goal and sentenced poor old Jim to a lifetime of mickey-taking about his judgement of players. Now we had to wait for the minutes to count down but when that final whistle sounded, the celebrations in Stockholm could not have been any more intense than those outside that Spanish bar. The locals looked at us astonished as we jumped all over each other and danced around laughing and shouting.

In the middle of all this joy and immense satisfaction, I had to get away and have a few moments to myself. And that's when I found myself strolling down a backstreet trying to take everything in.

Three months ago I had been manager of Wycombe, trying to keep them in the Second Division, counting the loo rolls, and doing my very best to make silk purses out of sows' ears. Now here I was, manager of Aston Villa. Appointed in a relegation panic and on a blind hunch and now qualifying for Europe.

I kept looking up, waiting for the roof to cave in on all this. But it didn't. All I saw was a brilliant, Majorcan night sky. Countless millions of stars. Everything we had done seemed pretty insignificant compared to that view. But I could at last reach out and touch something, a tangible reward, as a football manager. And it felt fantastic.

Well, Jim Gregory, Portsmouth and all the other doubters. Fuck the lot of you. I had done it. Up the Villa. And then I thought of my kids; I knew how much it would mean to them. And, of course, Michele. And I thought of Dad. Jeez, he would have loved this so much.

And I cried like a baby.

'Silly ponce,' the old man would have said.

CHAPTER 3

'I think I've made an unbelievable mistake.'

It couldn't go on like this, surely? Something had to happen. I mean, I'm not stupid. I was a rookie, still wet behind the ears. I knew that I had not suddenly discovered a secret that had eluded everyone else in my profession. No matter how good a job I might have thought I had done, I knew that the game was always the master; when you think you have it licked, it suddenly tastes very, very sour indeed.

Sure enough. The waiters were still clearing up the champagne corks the morning after the night before when I finally suffered the kick in the teeth I had been waiting for.

It was delivered by the left foot of Steve Staunton. And he doesn't miss with that.

Staunton – a fantastic player, a super pro; one of those wonderful signings by big Ron I have referred to. He had not been quite fit enough to start the away leg of our Atletico tie but we eventually had to bring him on as a substitute for the injured Riccardo Scimeca. His ability on the ball instantly transformed the team and oozed confidence. It costs millions and millions to buy that. We had to keep him. The problem was he was out of contract at the end of that season – like, now – and due to become the first high-profile beneficiary of what has become known as the Bosman Ruling. Or, to give it another name, Every Good Player's Chance To Make A Killing.

But, with UEFA Cup football now in the bag, I was bristling

with renewed optimism when Steve came to see me the day before we flew home from Majorca.

There was plenty of heresay surrounding his future. Everyone assumed that he would be going to Liverpool, but the messages I was receiving suggested Newcastle and Tottenham were even more keen. I had already been given a salary figure that would be our last offer to him. 'That's it, Steve, I can't top that,' I told him. 'But look at us – we're going places. We're back in Europe. Last season's troubles have gone'.

I was convinced he would stay.

But he told me there and then that he would be leaving. I couldn't comprehend it. There cannot be anywhere else better to go to, I thought, apart from Manchester United or Arsenal. And I knew they were not in the frame.

That's when he said he was going to a bigger club with more potential and more ambition.

'Oh,' I said, 'I didn't realize Barcelona were after you.'

My sarcasm had a hollow ring to it. In truth, it was a barely-disguised attempt to cover up the sinking feeling in the pit of my stomach. Damn! I can't believe he's doing this to me. Is he mad? Can't he see what is happening here?

He didn't tell me who he was joining and I didn't ask. I just wanted to hit him. I was horrified at losing him. As soon as Zola's goal had gone in and Chelsea had lifted the Cup Winners' Cup the night before, one of my first thoughts was that it meant Staunton staying. Even if only for another couple of years. But now I had a job I didn't want – trying to replace him. I knew how difficult that would be.

That summer the club produced a video highlights of the season which, essentially, showed all Villa's goals. Check it out and see how many goal-scoring moves start with that left boot of Staunton's. And that's when he wasn't scoring himself. How do I replace this guy, I wondered. And what with? He's walking away for nothing.

Nothing could persuade him otherwise. Steve's words knocked the wind out of me – not for long because I didn't want it to over-shadow everything that had been achieved – but I knew a player capable of giving us an edge was walking out. Even more, he was walking out on me. Maybe I wasn't the overwhelming success I thought I had been so far.

Had replacing such a key player represented my only major problem of the close season I could not have complained. But his decision to walk out was a stroll in the park compared to what was to come. For that was horrible, truly horrible.

The World Cup in France in 1998 was underway and dominating the football globe's attention. Sitting up in bed on a lovely June morning, I switched on the TV news to be greeted by a disturbing story. It said Stan Collymore had carried out a physical attack on his girlfriend, Ulrika Johnson, in a Parisian bar full of Scottish fans.

It made for an ugly story. Once the shock had settled in, I thanked the Lord it was not my problem. Yes, it affected one of my players but, as I viewed it in my own naïve way, it was something that Stan had to sort out with Ulrika and his own conscience.

How wrong I was.

The phone started ringing the moment I arrived at the office as everyone pounced on the story. The media, women's rights groups, the civil liberties folk... they all wanted to know what I was going to do about it. 'Are you going to sack him?' 'If not why not?' 'How can you defend him?' 'How can you sack him?' 'There again, why should his private life have anything to do with his professional career?' The questions were relentless. Hang on a moment, I didn't sign up for this little lot.

It was that day, more than any other, that drummed into me the enormity of the job I had taken on. This game now is a monster and it was beginning to feel as if a day could not pass without something, someone grabbing the headlines and demanding a response from me. But I'm just a football manager. I am not the guardian of the nation's moral principles, I thought. I'm not equipped to deal with this.

This may seem cruel but I knew that had this happened to one of my Wycombe players, it would barely have rated a mention. Now the cameras were at Villa Park almost before I was. I left home thinking it was Stan's problem; by the time I arrived for work, I knew that whether I liked it or not, it was also mine.

The first thing to do was speak to Paul Stretford, Stan's agent and probably the biggest shoulder he had to lean on at the time. He and I had developed a good working relationship and I knew

I could count on him for a full and frank description of what on earth had happened.

He gave it to me in detail; detail that has remained hidden from common public knowledge. I think that's where it should stay because only the people in that bar at the time really know what happened. What Paul told me didn't excuse Stan but it helped me get to grips with what I was dealing with. I had to know everything because I realized the problem was heading for my copy book.

It would be three or four days before Stan and I sat down together to discuss what the hell we were going to do. By then the letters were pouring into Villa Park and the phone lines had turned red hot with fans demanding we sack him, others saying we must stand by him. I had some people warning me that not a single woman would renew her season ticket, that there were bigger issues at stake now than the mere hiring or firing of a football player.

But when we did speak, I saw genuine remorse in the man. He was practically in tears; I guess he knew his life and his career were in a mess and he was in a state of true regret over his actions.

I knew that whatever I chose to do, I would upset some people. I wanted to scream: 'It's got nothing to do with me.' But no one would listen to that.

And so I resolved to deal with the incident in the only way I felt equipped to – not in any kind of moral judgement but as a football manager with the responsibility of doing whatever was best for Aston Villa.

I don't think Stan feared I was going to sack him. I did not have any grounds to do so that would have stood up to legal examination. So if it wouldn't stand up in court why should I be beating myself up over the issue? No, I'm paid to get Stan the footballer back into the fold. I was having my problems before that as I have said; he was proving an erratic, enigmatic character who I was struggling to understand. I never knew what mood I would catch him in on any given day.

But this was something else altogether. Help me, Gaffer, he was saying and I had to respond. How he dealt one-to-one with Ulrika was a problem for him and him alone. But I knew Stan's only salvation in the eyes of a now highly-critical public could come through work.

We agreed on that much. He would come back early to training. He would use this terrible episode to galvanize himself to prove to Villa, once and for all, that he was the great player they thought he was when he was signed, the great player we had glimpsed in isolated but undoubtedly thrilling moments the previous season.

But I was deeply disappointed by the turmoil Stan had created for himself. Footballers need many attributes, not least of all the kind of rare talent Stan possessed. But they also need character, a discipline to ensure that those talents are properly fulfilled. It may be what has stopped Paul Gascoigne becoming the greatest player we have ever seen.

And this incident cast aspersions on Stan in this area. He had finished that season poorly and I already knew that he could never be a team person. He didn't really mix in the real sense of the word, as was patently clear when he didn't come to Majorca. No one was surprised. No one really expected him to. And that said a lot.

I have lost count of the times he and I sat down together at Bodymoor for a chat and a cup of tea. We would talk about anything – music, women, shopping, whatever – and Stan would always say the right things.

'I feel right, I feel fit, I'm enjoying this role,' he would tell me. Villa, Villa, Villa, he would say. That's all that interested him. And I would come out thinking, fantastic, we've finally cracked it.

And then I would ring up Stan at home every so often to try to gee him up. I felt we could do 'bloke talk.' 'Are you going out tonight?' 'What are you up to?' 'How are you feeling?' 'We need you Saturday, son, we need you big time'. He would come in the next day and say, 'Thanks for the call' and Paul Stretford would tell me that he was really 'made-up' by my attention. 'He's really up for Saturday,' Paul would say.

But, on Saturday, he would be nowhere to be seen in the match.

I had a truck-load of those sessions and it was only after a while I began to question what he was telling me. I suddenly found myself saying to him: 'But Stan, you promised me that last week.'

I was beginning to feel that Stan was always searching for an excuse. I likened him in many ways to a Villa striker of an earlier vintage, Dalian Atkinson.

Dalian was at the club when I first arrived with Brian and I remember remarking to him one day that he had not scored for a few months. 'Didn't you see the cup final then?' he answered as if affronted by the question. That was a reference to his goal and a superb performance against Manchester United in Villa's Wembley win in the previous season's Coca-Cola Cup. Unfortunately, that match was eight months earlier and yet there was Dalian apparently expecting to dine out on it. Similarly, Stan had played brilliantly against Liverpool and, I concluded, felt that was enough for the time being.

Now we had this Ulrika episode and and I felt I had this one final chance to rescue Stan from himself. Yes, he would come back early and work hard and prove that the world had misjudged him. But I was beginning to think that the world had not misjudged him. Sadly, I was beginning to think the world might have a point.

And of one thing I was certain.

If Stan was not going to do it for himself, he sure as hell was not going to do it for me.

I was busy enough as it was without spending countless hours trying to resolve this new crisis in the career of Stan Collymore. Too many football folk want it all ways these days and that includes commuting long distances to work despite the handsome salaries now on offer.

I've said all along that I was a baby compared to some of the managers I was now up against but when you take me on, you do at least get the whole darned thing – the whole nine yards as my dad used to say. And that includes a commitment to where I work. I had promised my chairman that I would have a house in the Birmingham area by July and Michele, Bella and myself moved in to our new home on the first day of that month.

That is something I do not think is too much to expect from players. I remember at Wycombe we had so many players travelling hundreds of miles for training that they could not stay for training after lunch because of the traffic implications for the journey home.

On the kind of salaries available at that level, I was not prepared to demand they move. But I felt I could at Villa and have done so, a subject that would come back to haunt me later that summer. To give a job your all, you have to move close by; you cannot have travelling problems at the back of your mind with the unsociable hours football demands.

But Michele and I were in, settled and able to enjoy a brief holiday in our favourite region, the south of France, to at least recharge some batteries. And while the Collymore incident had exposed one side of the coin, we were already starting to notice other, more enjoyable changes to our lives.

For a start the money was nice. Very nice. Football had always given me a decent living but in the 16 months since I had been away from the Premiership, the rewards had rocketed to even greater levels.

Many of the players were still earning more than me but, for the first time in my life, I was able to buy things without looking at the price tags. There is probably nothing more over-priced in the world than the hotel mini-bar but that summer in Cannes, little Bella was able to indulge herself on her dad's new-found prosperity.

She must have gulped down £500 worth of Coca Cola from our room – much to Michele's horror. 'You can get it at the super-market for a fraction,' she would moan at me, unable to change the habits of a lifetime.

We celebrated our 25th wedding anniversary shortly after and I was able to treat the entire family to a weekend at the Ritz to mark the occasion, courtesy of my new salary and bonus. I remember Michele and I strolling around Harrods and finding a bathrobe she liked. Cost? £220. 'No,' she said, 'they are just as good in Marks and only cost £45.' Bless her.

There were no such reservations for me, though. I was enjoying myself and after the events of the previous three months, and the turmoil I had just experienced with Stan, felt I had earned a few treats.

We were there while the World Cup went ahead which I

thought might be opportune if something – or, more pertinently, someone – should catch my eye. I would be a car ride or short flight away from having a closer look. But the truth is that unless you can afford the very best – and we were not in the Ronaldo league – I believe World Cup signings can be as misleading as a holiday romance. Sure, they feel great in the sunshine but by the time a wet, cold Wednesday night at Wimbledon comes along... well, you might find yourself wondering what on earth you saw in each other.

And anyway, by the time I came home, I felt I was beginning to make real progress in filling the gaping hole left in the team by Staunton's walk-out.

I had already been successful in signing Alan Thompson from Bolton for £4.5 million, the biggest transfer of my career so far. Thompson had been the outstanding player in a Bolton team that had just been relegated and possessed a sweet left foot at a time when quality players in that position were at a premium. He was now one of the best players outside the Premiership.

We had to fight off strong competition from Leeds for his signature but, again, I was thankful for our UEFA Cup qualification which played a part in clinching the deal.

But Thompson was a midfield player. Still the natural, left-sided defender was missing and at that stage I had no idea how good young Barry was going to be. No, we needed someone and the time was right to follow up the phone calls that had been telling me David Unsworth was available down at West Ham.

No questions about his ability, as his subsequent form has underlined. But West Ham's manager Harry Redknapp was having problems because David's wife was desperate to get back closer to her home city of Liverpool. I spoke at length to his agent, Hayden Evans, and we decided to go for it. A top lad, Hayden – a straight guy who I had always got along with in our dealings over his other Villa players, Julian Joachim and Simon Grayson.

And he was adamant that although there was also interest from Everton, his boy wanted to come to Villa. The Goodison club had not been having the best of times and he felt, career-wise, Villa represented much the best option. He cannot believe he is going to get out of this West Ham situation by landing a move to

Villa, Hayden told me. He was desperate to sign. That's what I wanted to hear. The only demand from me would be that David eventually find a home closer to work. No problem.

West Ham got their money back – £4 million was the fee – and David got his move. Everyone was happy.

Well, for 36 hours at least.

Hayden tells me to this day that when he dropped David off at his car on the night he signed for us, the player looked at him and told him: 'I just want to thank you so much for everything you've done for me. My family are just so thrilled by how it's all turned out.'

That was Thursday, 23 July. The following day we trained in the afternoon – perhaps the key to this whole sorry episode. David came down at about midday and left at around 4.30 p.m. He didn't get home until gone 7.30 – well, everyone in the Midlands will tell you what rush-hour traffic on the M6 is like on Friday evenings.

Saturday morning, 9.45 a.m., and big Dave wants to see me. And he's got a face like you cannot imagine…

'I think I've made an unbelievable mistake,' he says.

'What's that then?'

'I don't think I should have signed for Villa.'

The words echoed around my head for a moment while I tried to unscramble them. Is this a wind-up?

I thought something had gone off in the dressing-room and for one reason or another, it was not going to work out. But he went on to tell me that he had taken two hours to drive to training that day and he had broken all speed limits to do so.

'I've made a mistake. I should have gone to Everton,' he said.

Now I guess I'll never know the full truth. I imagine that he was already starting to think about the journey time from matches down south or in London.

But I tried to dismiss it. 'Don't be silly,' I said. 'It will be fine. You can buy a flat, move down, go home at weekends and then find a house for the family. Your wife will love it down here,' I told him.

'There's no way she will move down here,' he answered.

I felt insulted. The fact that she would not even be prepared to come down and have a look despite the fact that her husband had just signed for Aston Villa... well, that was a lack of respect for us all. I know Brum's reputation but I also know that you do not have to look very far for some beautiful places to live – especially on the kind of money David had just agreed to take from the community's collective pocket. He could buy as many houses as he wanted. This was just unbelievable. He's dismissing the idea without giving it a chance.

I batted it off one more time, hoping it would go away. 'Come in Monday,' I told him, 'everything will be fine.'

But Monday came, so did David – and then he went. Just as quickly. So much for my ethos about players wanting to work hard and mix in together afterwards. And after one appearance for us in a friendly at Wycombe – an appearance that had 'reluctant' stamped all over it – we ended up looking extremely foolish as we were forced to enter into negotiations with Everton about selling him on.

What on earth had I stepped into? This was ridiculous, completely ridiculous. It only seemed like yesterday that his father, his agent and the player himself were adamant he did not want to go to Everton. Now that was the only resolution to the situation that they wanted.

I kept hoping and hoping in the days that followed that it would go away; that he would realize what a good club he had joined. But by then, Everton were chipping away and to everyone's embarrassment, we eventually sold him, somewhat begrudgingly despite the tiniest of profits, to Goodison. I could not help but point the finger at Mrs Unsworth when I was cornered by the press about the whole, sorry episode. But I'm sorry, I still think his wife was too much of an influence.

But then I remember Arthur Cox telling me one day: 'Never – but never – be surprised by anything that happens in football.' Now I knew what he meant. But even Coxy would have been shocked by that one.

CHAPTER 4

'It's not bad news is it?'

For the first time since that phone call from Marion – God, that seemed an age away now and yet it was still less than six months ago – I was feeling the walls starting to close in.

The extra recognition that came with the territory was one thing. I could handle that; in fact, I quite enjoyed it. Tickets for gigs were easier to come by and the invitations to the party scene were forever landing on the mat.

But now there was no respite from the attention, especially from the press. There was nowhere to run, nowhere to hide and there was always a phone I could not switch off. The media were now virtually camped out at Bodymoor Heath wanting a reaction to all of these stories – and the others that lay ahead – and I realized that my pledge to always be up-front and frank about things could now aggravate some sensitive scenarios.

The trouble is, if they film you leaving the training ground saying 'no comment' they have still got something; at times, I could not afford to be seen doing even that.

Dodging The Press became a daily game, one of the ways to release some of the tensions that were now building – and, if I say so myself, I did come up with a foolproof wheeze.

They soon worked out that if they stood by my car and waited there was no way of my avoiding them. What they didn't know was that I would often slip out of a side entrance, straight into one of our vans, lie flat on the floor and be driven out of the training ground. Meanwhile, one of the staff would go to my car and, when asked by the press lads what he was doing, tell them: 'Oh, the gaffer just asked me to fill it up for him.'

He would bring my car to me and I was free to make the great escape while my pursuers were still hanging around in the car park! An hour later, they would still be there and I could never resist ringing one of them to ask why they were still waiting. It was a good laugh at their expense; most of all, it was good therapy.

But their relentless interest was understandable because, on top of all these other events, the biggest story of them all was about to kick off.

It seemed amazing to me that the club had allowed itself to get into such a vulnerable position over player contracts. Incredibly, we had Mark Bosnich, Gary Charles, Riccy Scimeca, Julian Joachim and Mark Draper all going into the final year of their agreements. In this Bosman age of football, that was suicide; financial suicide. All could sit back and walk out for nothing in 12 months time, just like Steve Staunton. The club could be looking at burning 20 million pounds' worth of talent.

Now I don't care whether you think I'm a good manager or a crap manager. But I tell you this. The work I put in that summer in getting those players to re-sign, when they knew they had free transfers and massive pay days beckoning a year down the line, IS one of my best managerial achievements. I saved my employers millions that summer and I am not sure that that has ever been truly recognized.

It was an exhausting business. Non-stop. Even just setting up a meeting was taxing. Mark and Gary both had the same agent, Kevin Mason, who again I do not have a problem with. But – as an example – I would meet him for an hour about Mark and then an hour about Gary. And then it was off to the boardroom to talk for an hour about Mark and an hour about Gary. Then it was back to Kevin for an hour about Mark and... well, you get the picture.

And this was day after day after day, for weeks upon end during that summer. I didn't need all this hassle, especially with our best defender walking out, our record signing and his girlfriend all over the front pages and one of my major signings not realizing precisely where Birmingham was.

But it was omnipresent and it was during all this that I wished I had someone else, someone who could take all this off my shoulders. But there I was, stuck in the middle. It was like a re-run of the day I got the job, as I went from talking to our financial people about what a particular player wanted and then back to the player to make him the offer. Which, of course, was refused and so we set off all over again.

I know this is what I am paid for. But the money involved at football clubs now has surely moved this kind of business out of the football manager's office. Most of us are in the job because we believe we can handle players and blend a team together that might win matches. But this sort of business? I mean, we are talking millions here. It's too much to put on a guy, no matter how many England caps he has. What's that got to do with decisions that could amount to financial suicide for a club?

All I wanted to do was get a team sorted out and prepared for our first game of the new season. But I remember one day having an absolutely blazing row with Gary Charles and throwing him out of my office. It all sprang from these contract talks and I regretted it immediately. I did not want to have bad relationships with my players. I didn't need that. In fact I liked 'Charlo'; I had a lot of time for him and believed he had the capability to play for England again. That's what I wanted to talk about with him. Not row over what his win bonus or appearance money might be.

In the end, those efforts have been rewarded. We got £4.5 million in total for Scimeca and Charles in the months that followed. And for different reasons, we can be thankful that we also struck deals with Draper and Joachim.

But I got nowhere with Bosnich. Not that that surprised me. From day one, I knew that Mark was not going to stay. That was just from conversations and impressions I had developed. I had got to know him well during my previous spell at Villa; I knew what made him tick. I knew he had visions of going to a bigger club, especially abroad, and the financial killing that he could make in the process. He was looking for twice what we were able to offer him.

And why not? He was at the prime age and, as we would soon discover, at the peak of his career – he was not going to let this opportunity pass. Let's face it, we would all have thought the same way.

I tried everything. I tried threatening to let him rot in the reserves for a season. But then I saw him in training and realized that would be cutting off my nose to spite my face. He was, is, a magnificent keeper and was still far ahead of his number two, Michael Oakes.

No, this was one battle I was not going to win. I've got him for a year and I might as well make use of him, I thought. Be content with that. Maybe we will do well enough to persuade him to stay a little longer. It was a long shot but the only way to look at it.

And, anyway, by then I was beginning to fret about another scrap I knew I would struggle to win.

I had barely been in the job a month when I was called to my first meeting with Dwight Yorke and his advisor, Tony Stephens. Hmmm, what was all this about? After the pleasantries had been exchanged, I soon discovered.

Tony said Manchester United were keen to sign Dwight, who still had two years of his contract remaining. Remember, this was back in the March of that season and the rumour-mill had not yet clicked into top gear.

Ah, I thought, they're trying it on. United had not long bought Teddy Sheringham; they had Paul Scholes, Ole Gunnar Solskjaer and Andy Cole all doing well and were now reportedly interested in Patrick Kluivert. Where did Dwight fit in all this?

No, I thought on reflection, Tony was angling after a new contract or, perhaps, to find out whether I would be prepared to sell him and, if so, at what price. United? Get out of here.

I wish.

Dwight was outstanding over those three remaining months of the season. Absolutely brilliant. If United didn't want him before, they sure as hell would now. He was that good. He was again our top scorer but I did not think finishing was the high point of his game. Dwight could control play with his back to goal – fantastic balance, surprising strength and wonderful skills. He threaded everything together for us. Lord please – I do not want to lose Yorke and Staunton in the same summer. That's too much.

The stories started rumbling with increasing frequency but still there was nothing concrete. And he came back to training in early July in fantastic condition and in a bright, upbeat mood. There was nothing to indicate anything was on his mind or troubling him.

I certainly had no complaints and despite all the difficulties, I still felt I had a good team at my disposal. We had finished the previous season like a runaway train and I felt we could pick up where we left off.

But then came the phone call; the call that I knew would change everything. United's chairman Martin Edwards rang my chairman to formally declare his club's interest in Dwight by tabling an immediate £8 million offer.

Shit.

I had been fighting fires all bloody summer but now here was a forest blaze about to engulf me. We called a meeting with Tony after this official approach, where it was confirmed that United were, indeed, intent on taking Dwight. We knew we would get big money – this first United offer made that clear – but if I wanted to keep Dwight, which I did, I would have to take on Man U.

So that's not a problem.

We held them at bay for a while but it became increasingly clear they were not going to go away. A day never seemed to go by without their making a call in some kind of capacity. And now, despite the fact that Dwight was still contracted to us, Alex Ferguson was talking about his interest openly in the papers. I didn't think you were allowed to do that. We started exchanging one or two side-swipes.

But all the time I knew he held the aces. He had the money. And he was offering Dwight Manchester United. Giggs, Keane, Beckham, Schmeichel, Old Trafford, the Champions League; probably the most famous club in the world. And there was me feeling pleased with my little UEFA Cup spot...

I had gone on record as saying that Dwight would not be available unless £16 million were offered. I meant it. That's what Newcastle had paid for Alan Shearer and Dwight was younger and in the same class. But the resistance was weakening around me.

I had to try to find a way out of this and figured there might be one other escape route.

Coxy, inevitably, was on the blower pointing to another solution. 'Is he...' meaning United manager Alex Ferguson '...really going to play Yorke and Cole together? Why don't you go and get Cole?' he was asking me. Arthur was convinced about the United striker. 'If you ever get the chance to work with him', he said, 'take him. Don't hesitate. If you can get him and some cash, do it. If you can get him in a straight swap, take that. Because Andy Cole will score you goals morning, noon and night. He is the kind of player who keeps a manager in a job.' Arthur was adamant.

Maybe that would be a way out. Cole at our place? His United experience had not been entirely convincing thus far. Maybe that would give us a chance, especially if we could get some money as well. And few people, perhaps even Fergie himself at that stage, were convinced that Cole and Yorke would be a workable partnership.

I rang Paul Stretford, Cole's agent, to make some gentle enquiries. 'If Alex makes it clear that Andy is no longer in his plans, there could be an interest,' he told me. 'But if he is still wanted – forget it.'

That Manchester United 'thing' again.

It wasn't to be. Fergie would have none of it. We spoke about other players possibly coming to Villa but Cole was never one of them. Every time I tried to bring him into the conversation, it was a no go area.

Just before we were due to depart for Spain and our final pre-season friendly against Seville, United faxed us a second offer... £10 million. And once again we resisted.

But now, Ferguson was flexing his considerable Old Trafford muscle more and more in the press and speaking constantly about wanting to buy Dwight. And quite clearly it was starting to get to our player. Perhaps Dwight's earlier calm had reflected behind-the-scenes assurances from his camp that the deal would be done. Now, suddenly, the season was bearing down on us and he was still a Villa player.

The chairman joined us on that trip and, when he boarded the coach to the airport, he told me of a conversation he had just had with Stephens. It seemed to contain a veiled threat, he thought, that Dwight was refusing to come. That was very unlike the Yorkey we all knew. Was he beginning to crack?

55

Still we had made our stand and I, for one, wasn't for budging. We've said £16 million and that's what we should aim for. If they come up with that, fine.

In the event, Dwight did turn up, played perfectly well, and even though his body language was not entirely convincing, I returned home wondering if we might, just might, fend this one off.

Make them go away, I prayed. Make United go away, get Dwight back into the groove and then he will forget about it all and remember how much he enjoys life at Villa.

But it wasn't to be.

I knew I had lost Dwight after our first match of the following season at Everton. He was quiet, brooding, coming alive in the last 20 minutes or so but... no, that's not the Dwight we know. We had lost him.

And I soon found out why. The following day, he went public in a Sunday newspaper article saying how he just wanted the chance to join United. He tried to dress it up in sympathetic language but whichever way you looked at it, you knew what he was saying.

It was the Tuesday after the first game that he came to see me and told me face-to-face for the first time that he did not want to play for Villa any longer. He wanted to go to Old Trafford. He wanted the chance to go and speak to them and could not believe that we were denying him that chance.

God that really hurt. I have taken stick for my 'If I had a gun I would have shot him' comment later that week but, I'm telling you, that's how it felt. Dead personal. To me and the players. That's it, I thought, they've bloody won. Dwight, United. All of them.

Well, what's the matter? I thought. Aren't we good enough for you any more? Oh sure, I know we used to be. But now you think you can insult me and the rest of the guys in the dressing-room by just walking out because you're too big for us? He wasn't really, I know; but that's how I felt at the time.

And while I was still reeling from that whammy, United made it a double. The next day a final, very last, take-it-or-leave-it, you-must-be-mad-if-you-turn-this-down offer of £12 million came in from Old Trafford. Now things were getting serious. This was a massive amount that made everybody twitchy.

United were in a hurry because they only had 24 hours before the Champions League deadline for signings passed. Any more delays and Dwight would be unavailable for the first batch of games. And so it was all round to the chairman's house that evening – Steve, Mark and myself – to thrash it out. We talked and talked it through. By now, I too was beginning to think Dwight had to go but I still felt we could get more money. Or that we should at least try.

The chairman's palms, understandably I admit, were getting a little sweaty over the kind of figure that was now staring at us from the fax machine. I think our 'hard ball' had already paid dividends because had I said 'Yes' at the start, I suspect the board might well have accepted £8 million. Nevertheless, the decision would be mine. I didn't have to sell him, they insisted. At the same time, they pointed out, Dwight's value might be halved in a year's time because he would be closer to the end of his contract.

There were big side issues at stake apart from the blunt choice over whether we should sell Dwight Yorke, our most popular player, for £12 million.

How do I replace Dwight? That was tough enough. But this was a terrible message to our fans on the eve of the season. We were saying, sorry, we're not big enough to keep our best players. OK, so we all might acknowledge the reality of the situation but you don't want it rammed down your throat do you?

We agreed to meet again at 10 p.m. that same evening after further discussions between the respective chairmen. In the meantime, I had been visited by my old pal Gordon Smith – yes, the one who should have scored and we all remember who against, don't we? – and we slipped away to TGI's in Sutton Coldfield for a bite to eat.

I used Gordon as my sounding board and told him of the latest developments. Earlier that week, the local Birmingham paper had conducted a phone-poll as to whether Dwight should stay or go. The result had been a resounding vote in favour of his leaving.

But still I was not convinced. Villa Park had been short of an authentic, goal-scoring hero since the League Championship-European Cup winning teams of the early 1980s. A succession of figures had laid a brief claim to the title – Dean Saunders and Alan McInally most recently – without ever pinning it down. Dwight was as close as anyone had been in recent years to continuing the line of Andy Gray and Peter Withe.

He was a fantastic player but his words from the previous day were still burning at me. And after fighting so hard to keep him, the thought of losing him now still ate at me.

What have they got that we haven't got? They had won nothing last season. They are yesterday's force; we're the coming force. Their time has passed. We are going to be hot this season. Couldn't Dwight see that?

I was kidding myself, maybe, but I was still so angry about Dwight's rejection. And we had gone to extraordinary lengths to try to keep him. We had come up with an offer that, for Villa, was mind-boggling. And I mean mind-boggling. By the end of the fifth year of his contract, he could be earning a king's ransom, the biggest pay cheque our chairman would have signed in all his years at the club. But it was that chance to play for United and step out into the Champions League. That's what we could not get around.

So I sat down to eat with Gordon with all this spinning in my head. Was it only five months ago I was trying to shave a few quid off my mobile phone bill at Wycombe or driving at the most economical speeds to keep the mileage charges down? Three times the mobile phone rang and on each occasion it was the man himself, Fergie. Each time, I went outside to the car park to take the call.

The figures that we were discussing were frightening but the wheeling and dealing with the Great Man was not a problem to me. This was what I wanted and what I believed I could do.

All the time I was trying to drive up the price; Fergie was trying to do a part-exchange deal. But Cole was still out of bounds and although I mentioned Solskjaer as a possibility, he was never actually offered to me.

After the third call, I came back to my seat, still in a quandary, still waiting for a sign, still not entirely sure which way to go. By then, the curiosity of the punters in the restaurant finally snapped. Two guys were in the booth next to us and one of them leaned over and said: 'It's not bad news is it?'

'And what would you consider to be bad news?' I asked tentatively, still unsure about the feedback that would come from supporters.

'Well, Yorke staying of course.'

That was it. I took that little exchange as a highly symbolic moment. It was like this guy, picked at random, was telling me what the Villa fans wanted. I don't know his name and I doubt he ever realized the role he played in that night's events. But sod it, I thought; let's stop messing about and let the bugger go. Who are you trying to kid? He's finished with us anyway. Let's do the deal.

The timing was lousy. Twenty-four hours later, the chairman was given a terrible mauling at the club's AGM. It's one of the few times I had seen him shaken. I tried to deflect the flak off him because, given the set of circumstances and Dwight's declared ambitions, it was difficult to imagine there could be another outcome.

But we had little to offer them in return. Despite all the traumas of the summer, I was still wildly enthusiastic about the approaching season. There was money in the bank now for new signings. I was not going to let the disappointment of losing Dwight shatter all the impetus we had built up at the end of the previous season.

And, to be frank, I thought we might have even pulled one over Fergie and United. I think when they paid that amount for him, the whole game issued a sharp intake of breath. I could understand why.

I was not sure that Dwight would be a success at United. Yes, I knew he was a great player. But a great finisher? I was not so sure about that.

I seemed to remember that some people used to claim Jimmy Greaves would only score his hat-tricks against the lesser teams, not the big boys. I am not sure whether that stood up to statistical analysis but I used to have the same reservations about Yorkey.

We would go up to Old Trafford and play United and he would

not have a shot. Then, the following week, we would be home to Southampton and he would score two. I did wonder if he was a big game player.

But maybe that was really a comment on Villa. We could beat everyone else but we couldn't beat the big boys when it mattered – Liverpool, United, Newcastle under Keegan. In my time at the club as coach, that had been the one thing to hold Brian's team back. And it is still the big trick we have to pull off.

And Old Trafford is an unforgiving stage. Cole himself had to come through some difficult criticism before winning over their supporters. As it turned out, Dwight scored twice on his home United debut. It was against Charlton; immediately I thought, see, it's only Charlton.

But those goals did the trick; they took all the pressure away. And we all know what happened after that, don't we?

CHAPTER 5

'Did you see that? Who taught him to do that?'

I love match days. I mean *really* love them. One of the things that puzzled me when I spoke to other coaches and managers was how they considered the day of the game the worst part of the job. They told me how they loved Mondays to Fridays; the training, the banter, the 'craic.' But come match days and the tension would chew them up. The result was now so much the be-all and end-all, all the pleasure of the big day had been spoiled.

But me? No, I love them. Even that tension. It is as close as you can get to feeling like a player again and, having had such a fantastic run since February, I was too in love with the thrill of it all to know any different.

When our opening game of the new season at Everton arrived, however, I was not as confident as I would have liked. Fair enough, we had sold Milosevic and two more of our foreign contingent, Sasa Curcic and Fernando Nelson, by choice. This, I reasoned, was no big loss to me.

Milosevic and Nelson, a right back Brian had brought in from Portuguese football, were talented, no doubt about that. But Savo had made his feelings clear from our very first meeting. Nelson, a lovely, amiable guy, lacked the essential quality I was demanding from everyone.

And Curcic? Well, we're talking about one of the game's authentic mavericks here. In fact, I quite liked the guy. You couldn't help but laugh either with him or at him. And, boy, there was a talent there. But in terms of building a team? No. That was never going to happen. Villa had spent £4.5 million on him and it was another costly failure.

I always felt that, to these particular foreign contigents, Villa were simply another port of call, the next place of employment to stick on their CVs. And that was not good enough for me. I wanted it to mean more than that. I wanted Aston Villa FC to be their life. I wanted total commitment. If it meant getting hurt in that tackle that had to be made or that header that had to be won, then so be it. That's how it had to be. I suspected – no, I knew – these guys would not go the extra mile for us. Their departures had left holes in the squad but not in the dressing-room spirit.

But by now the Yorke affair was coming to a head and had already brought some disruption. One of our most reliable defenders, Ugo Ehiogu, was unavailable, suspended. I still had big hopes for Stan. He had worked hard and shown up well in a pre-season friendly. We all knew he had a battle ahead against the taunting of opposition fans over the Ulrika episode, but he was experienced enough to cope with that. Maybe he would be able to use it, turn it into a positive as if to say: 'I'll show the lot of you.' But then, during a private match against Peterborough at the training ground, he suffered a groin injury.

So he was missing as well and, lest we forget, we had lost Staunton and Unsworth from the specialist left-hand side of our centre back line. We were short of bodies, experienced bodies. That was the big worry. I didn't want to change our system. But we were stretched and had no one of any seniority for that gaping hole in our back line.

It was time to play a hunch; to go with a gut instinct.

On my first night at the club, you may recall, I had watched the reserves play Preston, having already been told by some of the coaching staff: 'Come and have a look at this young kid – he is special.'

The 'kid' they were talking about was Gareth Barry, a 17-year-old we had picked up from Brighton the previous summer. Truthfully, I wasn't over impressed and I certainly didn't think he was a midfield player, the role he had taken on in the second string. But as the weeks and the months rolled by, and I saw more and more of him, I began to share their excitement.

Gareth had finished up the previous season figuring in those final games against Sheffield Wednesday and Arsenal and that had told me a great deal about his temperament. He looked even more impressive during the warm-up sessions and as the opening day of the new season neared, I decided to go with him for the role vacated by Staunton and then Unsworth. I thought he was going to be a good player but there was only one way to find out.

But as the minutes ticked down to that first match, I was doubting the wisdom of my decision. Surely this would be too much for him? Goodison was electric. Everton had brought down Rangers' former manager Walter Smith during the summer and had 20 million pounds' worth of new players in the side. They had big Duncan Ferguson and John Spencer up front, a partnership I fancied would cause problems to anyone, and the Scottish international John Collins new to their midfield. On top of this, Goodison was heaving with anticipation and excitement after their narrow relegation escape a few months earlier – they even had pipers on the pitch before kick-off to welcome Walter.

And into this frenzied atmosphere, I had thrown a pale-faced 17-year-old who looked as if he should be at home on his Playstation. I must be bloody mad, I thought.

Fifteen, maybe 20 minutes into the game I was convinced I had, indeed, taken leave of my senses. Everton were on fire and we could not get out of our half. And in the thick of it all, poor Gareth looked decidedly ill-at-ease, a little boy lost. At the height of the storm, Bozzy rescued the side by adding to his long list of terrific penalty saves for the club – ruining Collins's debut in the process – but we were being given a chasing and this did not seem to be the day on which to back a hunch about young Gareth.

But then something special, extra special in fact, happened. Something which told me deep down that I had been right, that no matter how this turned out, going with this kid Barry had been the correct thing to do.

This ball flew at him at about 80 mph, an absolute missile that most players would have been happy to stick a head onto and send it back where it came from as quickly as possible. But this kid brought it down on his chest, flicked it up, controlled it and then side-footed a pass out to our left wing back Alan Wright on the half volley.

'Christ,' I said to Harry next to me. 'Did you see that? Who taught him to do that?'

You would have struggled to see the great Bobby Moore in his first few years and with all his ability reproduce something like that. I knew at that moment we had a bit of a player on our hands. I suddenly saw a kid not frightened by the atmosphere, not wilting on the stage he was sharing with so many household names, but loving it and revelling in it. Gareth went on to have a terrific match; hell, we might even have nicked a win at the death. But a goalless draw after such a torrid opening was good enough for me. Especially when the bonus had been Barry.

But by the time the next match came along, a Sky TV home game against Middlesbrough, Yorke had completed his move to Old Trafford to further reduce our options. With Stan still unfit, I could get by for that game by asking one of our young defenders, Riccardo Scimeca, to play up front, the position he had held when he first came to the club. But I was beginning to think about who we could bring in with the £12 million.

One of my first thoughts was Dion Dublin at Coventry. A good player but one, I felt, who needed a bigger stage; someone who could be a real, 'big club' player. He always caused problems, was always in the game and every report I had on him suggested he was also a top guy. An excellent pro for whom everyone had a high regard. We didn't have an authentic No. 9 at the club, a leader, a focal point if you like. Yes, Dublin might be interesting. But he had just signed a new deal with Coventry where he was the main man. They were not likely to even consider a bid.

At Blackburn there was Chris Sutton. But same problem, he was their main man. And they were another club with big ambitions for the season. I had spoken to their manager Roy Hodgson about their goalkeeper, Tim Flowers, at one stage and he had treated my enquiry with something bordering on contempt.

To make any deal for Sutton happen I would have to offer stupid, stupid money. I couldn't afford that at this stage.

So what about Europe? Was this the chance to go out and buy a top European star? The trouble here was that everyone I fancied abroad represented anything from a £12 million to £18 million pay-out – and that was before you even got to salaries. But the experience I had had handling the team in those games against Atletico Madrid had really given me the European bug. Having had very different horizons at Wycombe, I was anxious to expand my knowledge and get into the European scene.

I had been to the UEFA Cup final that year and sat behind the great Italian players of my generation, Gentile and Albertini. Those guys were legends to me. I remember watching that game thinking, damn, this could have been us; this should have been us. The whole scene was compelling, exciting. I wanted to find out more about the players, the coaches, their training methods. I really was a rookie, a baby compared to some of my counterparts at other clubs. I had to learn and learn fast.

Was this now an opportunity to import a player who could really capture everyone's imagination?

I had also been back to see Atletico play the previous season after they had beaten us and struck up a relationship with the European striker I coveted most, Christian Vieri, who had played against us in both the quarter-final ties. I watched him score four goals against Salamanca and still finish up on the losing side. He was – is – superb, right out of the top drawer.

In our conversations, it became clear to me that he was dissatisfied with Spanish football; he felt it was a little sloppy. He acknowledged how fortunate Atletico had been in getting past us, how Atletico had trooped off the Villa Park pitch that night barely able to breathe having been given such a chasing. And it was clear he was not adverse to a crack at English football. Dare I think about Vieri?

That was just me daydreaming. Vieri was an £18 million fee and probably half as much again for wages. We just couldn't handle that at Villa. I would be expected to bring in three or four players for £18 million. Mind you, it would have been an investment wouldn't it? His last transfer fee was £32 million which led to accusations that he was little more than a mercenary so-and-so. Christian has Australian heritage, however, and they breed very fierce, very competitive sports folk. I was going to end up having more problems with an Aussie before the year was out.

But how much longer could we go without a new striker? My

mood changed a little after that Middlesbrough game which we won convincingly 3–1. For a start, Riccy played his heart out for us up front. He had to adapt very quickly but he had good technique and had been a prolific scorer as a younger player. He should have scored for us that night but Julian, who was really developing now, got us going with the first goal. I knew that his reputation was blossoming by the phone calls I was receiving from home and abroad.

And I was also being bloody-minded. So Dwight had gone – so what? Sod him. There's other players here who might get a mention now. Young Barry was looking incredible; Gareth Southgate was playing as well as ever and Bozzy was keeping fantastic goal. The dressing room was tight. Everything was ticking over and we already had four points on the board.

And we were keeping it simple, Harry and I. We had a laugh and a joke and mixed-up training with indoor cricket between the English and the Exiles. We didn't have them out there, day in and day out, going through the same routines.

I suppose part of me was silently waiting for the roof to cave in. But it didn't. In fact, we just kept going from strength to strength. We even had Stan back for our third game, at Sheffield Wednesday, and a 1–0 win – another Julian goal – took us to the top of the table for the first time, albeit only for 24 hours. Liverpool hammered Newcastle the next day to knock us off.

But I was pleased to get Collymore through his opening game and interested to see how he coped with his first high-profile appearance since he had 'lost it' in that Parisian bar. He got some stick but no more than he might have expected and was prepared for. And he worked hard, too, without perhaps, having as big an impact on the game as you would like. No, that was still a positive. Stan had coped. And we were winning and the money could stay in the bank until something which felt right took hold of my instincts.

And something did. The next day.

'Let's face it, Merse, no matter what we do, it isn't going to be good enough for you is it?'

Paul Merson smiled at me. And at himself.

'No, you're probably right Gaff.'

That exchange, one of many, still sticks out in my mind. It came at the height of Paul's traumas a year or so ago and perhaps illustrates the difficulties we would have with one of the game's most talented players. When Paul's world, both private and professional, collapses around him, there is very little you can do to keep him sweet.

He joined us in the early days of September 1998, a keynote signing as far as I was concerned. During our victory over Middlesbrough the week before, we had had one dodgy period in the game when, with my boys 2–0 ahead, Boro manager Bryan Robson had brought on two strikers as substitutes and moved Merse into his favourite role, just behind the front players.

I remember Harry turning to me at that point saying: 'This could be trouble. If anyone can play there he can. He's probably the best in the country at it.'

Fortunately, in Ian Taylor, we had a midfield player who is very good at tracking back and shackling that type of player and we limited the damage to Middlesbrough getting back to 2–1 – a goal Paul set up – before Alan Thompson killed off their revival with a third. But Merson kept plugging away to the finish and I was impressed with his attitude on a night when his team were largely second best.

To his immense credit, he had created one of the success stories of contemporary football. He had owned up, in a blaze of publicity, to drink, drugs and gambling problems that were wrecking his life at Arsenal. He had then had to face rejection by his beloved Gunners when the club sold him to Middlesbrough. But from all that despair, he had fought his way back and even revived his international career on Teesside. He had made it to the World Cup in Glenn Hoddle's squad. That for a guy who, by his own admission, had been in the gutter was some come back.

But by the early days of September, the game was buzzing with rumours that all was not well with Paul. He was looking for an 'out' from the Riverside and I was immediately interested. Could this be the one?

First check. I asked Gareth Southgate, who had spent time with him in England camps, for his opinion. Gareth gave me a highly positive response; he was full of praise and enthusiasm for the guy. This was getting interesting.

I remembered the night that Chris Sutton famously turned down an England B appearance and effectively ruled himself out of Hoddle's plans for France '98. The fixture had not been insignificant enough for Merson to captain the team. And he ended up going to the greatest football show on earth, which, most acknowledged, is where his ability belonged.

Other rumours and stories were finding their way back to me. There were claims that the player was riling against the culture at the Riverside Stadium, unsettling Paul because of his well-documented struggles against his addictions. I do not know the truth of them and they had nothing to do with us. But if that meant we had a real chance of getting him, then so be it.

And when I called Robbo it appeared we did – providing the price was right. A few days to-ing and fro-ing unfolded as the haggling over a fee began. Paul was a major figure at Middlesbrough, who had just been promoted back to the Premiership. If Robbo was going to lose him, he wanted a fat fee to offload the angry public reaction.

We struck a deal at £6.75 million. It was a lot of money. But it occurred to me that apart from his obvious ability, Paul had another priceless commodity clearly lacking in my camp. Experience. Especially championship-winning experience. He had done it all with Arsenal and then been the source of inspiration for Middlesbrough's climb out of the First Division. And the way that he had confronted the demons that threatened to destroy his career, his very life, suggested that the guy had a bit about him.

The kind of financial territory I was getting involved in now was mind-blowing. The deal for Alan Thompson, my first big incoming transfer, had been reasonably straightforward. But these negotiations would show that you had to keep your wits about you at all times.

When we got down to the brass tacks of Paul's salary, we were having a major problem meeting the demands. We had come so far down the road towards pulling off what I thought would be an exciting deal but, as the talks with his agent unfolded, the figures were a stumbling block. Damn, I was telling myself, surely I'm not going to lose him now.

Fortunately, when Mark Ansell checked with Keith Lamb, Middlesbrough's Chief Executive, we found that Paul's earnings were significantly lower than the figure we had been quoted. That kind of oversight could have been the difference between Merson signing or not.

I know agents generally have a bad reputation in football but I had had few problems in the past. In trying to get to the bottom of Stan's difficulties, I had built up a good relationship with Paul Stretford. Similarly, Kevin Mason, Hayden Evans and Strewn Marshall. I did not, however, enjoy dealing with Paul's agent, Steve Kutner, in all this and would not mind if I did not have to deal with him again. But he has since taken Ugo Ehiogu under his wing and it appears I may have to.

The excitement of Paul's arrival, however, washed away the sour taste of the preliminaries. I felt the signing was a significant breakthrough. In the past, Villa had not been able to land the big ones – the top internationals with a reputation and a profile. Paul had that and I think the deal made one or two people, both around and far beyond Villa Park's perimeters, sit up and take notice. In the dressing-room, it added to the excitement; the players, as much as anyone, needed convincing about my intentions after watching their mates Staunton and Yorke walk away. If I was to have any chance of re-signing Bosnich, for example, I needed to bring in players such as Merson. And three or four more.

This was all flying through my mind as Merse's signature neared the dotted line – and the immediate buzz was encouraging. Paul joined us on 8 September and, as the news began to spread, the queue of fans waiting outside began to grow. Some even went to the souvenir shop, bought a shirt and had Merson's name printed on it. Some even guessed right and stuck the No. 10 – vacant since Dwight's departure – on the back.

I broke with another tradition that day by inviting those supporters in for the signing in front of the local press. I don't think the 'journos' were happy but it added to the atmosphere and the excitement of the moment. Things were happening at Villa Park and I wanted the world to know it. And that instinct again. It just felt like the right thing to do.

Now I know what you're all thinking. What about the problems? Surely you knew handling Paul was nothing but trouble? You already have Collymore to sort out – why take on another?

Gregory is either a fool or a madman. I knew that would be the whisper behind my back.

Yeah, of course I knew about the baggage that came with him. All the indications at the time were that Paul was in pretty solid shape. He had never moved up and settled around Middlesbrough; now we were bringing him much closer to home. Eventually, he could rent a second place in Birmingham and have the best of both worlds. I felt I could handle it. In fact, at that time especially, I felt I could handle anything. I was buying him for his ability to win matches and whatever came with it I felt I could deal with.

By then, I had already been put through the mill and we were still top of the table. That old, cock-sure Gregory was feeling pretty pleased with himself. I had handled the whole Yorke saga, I was dealing with Bozzy, I had lost Staunton and I had Stan around my neck. But this was just part of the game, especially at a major Premiership club where the big names are to be found. It was what you had to take on and handle if you wanted to succeed.

And, as far as I was concerned, I *was* going to succeed. And the immediate impact of Paul's arrival was fantastic. He responded, the rest of the players responded. He gave us options and a dash of quality we obviously needed.

Now I'd be lying if I did not say there were times when I regretted taking on Paul. I have this thing about 'low maintenance' and 'high maintenance' players. Personalities like Stan and Paul required regular services. Like cars. Paul is one you constantly have to keep checking, handle with care. You can only do that if the bulk of the squad are low-maintenance; professionals you do not have to worry about.

He had troubles ahead of him that he would eventually bring to work. Days when, no matter what we planned or scheduled for training, he would kick against. Days when, because he was down, everyone else had to be down there with him.

But those are balanced by a lot of the positives; his abilities, particularly his exceptional passing range, spring immediately to mind.

It was all part of my learning curve. And the curve was steepening all the time.

CHAPTER 6

'I am *important you know.*
I am not a tourist.'

I had 'sold' Aston Villa to Paul Merson. Was there now a chance I could sell the club to an even bigger fish? Not just an England international. But the England captain himself and one of the most famous names in the European game.

For as soon as the formalities had been completed, there was no time to dwell on Merse's arrival. He had missed the deadline to be eligible for our match the following night when Newcastle, having just appointed Ruud Gullit as their new manager, were in town. Villa Park would be heaving. Fantastic. No wonder I was beginning to imagine even bigger and bolder schemes.

We had already made gentle but not ultimately successful enquiries to Newcastle about Alan Shearer. The Kenny Dalglish reign had just come to a sour conclusion and it appeared that things up on Tyneside were not exactly a bed of roses. I dared to wonder if Newcastle might let Alan go.

New managers sometimes have their own ideas about how they want to play, a fresh approach that frequently bring about changes in staff and direction. As everyone in the game knew, and took great delight in pointing out, Gullit was on record as saying he felt Alan had not been worth the fee Newcastle had paid for him. The subtext was clear: Gullit did not rate England's No. 9. If not, I knew someone who did.

I couldn't get the image out of my head the night before the game, the night of Merse's recruitment. Shearer in our No. 9

shirt. Christ, what a sight that would be. That would rip the lid off the place. We were big enough – or could be big enough – for him, I was convinced of that. In my dreams? Maybe. But...

Perhaps it was part mischief – God knows what my chairman would say if I brought the figures of such a deal to his door – but there was also a genuine desire on my part to really make Villa big time. To stop playing at it. To finally, firmly, conclusively announce our arrival on the Premiership's major stage.

And I knew from within the game that Alan had got wind of our interest. I guess he must have been thinking what was in store for him under Gullit.

So that following night became an occasion all about selling the club and the idea of joining us to Shearer, with Merse sat up in the stands watching. I was desperate that the boys show the Great Man they were not a bad side. If he had dismissed us as a club he did not want to come to, I wanted him at least to have second thoughts. I wanted us to play well and show him what we were all about. A real team. The stadium was packed, the excitement you could smell in the air. I didn't say anything to the players but perhaps they sensed something because they caught the mood perfectly.

Young Hendrie, now flourishing as a genuine international prospect, got what would be the only goal of the game from the penalty spot and, as well as we played in taking the game to Newcastle in the first half, it was what happened in the last 15 minutes that had my chest thumping with pride.

Newcastle laid siege to our goal but we just would not crack. The tremendous team spirit we were now enjoying really came home to me that night. It really pulled us through. The boys flung heads and legs in the way of everything; I remember little Alan Wright diving full length and getting one in the face to stop Shearer scoring. Everyone gave it everything they had and when the final whistle came, we were top again with 10 points from 12. Villa Park erupted. Incredible.

I was so proud and I wanted to tell the boys before such an intense moment was lost. Sometimes, moments such as those are gone too quickly. You go off; you shake hands with the opposition; you get down the tunnel to the dressing-room and the players begin to disperse; they start to switch off, to relax. So before that process began I wanted to grab them all and remind them what they had achieved so far. The only place to do it was out on the pitch where I pulled the boys into a huddle.

'Do you realize what you've done?' I told them. 'You've just beaten Newcastle, the first time Villa have done that in the Premiership. Sometimes, when you're in the thick of it you just don't realize what's happening. The next moment the season's over. And then you blink and your career is over. But you've just died for each other out there and you're on top of the Premiership because you deserve to be.'

It was impromptu stuff but I hoped it caught the moment. I think it did. We gathered more strength as a group from that night as the following weeks would underline. I knew Shearer wasn't watching but I also knew he must have felt this old stadium reverberating that night. He is a great player but I knew, more than anything, he loved the team ethos. 'Look at this mate,' I was saying to myself. 'How could anyone not want to be a part of this?'

I kept the huddle going a moment longer.

'What a feeling this is,' I added. 'Let's keep it. But it starts again now. It's Wimbledon on Saturday and we start getting ready – *now*. This game has gone. It's not about going out and getting pissed tonight. Get the right food inside you. Get the right rest. Warm down well. Together. Because if we want to keep this feeling, we have to do this all over again.'

Sadly, nothing would come of my Get Shearer campaign. I phoned Gullit the next day and dropped the Shearer idea into the conversation. He didn't say 'yes' – but he didn't say 'no.' But I imagine the coming weeks told him that to sell Alan Shearer would be the equivalent of signing his own death notice. And we were never able to get any more daylight out of St James's Park from our enquiries.

But that would be Shearer's loss; that was my attitude. The night had still been an intoxicating experience and the 'vibe' spilled over from one match to the next. Merse's debut arrived and we beat Wimbledon. And as I watched from the dug-out, I was given another hefty shove from the fates above. No matter what happened, I couldn't seem to do anything wrong.

The Friday before that game we were practising penalties and while Hendrie, our scorer from the Newcastle match, had seemed hesitant, Alan Thompson was smashing them in to all parts of the goal. He looked awesome. And that was still on my mind when, lo and behold, we were given another spot-kick in the first half against the Dons.

I felt Hendrie would be under massive pressure after scoring in midweek; Wimbledon would have sent someone to watch the match and they would have noted what side he put it. It would be a game of double bluff. The images of an uncertain session from Hendrie the day before flashed back into my mind. Impulse took over. From the bench I got a message just in time for 'Tommo' to take it. He did. And he missed.

Shit, I thought. That will teach you to be a smart-arse.

But before I had time to dwell on that cock-up, the ref gave us yet another penalty – a dodgy one too – and up stepped Merse to calm everyone's nerve. He stroked his shot to the top right hand corner; Neil Sullivan palmed it down but Merse followed up and tapped home the rebound. That was the kind of experience I wanted. It set us up for a steady convincing win, Taylor adding a second and our work rate restricted Wimbledon to a few bits and pieces but little more.

We were defending brilliantly. We had not played as well as we could but we had never looked like losing after going in front. And that was very satisfying because I knew there would be a lot of games like this coming up. Games you have to win but don't necessarily play well.

By now the media was getting an idea of its main themes for the season. Yorke and Cole at Manchester United. Would Arsenal do them again? And what about the galaxy of foreign stars Luca Vialli was gathering at Chelsea? Oh yes, and what on earth did that bunch at Villa think they were doing?

It was, of course, ridiculously early to be talking of a Championship challenge but the absence of any, shall we say exotic, foreign players in the Villa team was seized upon as a story worth following. I was genuinely happy to promote it because I felt that anything was possible with the camaraderie I was experiencing every day and in every match. It does make a difference when your mates will go the whole hog – and then some – in a game. It's the same in any work place. Why should it be different on a football pitch? If you see a pal dodging a tackle, then you automatically adopt the same attitude.

And Villa's experiences with their recent foreign signings, especially the east Europeans, had not been altogether happy. Ultimately, playing for Villa was a job. I didn't want that. I wanted it to be everything and all that mattered to them.

That's what I was getting and it continued to serve us well. For example, we started off on the UEFA Cup trail in the next game with a home leg against a small Norwegian club, Stromsgodset. This was important stuff. The one setback I still could not forgive myself for was cocking up in the competition last season. Having got to the quarter-finals, this lot could have won it, I kept thinking. I wanted to make amends. This tie, on paper, offered as good a start as we could have hoped for.

We knew little about Stromsgodset save for the fact that they were well organized and would raise their game at Villa Park. But they were a team who, to be honest, would struggle to hold their own in our Second Division. No problems, surely?

Well, we had a nightmare to begin with. We defended like amateurs and went two goals down. The Norwegians couldn't believe it; neither could we. I was hopping up and down on the touch-line and the fourth official, from Germany, was constantly on my case, telling me to sit down.

I snapped after a while. I told the guy to shut up in some fairly blunt Anglo-Saxon and reminded him: 'You are not important.'

Well, he did shut up. For about 10 seconds. And then he tapped Harry on the shoulder and said, 'I *am* important, you know. I am not a tourist.'

Oh dear, the shape of things to come.

Even Harry, who I had never seen 'lose it' with anyone, snapped that night. 'Will you shut the fuck up,' he screamed at him at one stage. For Harry to lose his rag like that meant something had to be wrong.

I wasn't panicking, though, because I always felt we could win over there. But we needed to get at least one goal back that night. Gary Charles obliged but then, in the last five minutes, our young substitute Darius Vassell popped in two more. We had turned the match upside-down and, again, that spirit, that will-to-win and give up nothing, the infectious desire not to let your

team-mates down… it swept everyone along and turned a potential disaster into an exciting victory. No, you can keep your
foreign mercenaries. I loved these boys and I wanted to stick
with them.

And so it went on. Leeds at Elland Road; a hard-fought goalless draw. Again the defence was outstanding. Southgate and
Ehiogu were immense and young Barry continued to surpass all
expectations. Behind them Bosnich was looking unbeatable.
After the match George Graham, then Leeds manager, claimed
both teams would do well to finish in the top six. Bugger that,
George, I thought when I heard about his remarks; I want more
than that.

Derby next, at home: a surprise top-of-the-table clash as we
went into the game first and second in the Premiership. There is
definitely something about being top of the League. It's pressure
but it's a lovely pressure, very enjoyable. I knew the fans were
loving it because after some early scepticism, they were beginning to be converted by what they were seeing. We were not playing brilliantly but we were proving bloody hard to beat.

And that's a start for anything.

I remember Derby knocking the ball around well to begin with
but without getting through a defence that continued to look
formidable. And then we got a break in the centre-circle and
Merse pulled away to come out on top of a one-on-one and score
an equalizer. Always the sign of a class striker, that. If I'm not
mistaken, Derby struck a sticky patch after that and dropped to
sixth or seventh and I often wonder whether the same would
have happened to us had we lost our unbeaten run.

The switch from domestic to European competition was proving a problem because Merson had arrived too late to be eligible
for our UEFA Cup team. But against Derby, we at last got Stan
back in the side after a long struggle against his groin trouble.
We eased him in for 20 minutes at the end in the knowledge that
he would be starting against Stromsgodset in the return leg.

This was feeling good now. I had two £7 million strikers in
Collymore and Merson, and young Julian continuing to blossom.
I felt that promised goals and I was still convinced at this stage
that I was doing quite a good job with Stan. Some of my reservations from the end of the previous season and his summer

trouble had vanished; he seemed to be mixing well and he wasn't causing any problems.

This image of his being distant and aloof was not a reality. OK, there were some training days when he did not seem to be 'with us' and there were occasions when I would speak to him and just find a vague, distant expression looking back at me.

I admit that at the back of my mind there was a nagging worry that something could happen at any time with him that I could not control. There was a grey area where I wasn't sure what he was thinking. I knew most of my players pretty well now; their strengths, their weaknesses, their likely reactions to certain situations. My previous spell as coach had helped in that regard. But I could not quite work Stan out. Still, I didn't find it hard to talk with him, which was the main thing, and maybe, just maybe, this excitement had got to him. I mean, he would not want miss out on this? We'll see.

The initial signs on his comeback were encouraging. He scored a hat-trick in Stromsgodset, including a first goal not too dissimilar to that memorable effort against Atletico Madrid. I was not really aware at this stage that he was having any off-the-field problems but during his long spell on the treatment table, he had developed a close bond with our physio, Jim Walker.

He was a top man, Jim, well-respected throughout the game, a physio first brought to the club by Graham Taylor but kept on by a succession of other managers because of his expertise and experience. And that says an awful lot about the guy, really. He had come to be regarded in a similar light by another Villa Park star whose injury problems required a delicate, understanding touch, the great Paul McGrath. So it was a nice gesture by Stan to dedicate his goals that night to Jim for helping him through a tough period of his life. Now he was ready to rumble and, of course, it all made for fantastic copy for the press lads.

Yes, it was a good trip, that. We won 3–0 which meant the tie finished exactly as I had initially anticipated – although I had had grave doubts after half an hour of the first leg – and we kept the mood light all along.

I had Harry to make sure of that. The hotel where we stayed had a promotional car in the foyer and I'll never forget the day of the game, coming down to breakfast and finding my entire first team squad in stitches. No wonder – there was Harry, underneath the chassis, legs only visible shouting 'Wrench' and 'Spanner' to an imaginary assistant. God knows what the good citizens of Stromsgodset made of it but the bloke's priceless, I tell you.

And another footnote – the fourth official that night gave a textbook performance of how that job should be handled. With a laugh. He took the mickey out of us all night but in a gentle, unobtrusive way which both benches warmed to.

It was pretty cramped on the touch-line – Stromsgodset had a Conference-style stadium – and both sets of coaches had to keep asking him to move if and when the play went into the corners.

When I asked him to step back for the umpteenth time he looked at me and said, 'Don't worry. Sit down. I'll tell you if anything interesting happens.'

Then it was, 'Come on, you see your team all the time. I want to look at them.'

He was a good laugh, right up to the point where both Stromsgodset and ourselves wanted to make two or three substitutions, all at the same time. His little board of lights couldn't handle it and he looked at me pleadingly and said: 'What do you want to change the team for? You're winning 3–0.' Priceless, that. Breaks all the tension. I wish we could have taken him home with us. At the finish, he asked us if he could have a shirt; we loaded him up with enough souvenirs to open a shop.

Proof, if any were still needed, that I was locked in some kind golden period of my professional life arrived over the next few days. I came home to be told that I had won the Manager of the Month award for September. It had still not been a year since I left Wycombe and yet here I was standing – briefly I grant you – over the giants of my trade such as Fergie and Arsene Wenger. With the ever-increasing influx of foreign coaches and managers, some folk in the press were getting really carried away by now and talking about me as a future England coach. What a joke.

Actually, being the big-headed sod that I am, I was a bit aggrieved that I had not won the award at the end of the previous season. In both March and April, we had won all but one of our games and yet each time 'The Arse' had stuffed us by winning all six as they put together their incredible double-winning run.

But it is an intensely personal moment. Yes, you know that you are just the figurehead; that the award salutes the players and the staff who have all played their part. But when you get home and sit down and look at the little trophy they give you... well, it feels personal and I was chuffed to bits.

I also knew straight away that this, more than anything, would be a test of the Gregory golden patch. By tradition, the award guarantees the recipient defeat in his next game.

Our's was at Coventry, local rivals who love giving the bigheads up the road a bloody nose. Happily, they had not done it too often but when they did, boy you knew about it.

But we even survived this test of footballing folklore. We played well and picked up a 2–1 win helped, I must admit, by a second goal created by Merson from a hopelessly offside position. It was ridiculous really but yet another signal of how things go for you when you get into a groove like this.

It also reminded me of one of my pet theories. I truly believe that, sometimes, decisions will go for or against you based entirely on who you are. Fans often complain about it and it generally gets laughed out of court. Well, I happen to agree with them.

During this spell, we seemed to be getting favourable decisions by the truckload. We had never had so many penalties for a start. If being at the top of the Premiership and having Paul Merson on your side could ever give you the benefit of the doubt, then it did at Highfield Road that afternoon. In that incident I was in line with the linesman and it looked to me that Merse was so far offside it was embarrassing. I didn't think it was a difficult decision to call.

Many managers have their own pet theories on what can influence officials. I remember Coxy advising me never, but never, to take the team sheet into the referee before the game. 'If you don't,' he would argue, 'they cannot form an opinion about you. They can't like you, they can't dislike you.' It's not something I agree with but I take his point.

But this was now the first game of October and we drove away from Highfield Road still unbeaten, still top. My elation would have drained away in seconds, however, had I known that night just how crushing a blow had been inflicted upon our season during that game.

Mid-way through the second half, Bosnich had saved at the feet of a Coventry forward and had to be treated for an injured shoulder. He got through the game in some discomfort and we figured that he might miss a couple of weeks. It was annoying but that should not be a problem.

Throughout this undefeated sequence, Bosnich had been in outstanding form, certainly the best I had ever seen from him. He had only conceded two League goals, against Middlesbrough and that day at Coventry, and was dominating matches. He had a great rapport with his defenders and was particularly commanding whenever he came out for crosses.

Defenders love that from their keeper. The English game probably delivers more crosses into the penalty areas than any other domestic football in the world and I like my keepers to come and catch them. When they take control, defenders don't have to head it; the attack is over; everyone can calm down. Pressure stays on you when central defenders have to head it.

But whenever Bozzy came for the ball, that was it. Panic over. He was loud, brash, arrogant and bloody brilliant at his job. And while there were times when he drove us all nuts, we could put up with it because we loved him. Loved him to death. Also, he had tremendous agility for a big man; in fact, I can still remember, clear as day, a breathtaking save he made in that Coventry match from Steve Froggatt, low to his bottom left-hand corner, as we clung to our points.

We didn't know the full extent of the problem that night. We had young Michael Oakes to go in and deputize and he had proved himself to be a more than able number two keeper in the past. But Mike had not been first choice for a long period and even he was unaware of how this was going to affect him.

Mike has a lot of attributes but he was not an all-round keeper of Bozzy's stature. He certainly couldn't dominate his area like his senior partner; neither was he the same brash character, constantly jabbering at the defenders in front of him. Mike is a great shot-stopper, and would prove that immediately in the next game at West Ham, where he helped us collect a goalless draw with some fine saves.

That was quite an afternoon. The Hammers were my dad's first love football-wise and it had always pained him that he had not made it there. I arranged for my mum to come to that game and, as I made my way to the press conference afterwards, I bumped into her.

Instead of leaving her waiting, I managed to slip her past the 'jobsworth' on the press door and took her with me. If I want to do something, I'll bloody well do it as long as it doesn't cause anybody any harm.

'This is my mum,' I said proudly as she stood next to me. It was a spur-of-the-moment thing but the press lads lapped it up. This guy's so relaxed he even takes his dear old ma to press conferences. You know the sort of thing. I think Gregory-mania possibly peaked that weekend. Some of the big hitters from the tabloids were there and Monday morning brought another dollop of 'FEC' headlines – Future England Coach.

That really was rubbish. You need massive experience and you need credible success for that post. It doesn't guarantee anything but it does mean you can stand in front of the best players in the country without them looking back at you and saying: 'Oh yeah, and what have you done?' I failed on both counts. I had only been at this a few months and was not stupid enough to believe my own publicity.

And what is more, they didn't know, and I didn't know, that the first seeds of our downfall had already been sewn. Mike performed superbly. But we didn't have that strong personality behind the defenders any more and, as the weeks without Bozzy became months, the impact was marked. I will forever wonder how things might have turned out if that big, daft, loud-mouthed Australian had not got injured.

CHAPTER 7

'Exit Doug – to the sound of breaking china.'

After our win at Coventry it was difficult to imagine that life could be any sweeter. This was turning into the club's best start for years and we had by then managed to iron out the one niggle that had been unsettling me. My contract.

I was effectively still operating as the 'chairman's gamble', the guy brought in on a hunch when the club were in a jam, the patsy who could still be jettisoned for next to nothing at the first sign of trouble should a big name present himself to the board. Behind all the excitement that was reverberating around the club now, it left me feeling strangely insecure. It was time to look after number one.

The contract I had originally signed was, not surprisingly, heavily loaded in the club's favour. I felt it was time to redress the balance. Target one – avoiding relegation the previous season – had been met. And we had thrown in a bonus of a UEFA Cup place that no one in their wildest dreams could have imagined the previous February.

Now here we were, top of the table and with Villa Park gradually running out of seats to accommodate the fans. All this despite the loss of two world class players, Staunton and Yorke, which had brought £12 million into the kitty and saved probably as much again in the wages we would have faced forking out had we been able to keep them.

No, there's no point hiding your light behind a bushel. I

wanted a rise and a longer deal. In fact, I was little disappointed that I had to go looking for it. I felt my efforts might have at least prompted an approach from the board. It didn't come.

I didn't particularly enjoy asking – I had no agent and was taking all this on myself – but I had to. Eventually, I was given my first offer from the chairman, a straight £50,000 increase with no time extension. They could still get rid of me at the end of that season if they so wished. I rejected it.

Fortunately, we kept on winning and that helped to strengthen my hand. Johan Cruyff famously remarked that the manager should always be the top earner at the club, even if it was by just one peseta. He is the man who has the job of keeping it all together – all those different egos, different personalities.

We were now signing players on five-year deals with £1 million salaries, but I was nowhere near that territory. I wasn't asking to be. But there were managers in the Premiership who were being rewarded at that level – some who were not winning that many games as it turned out – and I was expected to compete with them. I was not asking for £1 million a year or anywhere near it but I was asking for recognition of what had been achieved since I came in.

Negotiations went on a long time but I stuck to my beliefs and bit by bit, we got there. A three-year deal with dramatically improved guaranteed remuneration. If you want to know the figure research the newspapers because it was widely reported in the press at the time. But I had to fight for it and for some time I felt that represented a lack of appreciation for the job I was doing.

Still, it was sorted by the end of September and I felt much more relaxed. But did I say life could not get any sweeter? I was wrong. A knock on my door at our Bodymoor Heath training ground before our next game continued the avalanche of good news.

It was the skipper. Gareth Southgate.

'Can I have a word, Gaff?'

'Sure, come on in.'

The previous year, Gareth was one of a crew of leading players who had publicly expressed their concern about the club's direction and ambition. It had been unsettling, both for Brian and the team, and possibly contributed to the unease that settled on the dressing-room and, ultimately, my old boss's departure.

'Well, I've been thinking about a longer deal,' he said. 'I've known you as a coach and a manager for some time now and I like... '

'... Shut up. Don't say another word. I'll sort it out.' I did not need to hear any more. I didn't want to waste another second because this was a big moment for me, bigger than Gareth probably realized. If I had had to go looking for the seal of approval from my gaffer, here it was presented voluntarily, free of charge and without any prompting by the most respected player in the club.

The skipper believes in me, I thought. That was worth its weight in gold.

The negotiations were swift and painless. Gareth didn't want add-ons for England appearances or anything else, which a lot of players in his position would have claimed and probably been given. We offered him what we felt he was worth and he was not interested in haggling or bargaining. Instead, it was 'Yep, that's fine, let's do it.' He's like that. A very uncomplicated person and one of Brian's best signings, if not the best. My predecessor takes a lot of credit for bringing Gareth to the club and then helping him become one of the best defenders in the country. We also landed ourselves with a fantastic professional who commands respect from across the game. A five-year contract meant that we could count on his services for the foreseeable future and that was another terrific plus for me.

So we continued to keep our press corps busy. Gareth signed his new deal on 16 October; by then the fans were still catching up on another significant addition to the squad just 24 hours earlier.

Steve Watson was a player I had admired from a distance for some time. He was a typically tough Geordie – yes, he actually does train in a T-shirt in the middle of January, although not with a can of Newcastle Brown in his hands – who could play in a variety of positions. I wanted to start building up the squad's strength and flexibility and this guy seemed perfect to me.

But his strongest position was as a right back and I was beginning to get exasperated with Gary Charles, our current No. 2.

Not that I didn't rate him – quite the contrary – Gary is a big talent and a superb athlete. But I always felt I was waiting for him.

I told him he could get back into the England team if he played to his proper level. But he lacked consistency and was erratic. I also felt that he lacked a real desire, a real hunger to get back to the form he had displayed at Nottingham Forest earlier in his career.

Toss the pebble of Watson into the water, I thought, and see if the ripples bring out the best in Charlo.

I was surprised that Newcastle let Steve come to us because he was a hugely popular figure in his native city. But it was a very straightforward signing and Steve's commitment was evident from our first meeting. There were no demands for a big pay-rise and an immediate search for a new house in which to settle his young family was undertaken. He was going to throw his body and soul into the club and that was fantastic for me.

We did the deal, at £4.5 million, and I sat back to watch the shockwaves – hopefully – jerk Gary towards his best form.

It didn't happen. I thought I had chucked a bat up his nightie but instead he turned over and went back to sleep. He seemed to become even more laid back, as if he did not believe Steve was good enough to take his place. I held the new boy back for a few games before he took over from Gary, who never really fought for his place. A few months later, he would be sold to Benfica for £1.5 million. And I will always believe there was so much more to come from him.

Still there was money in the bank. Enough perhaps for one more big hit. We were up there with the big boys, United, Arsenal and Chelsea, but our squad by comparison was still painfully thin.

A couple of weeks later, another one of those 'instinct' moments arrived. Again, another knock on my door, this time at Villa Park. Stridey poked his head around.

'Have you seen Blackburn are in for Dublin?' he asked. He was talking about Dion Dublin, the guy I had initially thought about in the immediate wake of Dwight's departure.

'Yeah,' I answered, curious as to why Steve should bring this up. 'Why do you say that?'

Steve responded: 'Well, he's not bad him, is he?'

Now Stridey is one of the most discreet guys you can meet in this game. In fact, I must point out at this stage just how much I have appreciated his help during all my time at Villa. Whenever I was down or disappointed about something, I could go to Steve and he would always point me in the right direction. Usually after he had taught me the chords for some song or another. And he never interferes football-wise. Unless you ask him to. He gets on with his job and does not offer any opinion on the game without being invited. And yet here he was clearly itching to push Dublin.

'Do you think we should go for him, then?'

That was all the invitation Steve needed to put in his twopenny's worth, not realising that in doing so he was confirming my thoughts of a couple of months before.

'Oh yeah, I love him. I think he would be great for us.'

Shall we go for it? No question. Now that I knew we had a member of the board already in the camp, I was seized by one of those 'If it feels right, do it' moments. We went straight down to the chairman's office, conscious that we may have to move fast. Blackburn's offer was £6 million and the radio bulletins were telling us Dion was due for talks that evening. And, despite our financial success of the last 12 months, it was a fair outlay. I wasn't too sure the Old Man would go for it.

But we did not have to do any kind of selling job on the chairman. He was equally keen.

So think about it. OK, he's 29. But balanced against that was his track record. He has scored goals consistently for Coventry teams who have struggled to avoid relegation. That's a good sign.

Look at Villa teams who had been successful in the past and the type of players they had. Here was our 1998 version of Peter Withe. He led the line well, he was dangerous at set-pieces and yet excellent at defending from them. On top of that, he had proved himself repeatedly to be equally adept playing at the back. So there is a lot of mileage in him.

And he was a leader. A leader of men, a leader of a team. He was an authentic No. 9 with many of the old-fashioned qualities still revered on the Holte. He would be another string to our bow. Wow! Merson, Collymore and now Dublin at the club. With little

JJ as well. I was starting to get excited at the prospect of pulling off this transfer.

I felt that as soon as we could establish our interest with Coventry, we would have a strong chance. I thought we could out-flank Blackburn, who were struggling at the time. But I knew Newcastle were in there as well. And there will always be an appeal for players to go up there. Would Dublin want to go and play alongside Shearer? Who wouldn't?

It was that same day we heard about the clause in Dion's contract at Coventry which would cause so much trouble and discord. Their chairman, Bryan Richardson, was explaining on the radio why Coventry had to accept an offer for one of their best players.

Under the terms of Dion's new contract, he revealed, they were honour-bound to inform the player as soon as any offer came in at £5 million or above. He had the right to speak to the interested club.

So we went in at £5 million – and all hell broke loose. Richardson accused us of an illegal approach, claiming we had contravened the rules of approach, that by knowing of this £5 million clause we must have tapped up the player unofficially. He should have just kept his mouth shut instead of broadcasting it all over the media. It was nonsense, as was eventually acknowledged by the FA.

But there's something curious about the relationship between Coventry and Villa. We don't particularly hate them but, blimey, they hate us. And this seemed to fuel the enmity that was now dragging out the deal. Coventry would not allow us to speak to Dublin until we had matched Blackburn's £6 million. We stuck to our guns, insisting £5 million was all we were required to offer.

In the background, I detected some highly-competitive rivalry between the two chairmen. I must admit that as this impasse dragged on, I was still chuckling over a story that came back from the boardroom at Highfield Road following our win there a couple of weeks earlier. Legend has it that our man, scooping up the printed results and table sheet just before leaving, waited until he had everyone's full attention and then loudly announced: 'I'll just take one of these with me so I can check where we are in the table on the way home.' Ouch! And

'Do you know what you're doing?' Arthur Cox was, as usual, straight to the point.

©Allsport

'Anything catches your eye, jot it down – on the back of a bus ticket if needs be.' More invaluable advice from Terry Venables.

©Mark Leech

©Empics

'When the rest of the game treated me like something it had scraped off the bottom of its shoe . . .' Brian Little (above) rescued me from the scrapheap after the Portsmouth fiasco. My collection of rejection letters (right)

The chairman and his gamble. Invited to sit in The Big Chair by Doug Ellis.

'So Stan can't be the problem then?' Collymore delivers an epic performance and scores our first goal in my first game against Liverpool.

A contented man. Liverpool have been beaten 2-1 – perfect end to a perfect week.

Straight into Europe and Atletico Madrid. What I knew about the Spaniards could be restricted to two words – 'very' and 'little'.

We had a set way of playing at Villa and there was no reason to change. We would stick with a sweeper.

Alone again, naturally. Back into Europe and a walk on the beach before our tie with Celta Vigo in Spain. We won 1-0 but the tie had a sting in its tail.

'Let's do the deal – let him go.' An echo from the past – Dwight Yorke in claret and blue.

©Mark Leech

'No matter what time I get to my desk of a morning, I always imagine the Great Man has got there before me.' Sir Alex Ferguson, the guvnor.

©Allsport

'He had done it all with Arsenal and then been the source of inspiration for Middlesbrough's climb out of the First Division.' After signing Merson for £6.75m.

Dion Dublin joined to great effect and I still had Stan up my sleeve. Dion Dublin opened his account (above) with two goals on his debut against Spurs.

'So what's all the fuss about this management lark? It's easy isn't it?' The pride before the fall . . .

'I wish they would believe in themselves as much as I believe in them.' Embracing Dion after a 0-2 deficit to the mighty Gunners had been turned into an epic 3-2 triumph. Simon Grayson (left) and Ian Taylor show their support.

exit Doug to the sound of breaking china! You can imagine the last thing Richardson wanted after that was to sell his best player to us.

Had the conflict gone 'legal' I still maintain our lawyers would have had the easier time in court. But eventually everyone calmed down and sanity prevailed. We ended up paying £5.75 million for Dion – that was £750,000 more than we had to but it restored some goodwill into the proceedings.

Dion and his agent, Strewn Marshall, handled themselves brilliantly. All my theories about the player's character were quickly borne out. The money was not the overriding issue for him. He just wanted that stage, to push himself even further if possible. I knew from day one that we had signed a diamond.

And I've still got his shirt, stored away at my house, from his debut game against Spurs. It will be lovely when I'm a wrinkly old grandad to get it out and think back to the day 'DD' played his first game for me.

He scored twice in a 3–2 victory over Tottenham; he actually had a hat-trick because TV replays would later show that a third goal ruled out for offside was, in fact, good. But you can't have everything.

And he had a terrific effect on everyone around him, especially Stan. Stan scored the other, by the way, and made the valid point later of how much he enjoyed not playing the role of main target man. Now, with Dion taking so much weight off his shoulders, he was free to roam out wide. For different reasons, that partnership did not quite work out as it might have done. But for that moment, the weekend at least, we felt as if we were really in business. We had been solid and strong and effective, working like Trojans, playing at capacity. But Dion's arrival now gave us another weapon in the armoury. Now, I felt, we had real goal power; the opposition would not know where we were coming from next.

And we needed that lift Dion gave us because, two days before he signed, our European hopes had crashed against the Spanish team Celta Vigo. And that was the first real body blow the team had suffered.

Celta were another side I admit to knowing little about before we faced them. Neat and tidy, we were told, but with ageing players. Unfortunately, they were bloody superb ageing players and their team were to peak that season as we discovered to our cost.

I don't think I had ever been more relaxed before a game than our first leg, in Spain, a couple of weeks earlier. I felt I was surrounded by good players and even though I was having to chop and change the team for domestic and European matches, I was the happiest manager in the country.

The players reminded me why as well as they appeared to do all the hard work by winning 1–0 out there, Stan creating a goal out of nothing which was superbly taken by young Joachim. A tremendous defensive operation, topped off by that shot-stopping of Michael Oakes to which I referred earlier, did the rest. We could barely get out of our half for the last third of the game but... well, by then the bigger the challenge, the greater the odds, the more the players seemed to respond.

But they floored us at Villa Park. Our first defeat of the season, 3–1, closed the door to the excitement of Europe. I badly wanted another one of those Atletico nights – only this time with a different outcome – but I would have to wait. We had one or two moments early on which might have changed the tie, but I'm not going to deny Celta their due. They were terrific, gave us a lesson in keeping the ball and deservedly went through leaving us stronger and wiser for the experience.

A crop of their players had impressed me and we immediately took the opportunity to keep an eye on them. One player, Revivo, a left-sided attacking midfielder, particularly caught my eye. Was he someone we could go for? They eliminated Liverpool in the next round and I went to Anfield to see for myself. Revivo scored a fantastic winning goal. Yes. Keep your eye on him, I thought.

There are some moments that make this job the best in the world. And not just the obvious things, like winning games. There are quieter, more private episodes that you would not swap for the world.

Like, for example, the day I could call Lee Hendrie into my office and tell him he was in the England squad. The big boys club, that is; not the juniors. We also had Gareth Southgate, Paul Merson and Dion Dublin called up to play against the Czech

Republic that November and I had the three of them in my office at Bodymoor when I sent for young Lee.

I told Gareth and the boys the news and they were naturally delighted for the lad, whose face was a picture of puzzlement when he came into my office to find us all there.

'I thought you might like to meet your new team-mates,' I said to him.

I could see Lee wondering what on earth I was talking about. 'In the England squad, that is.'

God, his face was a picture. He only looks 12 at the best of times but when he realized what I was saying to him, his face lit up like an eight-year-old's on Christmas morning. Coaches and managers will tell you there is no greater reward than seeing young players develop to the point where they get *the* call.

But as our magnificent start unfolded, we were getting used to this kind of attention. On one occasion, though, it rebounded back on us big time.

Gareth Barry's performances had been so outstanding that not only had he continued to hold down his Premiership place but the then England coach, Glenn Hoddle, had invited him to join the seniors for training in October as they prepared for European Championship qualifying games.

The young man had become one of the stories of the season and rightly so. But back at Villa Park, we were still waiting to find out what we would have to pay Brighton, with whom he had started his career, for his services.

Well, when I say started his career, I am speaking in the loosest possible terms. For Aston Villa were about to be manipulated by today's transfer system.

Since the previous summer, we had been waiting to go to a League tribunal to sort out a compensation figure with Brighton. But the scheduled hearings kept being put off – you can imagine what these tribunals are like. Someone was having a pacemaker fitted, someone was having their hearing-aid sorted out – the usual stuff.

Of course, by the time October arrived, Gareth was rightly regarded as one of the brightest young prospects in the country. And of course, the more his reputation blossomed, the more Brighton seemed to expect in compensation.

Suddenly we were hearing all this talk from the south coast about how Aston Villa, those bullying Premiership big shots, had ruthlessly plundered poor, impoverished, little old Brighton to steal away one of their top young stars. I knew what was coming and I would have liked to have left out Gareth to try to save us a few quid but it didn't seem right. And the kid was doing so well.

So well, in fact, that by the time we did get the tribunal fixed, the compensation Brighton were seeking had reached astronomical levels. They wanted £2.5 million for him and the same for another player we had signed from their stable, Michael Standing. It was outrageous.

I said at the time that Brighton would not know who Gareth Barry was if they stuck a ball under his arm and a seagull on his head on Brighton Pier. I stand by that. They did not have a clue who he was.

As a 15-year-old, he had been a substitute on one occasion for their youth team. We have 15-year-olds who, if they display the slightest promise, will play a dozen games in our youth team. They then might, just might, get a YTS contract. Gareth was not even offered that by Brighton.

Ask Gareth himself. He is the first to admit they didn't know the anything about him.

I would wager that had he stayed there, he would still not be in Brighton's first team now. The principle of compensation was fine; he had been on their books since he was 11. But the sum total of Brighton's expertise and education was probably a Thursday night five-a-side session for an hour. We had imagined that £150,000 or maybe £200,000 would represent a generous acknowledgement, and helping hand, to them.

But all the tribunal heard was how this 17-year-old had now played a dozen Premiership games, trained with the senior England squad and become a fixture in the Under 21 team, and how Brighton had been powerless to prevent Villa stealing this player of immense potential from under their noses. It was a myth becoming fact. At the end of it all, we were presented with an £800,000 bill which, with extras, would rise to £1 million.

Now don't get me wrong – Gareth is worth that and much, much more. But he is worth it because of the work that Aston

Villa's coaching staff have done with him. His development as a top flight professional had nothing to do with Brighton.

But of course, we were picking up the tab for a club that was in deep financial trouble before this came along. I used to play for Brighton and I've had letters from supporters asking me how I could be so mean-spirited as to deny them their due reward for Gareth.

'You're an ex-player,' they wrote, 'surely you don't want to see your old club go to the wall?'

Well, I'm sorry, but I think it was matters off the pitch that led the club to the position they were in. Not us. I would hate to see any club go to the wall. But it was nothing to do with Aston Villa. Why should we bail them out with this pile of bull-shite?

No, we got well and truly tucked-up by that decision. I don't want to come away from the fact that Gareth is worth it. But there was a far more deserving case later on from Charlton, who must have been beside themselves that they we were only asked to pay £50,000 for taking JLloyd Samuel, a promising young defender, from their books. Gareth should have been, at tops, £100,000 and no more. And the decision still angers me – as you can probably tell.

Having got that off my chest, it is time to dwell on the climax of our amazing start. Although Celta Vigo had inflicted upon us our first defeat, we were still unbeaten in the Premiership by the time our 12th game came along at Southampton on Saturday 14 November.

If we were still unbeaten after that match at The Dell, we would have established a club record – the best ever start to any League campaign. Players do not normally take any notice of the anoraks with their facts and figures. But this one you could not ignore. Aston Villa has a long and proud history, littered with great teams and great players. The thought that we might do something to outstrip all of our forerunners, of whatever vintage, was astounding.

Two things struck me in the build-up to the game. The first was to make sure there was no complacency. I remember pounding on about treating Southampton, who were marooned at the foot of the table and being written off at the time, as if they were Manchester United or Arsenal.

'If you don't, they are quite capable of beating you,' I warned them. If we were not to reach this club landmark, then I did not want it to be because we got sloppy or complacent.

But the team, what about the team? Dion's arrival had given me all sorts of options, the boldest of which was his inclusion with both Stan and Paul Merson. It was exciting, full of goal potential; but would it leave us vulnerable in midfield? This was, after all, an away game; Southampton would have to press us at some stage.

But I couldn't resist it. I thought of Southampton's defenders going to bed that Friday night thinking: 'Bloody hell, Collymore, Merson and Dublin on the same afternoon.' They are only human. It must prey on their minds, knowing they had a handful the next day. That could be worth a goal start.

Stan was free to turn up wherever he could and Paul, too, was handed a free role. It was a gamble but I did not want my instincts curbed by the reward beckoning.

And it all turned out well. In fact, we not only won 4–1 but scored probably my favourite goal of the season, our third. I'll never forget it. It started on the edge of our own box with Barry, who drilled a pass out to Stan on the right; he advanced and put Merse in who bent his shot into the bottom corner. Box to box in two passes and a few seconds. It was what having those players in the team was all about.

That outstanding goal was one highlight; the other was a hat-trick from Dion in his second game. Five goals in two now. It doesn't get any better, surely?

It was looking good wherever I looked now. The fans were delirious, the subs' bench was getting a little stronger. I remember bringing on Joachim for Stan that day with 10 minutes left but I also had Alan Thompson, Mark Draper and Simon Grayson on the bench. Good players all. And the fact that I left out Tommo would, I hoped, be interpreted in the right way by the players – that, just because I signed them for good money, they did not get any special privileges.

As the clock was ticking down in that game, and I knew that our victory was secure, I noticed a photographer near our dug-out. I walked over to him and asked if he would take a picture at the finish.

'What are you on about?' he said.

I told him I wanted a team group photograph for us, on the understanding that I would have exclusive rights. It would be for my private use only, that he would not publish it anywhere and if we published it, we would send him a few bob. He was happy with that.

Maybe I was pushing my luck. Maybe I was just asking to come down to earth with a bump after that. But I wanted that afternoon captured for all time in some way. I wanted something that would bring it all back to me in another of those 'wrinkly moments'. That record was and is precious to me. It had been 120 years in the making and it might be another 120 years before it is broken.

As I called the boys together, I could see one or two of the senior pros were not enamoured with the idea. I took their point. We had not really done anything yet. I think they had visions of the rest of the country seeing it and thinking, flash bastards – they're getting a bit above themselves aren't they?

If you look at the picture, you can see Merse and Southgate, for example, looking very sheepish; a kind of 'We shouldn't really be doing this' look on their faces. But the point is that you won't see that picture because it was never meant for public viewing. It was something for me, that's all.

Scattered around the walls of Villa Park there are many, many photographs of the teams of the past and some of the big moments from the club's history. Maybe, at a suitable date somewhere down the line, they will hang that one up alongside the others in recognition of a terrific little effort. That would be nice. Until then, it's staying under lock and key.

I knew at the time that even with a club record tucked under our belts, we had only just started. It could not go on like this surely? But I didn't expect to have my worst fears realized quite so quickly.

CHAPTER 8

'Gaff, it's Jim. There's a problem with Stan.'

So there we were, rolling along, top of the table and still unbeaten. Little media darlings we were; the season's surprise package. Liverpool next. At home. My first opponents from that February day 200 years ago. Or so it seemed. Heck, maybe we could do them again. Thirteen without defeat – now that would be amazing. And Liverpool. They were *the* team when I was a player; I seemed to have spent most of my career chasing the shadows of Dalglish, Souness and co. It was a special fixture for me.

True, the deeper we went into this run, the more I braced myself for that first defeat. I mean this couldn't go on, could it? In some ways, I was looking forward to getting it out of the way. You know, get back to normality, people leave us alone, get on with our lives again.

Well, the defeat did come in this next game which I could accept. Grudgingly. But it carried with it some worrying omens. We lost the game 4–2 despite playing some fantastic stuff during certain spells. It might have finished 6–6 or even 8–6 to us. But Liverpool defended a little better than us, which probably isn't saying much.

It was a great game, great entertainment and, as I say, I could deal with the result. But some other things had disturbed me. And they nagged at me long after the final whistle. In goal, for example, Michael had a difficult time and made me anxious to get Bozzy back. He would stay on his line a lot and I began to have serious doubts that he could handle the Holte because we started conceding a lot of goals at that end.

I felt it began to intimidate him. When 17,000 people start murmuring because you haven't come out for a through ball it makes a heck of a racket. And that can get to you. Michael began to get a bit jumpy after this defeat and our defence began to lose its cohesion. I needed to get Bozzy back and that old arrogance restored. Trouble was, we were starting to get bad reports about him. He would need an operation. And an injury we thought would keep him out for two or three weeks was now going to take three months to sort out.

I was also annoyed that it gave some of our critics a chance to say 'I told you so'. One of the labels attached to us at this stage was that we had not yet beaten anyone of significance. This really angered me. People seemed to forget that we had claimed some pretty big scalps the season before – Liverpool and Chelsea sprang to mind – but this defeat tossed fuel on to that particular fire.

But the talking point of the game, yet again, was Stan. You may recall that in my first match there had been allegations of Stan being wound up, taunted perhaps, by what many would consider hurtful comments. To this day I do not know how true those allegations were. And I would tell you if I did because I'll have no truck with them. But if they were as Stan claimed, then I can understand entirely what he did that day. Which was to save his response for the pitch.

I think he definitely had a problem with the Liverpool player Steve Harkness, the guy at the centre of Stan's complaint from that earlier match.

After Harkness cleared the ball, Stan was late with a bad challenge. And I mean a bad one. Had I been the referee, I would have sent him off straight away. But over in the dug-out, I was thinking, Well, OK Stan, I can see where you're coming from. I would do the same.

I was very much in his corner at that stage. He was, after all, making a good contribution to our season overall and seemed very much a member of the group. He was winning his battle to leave behind the events of the summer. OK, he had not scored the goals I would have wanted but there were no real problems with him. He was turning up on time; everything seemed reasonably under control.

But that day would change everything for Stan. I think Peter Jones, the referee, realized he should have sent him off for that first tackle on Harkness. So when Stan reacted angrily in the second half to a bad challenge by Michael Owen I knew what was coming. His marching orders. When I look back on it now, I see it as a fateful moment; a major turning point in Stan's life and career.

His demeanour after the game was one of isolation. He had a wild, glazed look; I was talking to him and getting the odd 'yeah' in response but he was not with me. His mind was racing away, lost in other thoughts. It was so frustrating. I was desperate to get in there and find out what was eating at him. But he was pretty screwed up and stayed that way for quite a few days. Damn. Just when I had him, I'm going to lose him again. That was my fear.

But there was a hangover from that game which, although not immediately apparent, began to unsettle us. The players were beginning to pick up the papers and read how they were not good enough to win anything; even worse, I think they were starting to believe them. They were starting to believe even Rodney Marsh – not the world's best tipster – and his regular assault on our ability at Sky TV.

Those doubts were there again the following week when we went 2–0 down at Forest, who were having a dreadful time one way or another. And we were lucky not to go four down. OK, we pulled it back to get a point which showed the spirit was still there. But, I don't know, it was as if that Liverpool defeat had punctured our feeling of invincibility.

Stan missed the Forest match, and a return to his old club, because of flu. I have to say that one or two people close to me had predicted he would not be available for that game even before he called in to say he was ill. I didn't believe them. Surely he would want to go back and show them how well he had done? He was top of the Premiership for goodness' sake. And a better player than when he left Forest. But it wasn't to be. And we could not play him after that because of his suspension.

If I was beginning to worry about the possible after-effects of that Liverpool game on Stan, I could certainly do without it. Because, by now, the wheels were beginning to come off for Merse.

He was having a bad time with his back, his football and his life and he was bringing all of that baggage into work. It had started, really, soon after the Coventry game, a match in which with 20 minutes or so remaining, I had taken off Merse and left on Stan.

He wasn't happy about that and he came to tell me so. My point was that Stan had just got back in the side and I wanted to show him that he was still a big part of the team; that although we had signed Paul, he could still be taken off before him. I thought, psychologically, it was important for Stan to stay on.

Paul hit back with a fair enough point when he asked what sort of psychological damage I thought I was doing him by taking him off.

'That's the trouble with this place,' he was saying. 'Everyone keeps bending over backwards for Stan, Stan, Stan. What about the rest of us?'

He became increasingly difficult to live with after that. And if Paul is in a bad mood, it can tend to affect everyone else. His training, his game, everything. If we were doing five-a-side, Paul wanted to be doing running; if we laid on a running session, Paul wanted a five-a-side.

And, worse than taking part really, he would then just go through the motions. He became slightly paranoid about his position at the club, too. If I had missed saying 'good morning' to him, he would assume I had a problem with him.

There would be days when we would bring the boys in and just take them for a walk across the water park near our training ground. Stretch them out, get 'em in the bath, massage, a bit of lunch, a bit of banter, keep them together. In the teeth of an English season, that's all they often needed.

But Paul didn't take kindly to being dragged up from London for a bath. 'I could have one of those at home,' he would tell me. At Middlesbrough, they had given him plenty of time off. Maybe as much as three days a week. Paul could come up on the Friday and take Stoke or Tranmere apart the next day. But this was the Premiership. He could not afford to take those luxuries.

He was having rows with me and the coaching staff. But the biggest confrontation, I suspect, was the one he was having with himself as his life came off the rails again. But through it all I knew that Paul Merson was a player of immense quality – so you persevere and work with that.

Even so I could do without the hassle because what lay ahead right now was about to sort us out. United at home, Chelsea away and then the Arse – champions Arsenal – at home. The top three teams in the country; the established powers we had dared to challenge. Now, said everyone including myself, we would find out just how good Gregory and his bunch were.

From the moment I had walked in at Villa, I was determined to 'be myself.' Ask me the question, and I will give you the answer. I had formed an impression during my spell as coach that my club was a little subservient to the big boys and I wanted that to change.

I mean, there are a few big fish out there who patronize the game and tell you how things are going to be. It was always 'Yes, Mr Manchester United' or 'No Mr Arsenal' or 'Whatever you say Mr Liverpool.' I felt that we cow-towed to them.

But I thought 'I'm not going to tug my forelock to anyone.' Sod that. We're Villa, for goodness' sake. Aston Villa. You, know, the club that was there at the start. We're the same as you; we're as good as you. There's loads of 'Uniteds' and 'Citys' but there is only one Villa. Yeah, I even loved the name: Aston Villa. Perfectly symmetrical. Magical almost. Our name is unique and so is our club. Yes, I thought, I'm not cow-towing to anyone when I get in there.

I had taken that attitude into the job with me and I knew that it was winning me as many enemies as friends. I didn't care. To be honest, I haven't got that many friends in the world anyway and I don't go through life worrying what folk might say about me. The people that know me and love me are all that matter. I will go to the wall for them.

But, yes, the press were having a field day with this brash, cocky so and so from Aston Villa. It wasn't meant to be that way.

You might find this hard to believe but I never actually courted the attention I was getting.

I never ventured an opinion on anything without being asked first. But I think that when I was asked, I told it straight. Straight as I saw it. I hate it when something really major has kicked off in a game and a manager says: 'Sorry, I didn't see the incident.'

I mean, what's that all about? If you saw it, then say what you think. There's nothing to fear but the truth and the truth is nothing to fear. There's a lot of small talk and rubbish and skirting around the issues in football. Cut to the chase. Say what you mean. I get agents coming to see me who want to dance around a transfer for two hours. Sod that. They look taken aback when I say after two minutes, 'So how much is he looking for?'

But that was me. Brash. Straightforward. And, yeah, big-headed but with a purpose; I hoped the players and the fans would start to believe in the club and the team as much as I did. You know, stop assuming that the big boys will always have their way.

Now I am going to contradict myself totally. Because I decided to pull up the drawbridge in the build-up to the United game. I was going to say nowt.

We were still top and half an hour couldn't pass without my being asked to do one thing or another. Truck-loads of faxes came from the media every day.

And this was a game loaded to capacity with enough sub-plots to satisfy John le Carré. Had we seen the first signs of a Villa wobble? United: could they win the treble? What about the return of Yorke? The great pretenders against the aristocrats. This was the start of the big test and everyone was really winding it up. United, Chelsea, Arsenal. Back-to-back. I thought it would be best to keep my mouth shut until after all three. Then I could make a much more rational judgement as to how good we were.

Staying silent was lovely. And so was the match. A beauty. Villa v United was a good, old-fashioned English winter's afternoon football match. Our grandfathers would have recognized it as easily as their grandchildren. A crisp December day, the pitch perfect, weather cold and dry, fantastic for the players, two good teams, getting it down, playing football, thick tension, Villa Park crammed... ah, classic stuff.

Scoreless in the first half, I can remember thinking: 'If they go ahead we've got problems.' They did. Andy Cole got to the byline and Paul Scholes stuck in the cross. Shit. But my fears were not justified. The cat and mouse was over now and we had to go for it. We did. We took over at that point and Julian scored a fairly quick equalizer.

The momentum was with us; Tommo hit the post and Schmeichel kept United in it. Fergie paid us the compliment of taking off a striker to bring on Nicky Butt. He was happy with his point. We could, possibly should, have won. But we had finished really well and though I kept my vow of silence, I was glowing inside.

But when we lost in the 93rd minute at Chelsea in midweek, I was murdered by the London media for again refusing to show. I had said I wouldn't but no one took any notice of that. It was assumed that I was 'bottling it.' Not true, although that defeat annoyed me for several reasons.

Lee Hendrie scored my other contender for our Goal of the Season and it deserved to be rewarded. And Dion, with all his experience, committed a basic, fundamental error at the end, hurrying to take a throw-in which only gave Chelsea the chance to launch one attack too many. I also thought of Bozzy again as our defenders headed away time and time again in the final frantic minutes only for the Chelsea players to pick up the pieces and launch themselves at us once more. And Tore Andre Flo killed us in the dying seconds.

One point from the two games and after that sickening blow at Stamford Bridge, I reckon I was the only guy in the country still backing us when we reached half-time against Arsenal that following Sunday, 13 December. We were 2–0 down to the Champions, with Bergkamp imperious and Arsenal grinding on; I do admire them. Class, sheer class – the club, the team. Everything about them. And I was a Tottenham fan as a kid. No one, but NO ONE, comes back from 2–0 down against the Arse; not against Adams, Keown, Seaman and co. I still felt we could but I suspected the tough job would be convincing the players.

And then something both terrible and weird happened.

By the time I was back in the dressing-room, I had decided on the change we needed. 'Take a break JJ,' I said to Julian Joachim. 'Stan, get stretched, get warm. You're on.' Now JJ never unties his laces; he just slips off his boots. He did so, and sat there, lost in thought.

Meanwhile outside, there was an awful accident. The half-time entertainment had involved a parachute display with the airmen all supposed to land on the pitch. But one of them got caught up in the Trinity Road stand and eventually crashed down on to the cinder track, suffering dreadful, but luckily not fatal, injuries.

All we knew down in the dressing-room was that the restart would be delayed by another 10 minutes as they attended to the poor man.

The minutes ticked down and with 60 seconds left before we went back out, I had a change of heart. I don't know why; I don't know where it came from. But I was seized by the need to keep Julian on the pitch.

'Julian, get those boots back on. You've got 15 minutes to prove me wrong.' Had he been stripped and in the bath, I would not have said it. But he was still sitting there.

And he proved me wrong, all right. He brought us back into the game and then I decided it was time to really go for the throat. We may as well get beaten 5–1 as 2–1. It was time for Stan.

He had been struggling to get back since his suspension but I knew that when our lot saw him getting ready to come on, it would lift the roof. Hopefully, the team too. Everyone still remembered Atletico Madrid.

It had the desired effect. We went to three up front and Stan helped transform the game. Oh, what a player he could be in those situations. Dion scored two goals in quick succession. 3–2. Incredible.

'Your team should learn to win with more dignity,' grumbled one of the Arsenal players on the way back to the dressing-room. What did he want? A guard of honour or perhaps three cheers for the losers? Sorry. We had done 'The Arse' from 2–0 down. Jesus, now maybe they will believe me.

I had banned drink from the players' lounge to remove temptation and, that afternoon, I felt all my preaching about fitness and conditioning had paid off. In the end, they were just 11 guys like us but we had overpowered them. The fitter you are, the easier it is to play and that comeback was a perfect example.

So now, surely, we were back on track. To win the title, you have to do special things, dramatic things. Sooner or later, you have to win really big games. No one could argue that coming back at Arsenal fitted into that category. My nagging worries were put to one side. We were hot again. And what's more, we had an electrifying Stan back in the fold.

Thrilled by his contribution, I called him early in the week. 'Just so you know son, you're playing at Charlton. Get yourself ready,' I told him. Charlton, our next opponents, were having a tough time and I was determined to go there and try to pick up the momentum which had floored Arsenal.

Three strikers again, Dion down the middle, Stan and JJ either side, checking their full backs and supporting whenever possible. Three big hitters; I was back in the mood of a month earlier and sat back to watch the fireworks.

I couldn't believe what I saw.

Stan spent the first 45 minutes barely breaking into a a jog. Did we bring the right guy down with us? Was this really the player who had transformed the Arsenal match? It couldn't be. It was. I was pulling my hair out.

How on earth could there be such an enormous gulf between two appearances? Sure, you always get a player who, in the middle of a trot of great form suddenly has a stinker. That's human nature. But this was... well, I don't know what it was. Still don't.

After 10 minutes of the second half, I had had enough. The team was suffering. When one man isn't doing it, everyone's workload is up 10 per cent. I took Stan off, brought on Riccy Scimeca as an extra defender and we hung on to the own goal Charlton had gifted us. But we were camped in our own half and were lucky to get away with it.

So now I was totally baffled. Three times I thought I had this guy, and three times he has wriggled from my grasp, my under-standing. After that first game against Liverpool, I thought he wanted to play for me, that I was about to rediscover the £7 million player. And it all changed.

I thought I had cracked it again after the summer, only for

that second Liverpool game to take him away once more. And now this. I just did not know what to think.

Harry, as his coach, was still batting for him. He had worked with him once before at Crystal Palace and coaches are always closer to their charges. 'Stick with him, Gaffer,' he was saying, 'it's frustrating but it's the price you pay for that type of talent'.

But I had tried everything, everything I knew. I had loved him, cajoled him, flattered him, kicked his arse. I had had a go at him in the press, hoping he would stick two fingers up at me and ram the words down my throat. I had gone through every psychological trick I could think of.

Believe me, I knew there was a player there. I knew that if I could get Stan to produce for just two-thirds of the season what he had shown in those fragments against Atletico or Arsenal, he would have 10 or 15 more goals and we would have 20 more points. He could be our missing link; our extra dimension. Damn, he could win us the title or at least put us in the Champions League.

But I was failing miserably. I still did not have a clue about what made him tick. I could not find out what made him... hungry. Yes, that's the word. Hungry. And, as Merse had pointed out to me all those weeks ago, I had 20 or 30 more pros to think about.

Not that Paul was in any state to pass comment by now. His personal crisis had deepened, as he has since admitted, and his back problems required surgery; he had lost his focus on football.

It would all come to a head as we turned into the new year when Paul, his home life in a mess, missing his children, his career struggling, decided he needed an escape. On the weekend that we scrapped out a goalless draw at his former club Middlesbrough, he flew to New York on Concorde.

I only found out about the trip from the media, which hit me hard. I think I am a fair guy, ready to let people do what is best for them providing they go about it the right way. Paul didn't speak to me, possibly because he feared I would say no. I suspect that if I had done, he would have gone anyway. So maybe he was trying to avoid a conflict, hoping he could go and come back leaving no one any the wiser.

But it is difficult for Paul Merson to climb aboard Concorde and not be recognized. And easy for the person who sees him to tell someone else who tells someone else. So then we did have a conflict. Paul's like myself in that he speaks his mind. Ask him and he tells you. That's fine. But I told him he had done something behind my back. And I was not thrilled that a highly-valuable player with a back problem was stuck on an aeroplane flying over the Atlantic. And, no, I didn't care that it was bloody Concorde.

Well, it all got sorted. It does with Paul. But I did not feel now that I was coping particularly well. I was trying to keep a team on the rails, not just a couple of individuals.

And there was just so much rubbish to cope with. It was wearing me down. Collymore – every day questions about Collymore – Merson, Bosnich... was he going to sign a new contract? How do you feel about Yorke scoring all these goals for United? And all the time I was worried about how the low-maintenance players were dealing with it. I mean, I never had a problem with Southgate or Taylor or Joachim or whoever. Were they resenting all the extra time and energy on the other guys?

Sometimes, you might look ahead to games and think, uh-oh, it's United on Saturday. But for me, the games had now become my escape. I was thinking, thank Christ for that – we've got United on Saturday. I loved Fridays and climbing on to the coach and getting to the hotel to concentrate on the game. I was even letting the negative vibes bug me too; the smart-ass, know-all pundits telling me what to do and how crap my team was. No, I was struggling now. And not enjoying it.

When our FA Cup campaign started, Hull City were bottom of the Football League. And we drew them in the third round. At home.

Now when you play against lesser opposition we all know the rules. They come for a great day, their fans come for a great day, to give it their best shot, to make a few bob, to see themselves on *Match of the Day*, to keep the score down... and then get beat. That's what happens. That's what it's all about.

So I always feel you should show them the difference. Show them why you are earning in a fortnight what they might not earn in a year. Show them why you are a Premiership player. The last thing you want is for them to go away thinking: 'Call yourselves big shots – you're nothing special.'

Or to put it another way, you should not patronize them; you should rip their throats out.

Well, we took a while to put them away. Julian scored one, Stan got a couple. But it was a game we should have won by five or six. I wasn't satisfied. And again, Stan had confounded me. With two goals under his belt, he became complacent. Why didn't he want to get three? I kept wondering what Andy Cole would have done? Scored six probably. Or Bergkamp? Or Vialli? Or Anelka? They pay the opposition the compliment of not letting up. Great players remain hungry and they want to show off a little. But for Stan, it was, two goals, that'll do, now let's coast through the rest of the game. Again, I couldn't understand him.

But we had another problem now... Dion was struggling. He was playing with a hernia which would require surgery. Typically, he wanted to put it off until the summer. Cup matches gave me the chance to rest him and throw another opportunity Stan's way.

Our next draw seemed ideal for just such a scheme. Fulham at home presented a much tougher proposition. But they were still from the Second Division. And if we kept our wits about us, we should be good enough to take care of them. By the time this game came around, mind, I had another option because Merse was also fit again. And he needed to get playing, too; to take his mind off his problems.

I was aware by then that Stan was spending long sessions locked away with Jim in the physio's room. I knew by now the pair were developing a bond. As the fourth round tie approached, I recall Jim saying he felt Stan should 'see someone'. I took that to mean a sports psychologist, someone to help with his motivation. That was fine by me. But it would be something that could happen in a week or two. It wasn't urgent, was it?

But on the day of the Fulham tie came a development I was never expecting. Three hours before kick off, my phone rang.

'Gaff, it's Jim. There's a problem with Stan.'

Maybe Stan suspected I was going to leave him out. Players always try to read things. If you are not trying to charm the pants off them, they think there's a problem; perhaps Stan was getting in his retaliation first. We had beaten Everton comfortably earlier in the week to retain our place among the title contenders. But Stan had been substitute and, knowing that Glenn Hoddle was there, had a pop at me afterwards in the local press. This wasn't good enough for him, he was saying. Did he think it was good enough for me?

So maybe he thought I was going to get my own back by leaving him out. Oh, I had wanted to play him – it was a genuine toss-up between Merse and Stan. And I had been sitting at home on the Friday night before the game hoping there would be a knock at my front door. I would open it and there would be Stan, champing at the bit saying: 'You've got to pick me tomorrow, boss, because I am going to be sensational.' God I would love to see that kind of *desire* from him. Come on, Stan; give me a sign.

Sadly, that was a fanciful notion. Instead, I had decided I was going to play Merson with Stan on the bench. But I never got the chance.

Jim told me that Stan was simply unfit to be considered that day. He was not in the right frame of mind. A psychiatrist had seen him that morning and declared Stan to be suffering from clinical depression.

I was shocked. Totally shocked. I never knew for a minute it was anything serious, anything for which the medical profession would have a label.

But it seemed it was. There was little time to think about it then. We had a game to play, a game that turned out disastrously with Fulham winning 2–0. Out of the Cup and with the Stan story starting to hit the headlines, the dark shadows began to descend.

Perhaps my mood was affected by our performance against Fulham. We could have done with Stan coming off the bench that day. But I was pretty scathing about the episode when we all met to discuss the next step on the following Monday. Clinical depression? Well, I thought that was mothers with six kids, 25 going on 65, run off their feet, part-time job, old man earning £150 quid a week... that was clinical depression. It was me being my old man. 'What's the matter with you, silly ponce?' he would be telling Stan. 'Get off your backside and get on with it.'

Stan had the greatest job in the world. Playing football. The salary, the lifestyle... it did not get any better than this. I simply could not comprehend what I was being told and just suspected Stan of working a flanker. Especially when he made it clear that the only place he would consider for treatment would be the Roehampton clinic that they had all attended – Adams, Merson, Gascoigne, the big-time crew. It was the clinic for the rich and famous. I thought Stan was just being trendy.

My relationship with him was by now, I guess, strained. Stan wanted to go to the clinic on Tuesdays, Wednesdays and Thursdays, and train with us Mondays and Fridays. I suggested this was no good to anyone. If he was ill, then he should go away and get better. Then maybe he would be fit for football again. But I was aware that there were other forces at work, other pressures. The chairman, for example, was quite rightly desperately trying to protect the club's investment. At £7 million, Stan was still Villa's most expensive signing. Something like this threatened to wipe off at a stroke what remained of that value.

So I agreed to his idea but I wasn't thrilled about it. I thought it would have a negative effect on the dressing-room. But by now, I just wanted the Stan factor to go away.

With all this in the background, we were then given a terrible mauling at Newcastle in the next game. The scoreline was 2–1 but it was a heavier set-back than that. Alan Shearer gave us a thorough working over, particularly young Barry who I was now anxious to get out of the team.

He desperately needed a breather, having exceeded all expectations in coming this far.

But on that same day, unfortunately, Shearer's boot smashed into Ugo Ehiogu's eye-socket and splintered it into several different pieces; another key member of our defence joined the recovering Bosnich and the suffering Dublin in the treatment room.

Ugo is a giant at Villa, the one truly physically intimidating player we possess. But I watched our colossus being led away by the medical staff that night as if he had run into Tyson in a bad mood – poor Ugo could barely walk.

The symbolism was both unmistakable and worrying.

CHAPTER 9

'The sound of self-doubt.'

Some people set their watches by Wimbledon. Others, the Lords Test or the British Open. But me? I know it's summer when Ugo comes to see me.

I've got him booked in again for early July 2000 and I am pretty sure I can guess what the conversation will be about. The details must remain confidential but I think he has himself revealed the broad thrust of his feelings. Ugo is a terrific defender who knows he is perpetually on the brink of the England set-up. Unfortunately for us at Villa, he is wondering if playing for a more fashionable club might clinch the breakthrough he craves.

He has openly questioned our ambition and, let's face it, he has seen two of his great pals in Dwight and Bozzy follow the yellow brick road to Old Trafford. He is inevitably wondering if he has also over-stayed his time at Villa Park; that he should now be looking to stretch out into the wider world.

In some ways I am hurt by his suggestion. I remember him talking in the press about needing a bigger stage when we were top of the table with Villa Park crammed, the best defensive record in the country and, so it seemed, the entire British media corps camped at our training ground.

What more could I do for him? If that was not going to help him then nothing would. Maybe, at that time, Ugo was plain unlucky in that Villa's purple patch coincided with an England manager who, for one reason or another, did not fancy him.

But there again, I know what he is driving at. Aston Villa won the league championship in 1981 and the European Cup a year later. But they were not the dominant force of the seventies or the eighties. The players at the club are of a generation who would have been hooked on the great Anfield teams as kids. Unless you lived in Birmingham in the early 1980s, Villa were probably not that big a deal to you.

The only answer, the only way we can change that perception, to make Villa the heavyweight it ought to be, is to win trophies. Get into the Champions League. Consistently. And yeah, if it is not asking the impossible, make our place 'sexy', in the Gullit sense of the word.

It irritates me that anyone would want to go anywhere else. We could not afford to let another Dwight Yorke leave. We had to make Villa Park a place players wanted to stay. We had to make it a fortress, sold out every week.

I was determined to keep banging on the door and asking for money for my players. If I was told 'No' then fair enough – I would come back next week. But I saw my job as making Ugo want to stay.

And as we looked down from the summit of the Premiership, a place Villa had rarely visited since 1981, this was something that I was now seriously thinking about. One of the points Merse had made when he first arrived was how we could not afford to squander the excellent start we had made. Sequences like this do not come along all the time, he was saying, we had to cash in. Make it count. I agreed. We were top of the table and hanging in there. People were talking about us, not just in England but across the Channel as well.

Was this the moment to really go for it? After all, I had already dared to dream of bringing in Shearer. I still tingled at the thought of what someone of his presence or stature would do to our place.

Had the time come to abandon a little caution and recruit a player who would not only give us the extra dimension we still needed on the pitch, but give the club some sex-appeal? After all, we were top of the table and showing a leg at the time. If we pulled this one off, we might be accused of flashing our knickers...

And so there I was, three quarters of the way through

January, sitting in my office at Villa Park and sharing coffee and conversation with the player I thought might help us make this breakthrough. The little Brazilian midfield playmaker, Juninho.

He had arrived in Birmingham earlier that morning in a cloak-and-dagger operation that had seen his representative in England, Gianni Paladini, and myself literally drive on to the tarmac at Birmingham airport and whisk him to the ground.

And what's more, I knew he wanted to sign. Oh yes. The effort he had made getting there told me that. Juninho was due to play in a benefit match that night in Barcelona and had been given the use of a private jet to take him there from Madrid, where he was playing for Atletico. Except he wasn't. He was not getting along with their new coach, the legendary Italian Arrigo Sacchi, and was out of the side. This was causing problems at Atletico. The little guy was hugely popular with the supporters but Sacchi was having none of it. This split in the camp was, I hoped, something I could widen to the point where we could nab him. And the fact that he had taken the opportunity at his own expense to divert to Birmingham suggested he was on the hook.

It had been an elaborate, complex chain of phone calls and conversations and contacts and exhausting legwork to get this far. The player's Italian-based agent Ernesto Bronzetti had been a major help along with Gianni. And I had seen him play and, despite his injury problems of the previous year, still thought he had much to offer. The lad's character was impeccable, as the supporters at Middlesbrough would no doubt testify. Although some of Robbo's foreign contingent would eventually leave the club under something of a cloud, tears were shed when Boro's relegation the year before cost them this player's services.

He had been a wow in the Premiership and despite his frail physique, had shown he could cope. He was a wonderful player, no danger.

And I felt we were a better side than Middlesbrough. Put him in with our boys, it seemed to me, and we would have an even better player. My excitement at the thought of pulling off this deal, the biggest in the club's history, was limitless. This felt like a defining moment. This felt like *the* moment.

It wasn't just the idea of Juninho joining the team. It was all the knock-on effects I was imagining. He would instantly sell another 5,000 season tickets, maybe more. And he would make other world class players look at Aston Villa seriously. Roberto Carlos, the brilliant Brazilian left back, was one of his biggest pals. If Juninho comes here, maybe we can get Carlos to follow next year?

Such has been the dramatic transformation in their image, people may have forgotten that not too long ago, Chelsea were very second-class, humdrum citizens of the capital. But then Gullit begat Vialli who begat Zola who begat Di Matteo who begat Desailly... and so on. And that led to Chelsea fans strutting down the Kings Road with 'Zola' on the back of their souvenir shirts.

And I knew the effect it would have on my dressing-room. Although the outside world was unaware of Juninho's presence at Villa Park for a few hours that morning, the stories had been rumbling along for weeks. 'Is he coming Gaff?' the players were asking me. 'Are we having Juninho here?' And this barely a year after so many of the senior players, respected voices all, had been openly criticizing the club's lack of ambition. Now they were saying to themselves, bloody hell, maybe we do mean it this time. Who knows, if I could clinch this deal maybe I wouldn't have to pencil in that regular summer meeting with Ugo?

And this was all spinning through my mind as we sat there talking about anything and everything with Juninho and his father, Osvaldo, who looks after his son's interests. They liked Villa Park. They liked the fact that I believed so much in Juninho's talent. They clearly wanted to leap aboard.

But then the alarm went off. It was time to wake up.

We were staring at a barrier that, no matter how we tried, we could not smash down. Juninho was owed a lot of money by Atletico. Two million quid, in fact. Net. That meant £3.3 million to you and me over on this side of the water. Osvaldo was adamant that his son would not give up that money.

Atletico were equally sure that they were not going to cough up; the money would have to go on to the transfer fee. We knew before this that we were dealing with an £8 to £10 million asking price. On top of that was the player's contract at £1.5 million a year. A package in the region of £15 million was something we were braced for. But now this could send the whole thing up into

113

the region of £20 million. And that was an outlay of mind-boggling proportions.

We hammered away. Hours and hours, call after call. Not just that day but on subsequent days. I urged myself on, trying to make a breakthrough. I told myself how Napoli had been a bog-standard Serie A club in Italy until Maradona went there and transformed them into a championship-winning team. That was not a coincidence. He left and they returned to their previous identity. In fact, even worse; they were relegated.

The deal had caught the public's imagination just as it had mine and the players.

But the figures were frightening. Villa spend what they earn and as crunch time arrived, the moment when we would have to make a decision one way or the other, I started to feel it was becoming the impossible dream.

I was looking around for one member of the board to say, 'Come on, let's do it'. But I began to get the feeling that their enthusiasm was waning. I sensed the decision was starting to rest squarely on my shoulders – which also meant that's where the blame would fall if it didn't work out. I understood that.

I kept thinking about the £20 million. We had already commit-ted £11 million to the Collymore deal and so far that had not been a success. The doubts were creeping in; it did not feel right any more. I could not push it any further. And neither did I feel the chairman nor Mark or Stevie were really pushing it either. I could understand their reluctance. I wondered whether to call it off. In the end, I didn't have to. Atletico tired of waiting and announced that Juninho had been taken off the market. They did so on the day that the chairman made plans to fly to Madrid to try for one last breakthrough. But the chance had been missed.

I was deeply disappointed at the time. Weeks of meetings and hours of phone calls... and then this huge deflation at the end of it. I had put a hell of a lot into the Juninho bid and it had all been for nothing. You would have been better off staying on the train-ing ground than chasing dreams, I chided myself as I headed back to the real world.

But I also knew I had to respect the enormity of the deal.

I was worried about the impact this might have on the play-ers. They were no different to the rest of the public. They thought they were going to have a hugely-respected, world-class player as a team-mate. They thought that the club was about to prove, once and for all, that it really meant business.

I knew that the team would have benefited had we made the signing, but at a cost of £20 million? I had to be sensible. It was not my money, after all. Do we risk bankrupting the club with a lot of star names or do we continue to strive for success but at the same time respecting our means?

One or two have tried to buy success and got their fingers burned. They have paid the price since then and we didn't want to get into that situation. I don't think my chairman would ever allow that to happen.

But, yes, I was also a little exasperated at the way it had concluded. I was frustrated that we, Aston Villa, had not been able to pull off such a deal and I did a lot of soul searching.

Most of all, I guess, I was getting frustrated with myself. What did you really expect? 'Yes John, here's £20 million, after all it's only three times bigger than our biggest ever deal.' Don't be daft. I know from speaking to the man that Alex Ferguson has had some of the world's top players sat in his lounge ready to sign for Manchester United and he's not been able to pay the salary his man knew he could command elsewhere.

If it happens to him, why should I not expect it to happen to me?

But there was something else.

I thought up until then I had been bullet-proof. That nothing could stop me, nothing could touch me. But I just wasn't handling things as well as I thought I should have been. I drove away from the Juninho deal with a sound in my head that disturbed me. I didn't know for a while what it was because I had never experienced it before. But then I realized.

It was the sound of self-doubt.

CHAPTER 10

'Oh Christ mate. Turn it off, will you.'

When I was 14, I quite fancied myself as a good cross-country runner. I won the school championships. Then I won the county championships. On to the nationals. And I remember the winner was so far ahead of me that I was looking for a way out. I was trying to find a kerb I could trip over, feign an injury, and not finish.

The point of the story is that I was, and probably still am, a lousy loser. I would have done anything in that race to avoid finishing so far behind the winner; give me an excuse to say 'Well, I would have caught him but I got injured.' As he sped away, the race meant nothing to me. All that Corinthian stuff about the 'taking part' being more important than the winning was nonsense to me. Winning mattered. And I just couldn't accept in the cross-country race that I was so far behind. And although I avoided the kerbs and reached the finishing line, I had already forgotten it by the time I was getting changed. I didn't win, therefore it was of no relevance.

I tell you this to explain, partly, why I might be a little sketchy in detail over what happened next at Villa. It's all a bit of blur, you see, mainly because I have made it that way. It was all such a nightmare, it was all so terrible, that I erased it from my memory banks a long time ago.

I have looked at people in the past when they have asked me

116

if I was ever in charge at Portsmouth and said, 'No mate, you must be thinking of someone else.'

It didn't happen.

I wanted nothing to do with it.

It was nothing to do with me. That was how I dealt with it.

But, of course, the truth is, that what happened at Villa was everything to do with me.

It was all my fault.

If you look in the books they will tell you – and it pains me to agree – we lost nine of the next 10 games. But the details? I honestly don't want to think about them.

We had not really had a setback from which we could not recover until this point and I was pretty pleased with myself. From the moment I had stepped into the manager's shoes, I seemed to be fighting fires. Now, no sooner did I put one out then two more started.

But I didn't handle what happened next very well at all. Part of that was sheer stubbornness. I kept thinking that we had won 17 games out of 23 up to that Southampton match and that it couldn't all be a fluke. I had to be doing something right. So I refused to change. I refused to alter the way we prepared for games, the way we approached them. If it was good enough before it would be good enough now. But it wasn't. No matter what I tried, we kept losing and losing and losing.

It all took place between 23 January and 21 March; if my life was a website, those two diabolical months would be spiked straight into the wastebasket and then emptied. Immediately. I've looked it up and the record tells me there were defeats by Fulham, Newcastle, Blackburn and Leeds, a draw at Wimbledon and then four more beatings on the bounce – Coventry, Derby, Spurs and Chelsea. Honestly, I remember the Coventry game because that one is just too awful even for me to forget. But the rest?

Looking back now, I know I should have reacted differently. When those first cracks became obvious in, say, that Fulham game, I should have acted *then*. Got it sorted. Changed things. But it's too late now.

I spoke to Coxy on a couple of occasions because his was the only outside voice I really listened to. He was, as always, asking the pertinent questions. 'What's going on?' 'What are you doing that's different?' And a few observations too: 'Have you thought about getting such and such?' 'You know, I don't think so and so is doing it for you at the moment.'

But he would only go so far. He wouldn't step over the line. I was a big boy now and it was my team. I had to find the answers.

But the answers were driving me to distraction. I was never a man for team meetings; never one for sitting there, bringing the players to attention, getting the video on, and making them sit through it like naughty schoolboys. I knew what their reaction would be to that: oh yeah, this is really going to make us better players.

And as I had never staged them before, I didn't want to start now. It would be a sign of panic. It would be another dollop of negativity. 'He's never held a team meeting before – he's losing it,' I could imagine being whispered from the back. So I was desperate not to go down that road.

And our opponents. Never bothered with them that much before. We might point out their set-pieces or one or two other things to look for. But all our preparations were about us. What we were going to do. Accentuate the positive. Not worry about the mob we wanted to beat. Again, I didn't want to change that.

There had been another trap I was always determined to avoid. There is nothing worse than the player who hangs up his boots one day, switches to coaching, and then suddenly becomes a power-hungry monster, screaming and shouting at his old colleagues. Suddenly they are in front of you ranting: 'Right you bastards, I'm going to run the legs off you this morning.' It never works. Surely, the trick is to make them *want* to run for you.

I've seen that happen to a few in my time. I remember Frank Sibley being caretaker manager at QPR and bringing in Bobby Campbell as his coach. Remember Bobby? He later went on to lead Chelsea to a promotion but, on those first few days with us, he was keeping quiet. So there we were at Old Trafford, slipping 1–0 down just before the break, and we trooped in, Frank having his say before asking Bobby if he wanted to add anything.

And I'll never forget it. He said, 'Right – do you want it from the lip or the hip?'

Well, that's a great line I must remember.

Of course, we all looked at each other, giggling, thinking what on earth is this guy on. And then he just goes berserk. Ranting and raving, screaming and shouting. And I'm thinking, yeah, this is good. This is really motivating. This is really going to help us play better. After Bobby's magic touch, we went out, conceded two goals in the first two minutes of the second half, and the game was up. Too many coaches and gaffers think like that and I was anxious to avoid it, no matter how desperate I became. I *knew* it wasn't right.

Back to Bally, for another example. Now he loved his players; he was a totally passionate football man. And he could make you feel fantastic as a player. No question. But he was too Jekyll and Hyde.

We played at Leicester, lost 2–1 after being 1–0 up, and in the dressing-room afterwards he screamed the place down; called us all the names under the sun. We were crap, useless, not fit to wear a Portsmouth shirt ever again. You know the sort of stuff.

We left the ground, got on the bus, and there he is, sat at the back, joking, laughing and drinking with the lads. What was the point of it all?

In the same way, I always think that coaches and managers forget too quickly what it was like to play. They forget how much it hurts or how painful a dead leg can be or what it is like, 15 minutes to go, when you've given everything, absolutely everything, and you are running on reserve, playing by memory. I wanted to keep sight of that, too.

Yeah, I shouted at the boys but I always tried to make it specific and not just rant and rave with sweeping generalizations. I tried to dig out the ones who were not doing it. The players know who they are and they are looking for you to sort them out. It is up to the manager to identify them. That's the job. Tarring them all with the same brush in a fit of temper does no one any good.

All these things, memories of what *not* to do, were flooding through me. But where were the answers? What should I do? Barry desperately needed a rest, but I couldn't get him one. Ugo was ruled out for the season. Dublin was limping along, sticking it out with a hernia but he was not the player that joined us.

Michael in goal continued to look uncertain but Bozzy was still not ready.

I had resolved that two training sessions a week was not the requirement necessary for Stan to play, but as our plight grew worse, I even called him up. A three-match sequence against Derby, Spurs and then Chelsea.

I still wasn't happy about the situation. And neither were the players. They were shocked when they walked into the dressing-room and found Stan there, getting ready to play. One senior player pulled me to one side and said: 'What's he doing here?' I understood that reaction. He was apart from them now, effectively a part-time footballer. He was not hurting with the rest of them. They were finding it difficult to understand why they should be in training every day, facing the flak so to speak, and this guy rolls up when he feels like it to have a game. That's not what it was like. I am sure Stan wanted to do his bit. But that was how they viewed it. We were all suffering, like an open wound. But to the rest of the boys, only 10 of them were bleeding.

But I was desperate for a win at that stage and willing to try anything.

It didn't work.

Stan hardly got a kick in those games. We might have been unlucky to lose at Spurs in the dying minutes but it was after the Chelsea game that I decided I had had enough. We had a meeting over at the chairman's house and I put my foot down. This arrangement was doing no good to anyone. We had a part-time footballer, the clinic had a part-time patient. It was time for Stan to go away, get better and come back when he could train every day and handle the matches.

By then, I was also weary of the Collymore circus and anxious for it to leave town. Stan does have an awful lot of rubbish to put up with and, as a consequence, so do his employers. Or, more accurately, me.

The lad can't park on double yellow lines without it making the news. If he forgets to say 'thank you' at the bar after being served, I get an angry letter from the barmaid's mother about over-paid, pampered, ungracious, don't-know-they're-born footballers.

And the press conferences. Interminable questions about Stan, Stan, Stan. Never can so much time have been wasted and so much written about a guy who, for whatever reason, just was not having an impact on the fortunes of Aston Villa Football Club where it mattered. On the pitch.

It was a relief to get him out of there and into full-time treatment. As far as I could see, it would do us both the power of good.

I think Merse hit the bottom of his trough in the middle of all this as well. The match at Spurs, always a special fixture for him because of his Arsenal career, found him in a terrible state.

When the wheels come off, it's natural for players to look around for any excuse – the colour of the grass, the air in the ball, the hotels we were using, the so-called unlucky away strip. Seriously. I've heard them. 'Oh no Gaff, not the white kit – we never win in the white kit.' Just like school.

But I think that Spurs match was a wake-up call for Merse. He felt that day he couldn't do it any more. The game was passing him by. He had to get himself sorted or he was staring at oblivion.

And the press were having a field day. We had been everyone's darlings before Christmas. Now we were a crisis story. They loved the fact that some of my big signings were out of the team because it was easy copy for them.

'How do you feel about being out of the side?' they would ask.

Well, the reply is not going to be 'I'm thrilled' is it? The stories were flying thick and fast. Villa had lost it. And so had Gregory. They were probably right.

Around the city, the reaction from the fans during these long dark weeks was pretty good, pretty sympathetic.

'Bloody hell John, what's going on?' they were saying, or 'Sort it out Greg – it's all going pear-shaped.'

But I knew there would be others enjoying my discomfort. As a player, I had been a horrible sod. We have a word for it around the London clubs: 'leery'. It was just the way I was. Looking back, I know it wasn't big and it wasn't clever. But that was me.

Ask Joe Jordan, the Scottish international and former Leeds and Manchester United striker. Later in his career, he was playing for Southampton at Loftus Road when we were giving them a bit of a hiding. Three-up and I was taunting Joe on the ball; standing on the edge of the area, motioning him to come and get it. He had to, they were chasing the game. And when he did, I would knock it back to our keeper, this being an era when the back-pass was allowed.

Joe got so steamed up with me he came roaring into our dressing-room after the final whistle to punch my lights out; he was met with a chorus of mocking abuse.

Ask the Birmingham City lads, too, from the same era. We were beating them comfortably at St Andrew's when I was presented with the ball on their goal-line and not a defender in sight. It was a tap-in goal. But oh no, not old big-head. I stood there, ball under my foot, beckoning their goalkeeper Tony Coton and centre half Billy Wright to come and get it. They knew what I was going to do and they refused to break into a sprint. But I kept taunting them until they had to – and just as they homed in on me, I stuck the ball over the line. Brilliant.

Everyone thought I was having a go at their manager Ron Saunders who, as Villa's boss, had moved me out of Villa Park by selling me to Brighton in 1979. I wasn't. I was just being me. Leery.

I've spoken to plenty of these old opponents since and they all agree: I was a right cocky, full-of-myself, arrogant sod to play against.

But their feelings towards me never worried me. They didn't know me. They just knew the player. I will not let anyone harm the people who matter most to me. But the rest of it has never got to me.

Remember I was telling you about those early days at Portsmouth after Bally had been sacked? That first morning at the club, the receptionist would not even look at me. The laundry lady, I recall, was much the same. They loved Alan and felt I had knifed him.

I walked into the club to be greeted by permafrost. But it never bothered me. You cannot spend your life worrying about what other folk think of you.

All of them, mind, were probably enjoying seeing the big-head get his comeuppance during this free-fall.

'That's shut that big-mouth up hasn't it?' I could hear a few saying. 'He's not being quite so smart now, is he?'

Within the game, I knew that the Southampton picture had come out wrong. I knew some folk were laughing at what they perceived to be another display of Gregory arrogance. I got a few letters. Mainly from Manchester United fans, actually, who were having a go back at me because I had said they could not do the treble.

I wouldn't have said anything at all if I had not been asked. But it wasn't that I didn't want United to do the treble, just that it seemed such an impossible task. Even that fantastic Liverpool team, in 1977, had come unstuck at Wembley in the FA Cup Final against, ironically, United.

But, yes, there were plenty enjoying it.

I could handle that but one of the big sadnesses was the way it savaged the 'Little England' success story we had developed during the season. That had been something that was really semi-accidental. I didn't sign Dion or Watson or Merse or Thompson because they were English; I signed them because they are all good players.

But suddenly, in an age when foreign players have swamped our game, here we were, a little corner of England and doing very nicely, thank you. I was not anti-foreign or anything. I know, even now, that for Villa to make further leaps up the ladder we have got to bring in extra dimensions we might only be able to find abroad.

But I am a footballing patriot. I love my country, I'm proud of it and proud of my profession. And, yeah, it felt good to be up there, muscling in on the territory that was becoming increasingly influenced by Continental flavours. It was a tall order, but we wanted to prove that English was still best.

And we had glowed with the same pride as the national recognition came our way – Dublin, Merson, Southgate, Hendrie and Barry had all been linked with the seniors. The club definitely gleaned great kudos from it all.

Unfortunately, by the time Chelsea came back to Villa Park, we were shattered. Collectively. We were in awe of them that day and couldn't get near them. They murdered us and dented some of that patriotic pride.

But nothing hurt quite as much as the Coventry game. They had never beaten us at Villa Park in the League before then. They were from the bottom half of the table and their supporters seemed to live for the day when they could come to Villa Park and win. They thrashed us 4–1; the worst performance of a pretty dire sequence and probably the worst I have ever experienced as a manager.

I had to do something.

In the end, we made a couple of signings that helped steady the ship, bringing in Steve Stone from Forest and Colin Calderwood from Spurs. Stone was a player we knew well, and someone who I thought would just be a good addition to our squad.

People had made much of the number of signings; they had conveniently forgotten that we had also moved on a few – Yorke, Staunton, Milosevic, Nelson, Curcic, Charles. By the time we signed Steve, we were still making up the numbers.

But Steve was a versatile lad, fit, lived just up the road, and was highly-regarded as a specialist right-sided midfielder. At Villa, our whole squad had been shaped and prepared in the last three or four years for a different system, one using three centre backs and playing with wing backs. One of the answers I went looking for during this calamity was a switch to 4–4–2. It did all right but it was never convincing.

And after that mauling by Chelsea, we desperately needed help at the back. Ugo was still out, the skipper was struggling because of the lack of support and Barry needed protecting. My chief scout, Ross MacLaren, threw in Colin's name – he was near the end of his contract at Spurs, not in George Graham's plans, and just the right guy to steady the ship. Which is precisely what he did.

From the moment he arrived, Colin has been one I have never had to worry about. He looks after himself superbly and does not need to be fussed over or pampered. I'm sure we'll miss him but it was important at his age to play regular first team football.

And, yeah, better late than never, we got Bozzy back. Well, sort of. I knew that these would be his last few weeks as a Villa player; his contract was up and although we had our meetings and outlined our offer... well, it was nowhere near the kind of salary territory the kid had his eyes on.

And why not? Peak of his profession, free transfer, clubs in the queue and the Big One, Manchester United, about to lose Peter Schmeichel. You didn't have to be a rocket scientist to work it out?

He eventually returned powerless to prevent Chelsea scoring three times as our slump continued before he was placed in an impossible position by one of the most disturbing elements of the freedom of contract, players now enjoy.

Okay, picture the scene. Our next two games are Forest at home and then, the following Saturday, United at Old Trafford.

Two days before the Forest match and a routine training session finishes. With Bosnich limping. None of the coaching staff had seen anything untoward.

'What's that all about?' I asked Paul Barron.

'I don't know. I didn't see him do anything. Did you?'

'No. You didn't either?'

'No. Nothing.'

Bozzy explained that he had gone over on his ankle. But he was now an innocent victim of an embarrassing position and, through no fault of his own, one which was bound to make us suspicious.

Especially me. And especially at a time when I was feeling vulnerable, desperate to get a win, any win, again. I couldn't help but start to map out a mischievous scenario in my mind.

Oh I get it, I thought, he's going to United next season ... we're playing them in a week's time ... he can't get an injury before that game because it would be too obvious ... so if he gets an injury now, misses the Forest match, doesn't recover for the United game ...

My thoughts were racing away with me.

Yeah, that's it, I bet. He can't win next week, not if he's signing for United. He plays well, he might stop them winning the title. He plays poorly, then Fergie might decide against him. And our fans could accuse him of thinking more about United than Villa. Oh yes, I can see it all now. He doesn't want to face United.

My dark suspicions had got the better of me, I'm afraid. When he did eventually rule himself out of the United match, it led to a bust-up with Mark in which I effectively told him to go away and not bother to darken my door again.

But, of course, he was in an impossible position. The football industry is awash with speculation and Bozzy's summer move to United was a story regularly filling the tabloids throughout all this period. No matter what happened that day at Old Trafford, he could not win. Whether he played, whether he didn't play, whether he was brilliant, whether he was poor. No matter what happened, everyone would be whispering one thing or another. And the fact that the lad got injured and couldn't play just made the whole thing worse. It is one of the unseen side-effects of the Bosman system and one which needs to be tackled by the authorities.

I remember going up to United on a couple of scouting missions earlier in the season dreaming of the day we would go there. It would be an awesome occasion. The title at stake. But our fade-out meant that it was all a little flat even though I felt we did quite well despite getting beaten.

I'm happy to say Bozzy and I soon resolved our differences. I think he understands that my accusations sprang out of the sheer frustration of seeing him miss so many games in the knowledge that he would soon be slipping through Villa's fingers and on to a new future elsewhere. But I had my say, he had his. I don't believe in letting things linger. You say what you say at the time, get it out in the open, clear the air and then, the next day, it's business as usual. I have always liked Bozzy and, as a keeper, he is second to none.

I phoned him the day his transfer went through, to wish him well. In fact, he called me shortly after that to see if he could use Bodymoor Heath for a training stint. No problem – although a woman spotted him and wrote me a stinking letter about how disgraceful it was to see Bosnich working there having turned his back on Villa. Yours Disgusted of Erdington. She would be equally outraged, I'm sure, to know I sent him a telegram on the day of his debut to wish him all the best.

But I don't believe in feuds. You never know in this game. Maybe it won't work out for Bozzy. Maybe, at some future date, we might be looking to try to bring him back. I bet Disgusted of

Erdington might even welcome that. You never say never in this game.

I look back now and recognize the pitfalls I went clattering into in hobnail boots. I knew when I was appointed I was signing up for the most demanding job of my life. I even thought I knew what I was letting myself in for. But the long, bitter and lonely weeks of our desperate decline showed me I was still learning.

The demands on the manager shocked me. The sheer slog and tedium of some of the things I was having to do wore me down. There I was in mid-March, unable to win a game for love nor money, but being dragged from the training pitches by peripheral stuff. I always tried to make 9.30 a.m. to 12.30 sacrosanct. That's my prime time with the players.

But come 1 p.m., I had not had the chance to speak to half the staff I intended to because of the number of people wanting five minutes of my time that became half an hour that then became an hour. Agents especially. Agents trying to sell me players when I really needed to concentrate on those I could pick for the next match.

Without doubt, the system on the European mainland, where a general manager works in tandem with the coach, is preferable. All the foreign coach has to worry about is tomorrow's session; his entire focus is the next game.

I'll let you into a secret. I managed to squeeze in a trip to Italy on one occasion to see Udinese play Roma. Oliver Bierhoff, the German international then playing for Udinese, was the principal source of interest. But the beauty of those excursions is that you can go watch a game, take in 22, maybe 26 players, even maybe a training session, and still be home for the next day's training.

Anyway, on that day I saw Bierhoff lumbering around; his touch was awful and clumsy. But stick it anywhere near his head and Bang! it was a goal. Sure enough, he scored twice that day,

But I kept picturing him in front of our Holte trying to control it and thought, naaah. Of course, he was sold for £18 million a few weeks later. Maybe I had the same problem as Cloughy in recognizing strikers – he signed a few cart-horses in his day.

But the point is I needed more of that experience. I had come from Wycombe, don't forget. This was all so new to me. I needed to build up my memory banks; I had so much groundwork to catch up on. And instead, I was stuck in my office, thumbing through a Rothmans, waiting to do an interview for our Clubcall before carrying out an unnecessary personal appearance.

And the media demands are insatiable. When I first arrived, and everything was new and fresh, I adopted an open house policy at Bodymoor. In fact, we're still pretty open. But I think our free spirit was abused; it all got a little out of hand. Journalists waiting by your car when you have to dash off; others stopping the players in the car park.

I've since spoken to journalists working the London patch who have told me they might as well try to speak with the Pope as interview Arsene Wenger, Luca Vialli or George Graham during the week. No chance. I was in the middle of all this thinking it just had to be done. It was more invaluable experience which I would put to good use in the future.

Sometimes, you have to just go through these patches in your life to learn; to make sure you don't make the same mistake. It was like finding out about Gareth Barry. I *thought* he was a good player; I *suspected* he might be a little special, that he could handle that opening game at Everton. But the only way I could find out was by sticking him in there. And the only way I could unearth and identify the huge problems that hit me during this period was by going through them.

During the dark days of my post-Portsmouth experience, I always used to wonder why the same old guys used to get the jobs. Guys who had failed at one club after another. But the answer was always that they had the experience to cope with everything.

The arrogance of youth sometimes leads you to believe otherwise. But there never will be a short cut to experience.

So, anyway, in we limped without Bozzy, without any of the fizz and snap and sparkle that accompanied the first half of our campaign. We went staggering past the finishing post like that 14-year-old cross-country runner all those years ago, desperately seeking a kerb he could trip over to declare the race null and void.

Even though we stopped the rot, even pulling off a win at Liverpool during the run-in, we were given one final kick in the whatsits by not even qualifying for Europe. And this after I had been so certain two or three months earlier that we could make the Champions League even if the title itself was out of bounds.

You never take much notice of fixtures that are too far distant. But for the first months of that season, I had not been able to help myself. Our last three away games were at Anfield, Old Trafford and Highbury.

It felt like an omen. After all, the last time Villa won the Championship, in 1981, their final, conclusive game had been at Highbury. And in contrast, our final three home games were all against teams in the wrong end of the table – Southampton, Forest and Charlton, teams we would be expected to beat. What if, just what if, we had to go to Liverpool or United or Arsenal with the big prize at stake? What incredible occasions they could be. That was the climax to the season that, for so long, was in my dreams. Unfortunately, that's where it stayed.

When I stood on the touchline at Highbury on that final Sunday, 16 May, it was Reality Bites. What a despairing anti-climax. We had cocked it up so badly that, having allowed Charlton to come from behind and beat us 4–3 at Villa Park the week before, we were now in danger of missing a place in the ruddy InterToto Cup. I ask you; the InterToto Cup. Here were Arsenal, hoping Spurs could beat United at Old Trafford to give them a last-ditch title chance, and here we were struggling to get into the Inter-bloody-Toto.

It was desperate. I remembered that astonishing comeback against the Gunners. We had seemed so right that day. Anything had seemed possible. Now look at us. The reality of our decline had slowly been seeping into my system but, boy, it kicked in that day.

West Ham, our rivals for the one last European spot in the InterToto, duly beat Middlesbrough and we did OK at Arsenal but conceded a soft goal near the end. A 1–0 defeat to finish with. Sixth place, one spot higher than last season, but not good enough for Europe. It didn't make sense. Very little did at that time.

I had told the players beforehand that I could not have asked for more. For 95 per cent of the time from 95 per cent of the staff,

I had been given everything. It is difficult to get much more. I still had a lot of love for them. It wasn't their fault. It was me who had got it all wrong. I had picked the wrong teams. I had maybe asked one or two to do things that were beyond them. I had not handled things as well as I should have done.

I had got it wrong.

I clung to a few positives. Yes, we had finished a place higher. And I remember reading how Lawrie McMenemy had taken 12 years to get his club the way he wanted it; how Alex Ferguson had taken four years before winning a trophy at Old Trafford despite having the weight of Manchester United behind him. We can't imagine it now but Fergie's early United teams finished in the bottom half of the table.

I had been at Villa 15 months. Maybe I wasn't doing so bad after all. And the squad was stronger, I knew that. And so was the manager. What an experience that had been.

But when that final whistle blew at Highbury I was shot. Knackered. Physically, fine. But mentally exhausted. If the truth be known, I had wanted the season to finish some time back in March; the last couple of months had been torture.

The daily media grind had worn me out as much as anything. I did not want to answer any more silly, inconsequential questions. You have to do it, I know that. The club demands it, the job demands it and if you don't, then the reaction is going to be: 'Huh, he's changed his tune now hasn't he? Lose a few games and suddenly we can't get hold of him.'

But I was shattered by it all and couldn't wait for the release that would be the end of the season.

When it begins, you steel yourself. You know it's head down for 40 weeks, constant, relentless, incessant. For 24 hours of each of those 280 days, you are at the beck and call of 20 or 30 players, and their little envies and jealousies, strengths and weaknesses, their wives, their girlfriends, their mums, their agents, their ambitions, their fears and the chairman, the directors, the fans, the press... the whole darn circus.

You have to pick your way carefully through that minefield and try to find a team that will win a few games to keep you in the job; even better, win a trophy. It is what we are paid for and, yes, paid handsomely.

But then comes that week, just one week, at the end of it all; the one week in the year when the phone gets switched off and for the seven days spent with the staff and the boys on our end-of-season trip to Majorca, I am answerable to no one. Heaven. Sheer heaven.

I collapsed on to the beach and knocked the top off a bottle of beer, ritually breaking my self-imposed embargo – no alcohol during the season. Another ritual is to sack all the staff by 6 p.m. for cocking it up and then reappoint them by 6.30 p.m.

But still the recriminations wouldn't stop. That bloody Charlton game, for example; that was reasonably fresh in my mind and kept chewing at me. If this hadn't happened, if that didn't occur. Sod it. Sod it. Sod it. The stakes are so big these days and there you are, right at the heart of it, with millions upon millions resting upon whether you pick the right team. That match had cost everyone money – the players and manager in bonuses, the club in terms of European revenue. And not just the money, the prestige.

A walk with the staff, past a few bars dominated by the English football fraternity, or so it seems. And there, on all the satellite TVs, are the highlights of the Premiership season just completed. You can't escape it.

I remember briefly steeling myself to glance up.

Who was that idiot jumping around in excitement at Southampton?

Oh Christ mate, turn it off will you? Just turn it off.

CHAPTER 11

'What – you mean Boateng and *Keane?*'

'He needs to get away from Liverpool. If you can do that, I don't think you'll regret it.'

I had bumped into Steve Staunton, the man who had walked out on me the previous summer, at a hotel complex in Sardinia, a complex the English footballing establishment had discovered during Italia 90. It was now a popular destination for the family holiday. And after the 10 months I had just survived, it seemed a perfect place to reintroduce myself to my nearest and dearest.

'Hi, I'm John, and I'm your father in case you had forgotten,' I felt like saying to little Bella.

When I arrived there with Michele and Bella a couple of weeks after that Arsenal game, it was no surprise to find the 'village' liberally sprinkled with football folk.

Not just those from the Premiership, either. Italians, Dutch, German players – they were all there. Michele might well have suspected that we could not complete a two-week break in the Med without the game invading our peace and quiet.

But Steve was a guy whose opinion I respected. I go back to that point about having your say, getting things in the open, and then shaking hands and getting on with life. Since he had decided Villa and John Gregory were not big enough for him, we had spoken a couple of times without any rancour.

Now I was actively seeking his views and thoughts on one of

the best-known characters in the English game. Liverpool's goal-keeper David James. For months I had been thinking about his suitability in replacing Bosnich without being able to reach a firm decision. But it was common knowledge that he would be available at the right price; Gerard Houllier, the new French manager at Anfield, was planning a big turnaround in staff.

In fact, no sooner had Steve and his family touched down for their break than they bumped into Stephan Henchoz – who, having just signed for Liverpool, was now a direct challenge to Steve's first-team place. But I knew the goalkeeping position had to be sorted out as a matter of some urgency. Bosnich was gone. The most I had ever hoped for as the season had unfolded was that we might just get him to stay for one more year; he had missed such a chunk of the programme, he might not have attracted the big fish he was looking for. But, deep down, the whispers from Old Trafford were always telling me that was a forlorn hope.

Michael was a good deputy – but he was just not my kind of keeper. I like mine big, dominant, bossy, with a touch of arro-gance and, most of all, happy coming for crosses. Michael was a shot-stopper, a bloody good one, but a shot-stopper all the same. And I think he might have had a credibility problem with the Villa fans who were simply never going to forgive him for not being Mark Bosnich. Not only were we looking for a new No. 1 but very probably a new deputy. Michael was in the last year of his contract; he was not going to hang around unless I moved him up into the senior slot.

So we had spent much of that season scouring the Continent in search of 'the next Bosnich'. Particularly in the Scandinavian market, where one agent after another assured us they had found 'the new Schmeichel'.

Sometimes fate lends a hand. One guy strongly recommended was Thomas Sorensen, who was playing in Danish football. I've got one of the best goalkeeping coaches in the business in Paul Barron and it naturally fell on him to scrutinize the candidates.

Competition out there is feverish and if a strong tip comes in, you have to act quickly. One weekend, Paul worked out that he could catch a 6.30 a.m. flight out of Birmingham and then a connection to Copenhagen. With the help of a 90-minute car journey, he could get to see Sorensen and be back in time for our game the following day.

But the plan was scuppered when Paul arrived to find his flight cancelled. An alternative route via Paris might have got him there 10 minutes before the end of the game. And Paul is very thorough. He even likes to check their warm-up routines.

The trip was abandoned, although there would be another chance to watch Sorensen two weeks later. Two weeks later, however, we wouldn't have to go to Denmark to see him play. We could just nip up the motorway. He signed for Sunderland in the meantime – and he does look a bloody good recruit for Peter Reid.

Paul was flying all over the world in search of our man; we were facing a key decision of vital importance to our team's future. We had to get it right. Paul took a strong fancy to Carlos Roa out at Real Mallorca – but conceded the guy was perhaps a bit too eccentric, even for a goalkeeper!

Who else? Oh yes, we had the Colombian Farid Mondragon over for a week's trial from Real Zaragoza. He was how I liked my keepers – big enough to fill the goal – but to be blunt, I was disappointed in what I saw during his stay.

And I do have a little worry about keepers coming in from Spain or Italy because the game is so different out there. Crosses are whizzing in from all angles in England; it is the single most constant source of assault on the penalty area. They have to be able to handle it, mentally and physically.

So I binned that idea. Paul had already unearthed a little gem, mind. We had been tipped off about a Finnish lad, Peter Enckelman, their Under 21 keeper who was playing for a little-known club in his homeland, Turku. Paul wanted to sign him after six minutes of a game in Ireland. I wasn't quite so impulsive – for once – but I have since taken his point. The lad could be very special indeed and we eventually signed him for £200,000 late that January.

But he was still a baby; he was for the future. We had to find the man to take the senior spot. To handle the pressure; to stand in front of the Holte and take it on, win it over. And whenever I asked Paul to name the three most talented goalkeepers in the country, his answer never wavered. 'There's Schmeichel, there's Bosnich and there's James.' End of story. No others need apply.

But James? I wasn't sure. Oh, I liked him as a keeper well enough. In that 4–2 home defeat by Liverpool, I mentioned that they had defended better than us. James was one of the reasons why. He kept coming out to take crosses. It never fazed him. And he was so big, so athletic, with bags of natural talent. But it had been reported at the time that he was supposed to be trouble.

People in the game who I spoke to initially seemed to confirm that popularly-held view of David as a talented but flawed individual. 'Stay away from him,' they were saying. 'He's a bad apple; in with the wrong crowd. Bring him in and you'll be asking for trouble.'

But none of the people telling me this actually KNEW him. I had to find out more.

So here I am, sitting over a glass of wine with one man who does. Staunton. And during that holiday we spend a lot of time talking about James. And Steve's version of the guy is very, very different.

He starts telling me about this fantastic trainer; this guy who is so awesome on the training pitch that they can't get anything past him; this guy who is so brave and talented. Steve is describing a phenomenal goalkeeper to me. And Steve also knew Paul Barron and how good a coach he was. Stick the two of them together, he was suggesting, and you could have a hell of a combination.

Yeah, that's true. Paul's coaching is spot-on. Ask the guys who have worked with him. It's all game-related. And it's all about keeping the strengths ticking over and working on those weaknesses. If you think Bozzy is a poor kicker now, you should have seen him before Paul got to work on him.

Steve always – but always – speaks his mind. If he thought David was a prat, he would have said so. If he thought him crap, he would have told me. No, he was giving me his honest opinion and I was hooked. I even asked him to speculate over the price. What did he think they would want for him? Somewhere between £2 million and £3 million, he thought. And if so, it could represent a heck of a bargain.

But there was that one proviso. You do need to get him out of Liverpool; there were one or two influences there that were not helping him.

So there was a good deal of that holiday spent pondering over our next keeper. There was one other outstanding candidate. Blackburn were ready to take money for Tim Flowers and his credentials were pretty impressive, too – in the last England World Cup squad, experienced, great pro, good dressing-room influence. He was also a West Midlander who had started at Wolves. He knew the patch; he would relish Villa Park.

I called him from Sardinia and checked a few things out. He was not going to be available for long; other clubs were sure to be ringing him.

So Flowers or James? No, I've got this hunch about James. I want to go for him. I spoke with the chairman worried that I might get some resistance. Labels are hard to shake off in football; I fretted that the chairman would give me that big, sharp intake of breath and say, 'Are you sure about this John?'

But to be fair to the boss, he was very supportive, very pro-David. 'Yes,' he said, 'let's do it. Find out what we're talking about.' Back from Sardinia, refreshed and now settled in my mind that I was going to take the plunge with James, I rang his agent. Check out his position – word is he can go, do you think he would fancy our place? The vibe was very positive. Liverpool cleared the way. Time to speak to the boy himself. It was now mid-June. I got in my car the next day, headed for the M6 North, and dialled his number.

'I'm coming up there to sign you,' I told him with vintage Gregory cockiness.

'When?' he asked.

'Right now. Today. I'm not letting you out of my sight until you're an Aston Villa player.'

And I stuck to my word. I sat with him in that hotel room at Manchester Airport until he had signed on the dotted line. To be honest, it wasn't that difficult a negotiation. I liked the guy the moment we started talking and it was clear he wanted that fresh start, too. He was dying to get cracking at a new club. Perhaps there is a hint, just a hint, of proving one or two people wrong. Not too much, though, because David has got a very good record if you care to examine it.

But he had played in a transitional Liverpool team at a time when the club was beginning to see the passage of power switch from Anfield to Old Trafford. That was difficult for all of them, fans and club staff, to accept. And it seemed to me a couple of errors in some big matches had stuck with him long, long past their sell-by date. I felt we were getting a major bonus from that in terms of the price.

And his wages were not an issue and were swiftly dealt with. It was not significant. He'll do for me, I thought.

And I was getting such a strong, optimistic feeling about this. It *felt* right. And the price was terrific at £1.7 million. Oh sure, I knew people would be laughing and giggling. They would be sold on all that 'Calamity James' nonsense. Predictably, there were the letters in the local papers and the phone calls to the radio phone-ins – 'Gregory's lost the plot,' they were saying. 'I cannot believe we have signed this guy.'

But from the moment David arrived, I knew, we all knew, we had a good 'un all right. The best we could have hoped for.

I realized that I was back into the swing of it. All the fatigue, all the jaded emotions of that battered and bruised figure on the Arsenal touch-line a few weeks earlier were gone. I couldn't believe it. Football's powers of rehabilitation are remarkable. A few weeks away from the training ground had transformed me. I was no longer desperate for the old season to end; I was impatient for the next one to start.

I knew there was more work to be done with the squad, though. We needed freshening up, we needed strengthening. We had been caught out last season; I was desperate to avoid that again. I wanted a squad where two or three could be missing and the changeover to other players would be smooth.

That's what United and Arsenal can do. They can have three or four out and they don't even notice it. And I wanted the players sitting on the bench to be capable of changing games, not just filling in the numbers.

I could not stand in the way of two of our 'support staff' when they were offered good moves. Simon Grayson went to Blackburn for £1 million – smashing lad and a great pro. He had spent all last season sitting on the bench and not whinged once. That kind of loyalty is priceless and meant that, when Blackburn came in, I was determined to help the deal along as smoothly as possible.

The trouble-makers might not find gaffers quite so accommodating.

And Riccy Scimeca went off to Forest for £3 million, giving me the chance to pat myself on the back for getting him tied up to a long contract the previous summer. Without it, that was £3 million that we would never have seen.

But I was still operating on a limited budget; I was paying the price for our failure to qualify for European football in different ways. The club had made record profits over the last 18 months but now, with some big wages about to kick in for the new financial year, I understandably had my wings clipped in the market. There was enough for maybe one more big hit. But not the big hit I had been dreaming of the day I sat sipping coffee with Juninho.

European football was off the agenda. I was not going to be able to call up Gabriel Batistuta and offer him a season in Brum playing domestic football. With the Champions League long since removed from view, the wage demands of the big-time superstars took them off my agenda.

There had been times last season where I had dared to dream of asking Del Piero or Baggio or Weah to pull up a chair and have a chat about joining Aston Villa FC. Manchester United and Arsenal offer a good wage but they have an even stronger attraction to pull in big names – the kudos of joining such famous and fantastic clubs.

It was still my dream to make Villa equally special in global terms; I still felt the traditions, size, the whole feel of the place made it a possibility. Still do, of course. But we had to get up there on to the big stages. After the collapse of our season, even the second tier of players was out of reach now. They would not be interested in coming without European football on offer.

But who?

I wanted more energy and drive in midfield. Stand still in this game and you go backwards. It is getting faster and faster. The key to it all in England remains how well you can get around the pitch. Yes, Arsenal and United have the best players but they still worked like Trojans. Check out Scholes and Keane and Vieiri and Petit. We had been overpowered at times during that fateful second half of the season. Maybe some of our guys were now a little bit too comfortable – you know, rolling along, happy to finish sixth or seventh. I had to shake that up.

One Premiership player I had serious thoughts of trying to buy had already ruled himself out without knowing it. During that break in Majorca, I had wandered into a bar – like Sardinia, the area was crawling with partying footballers – and caught him smoking. I'm not a rabid anti-tobacco man, I should point out. I just don't like to see my players with a fag in their hand. The demands today are just too high and you cannot take any liberties with your physical condition. So no thanks.

By the time the players were reporting back for training, I had narrowed the choice down to two. The performances of George Boateng for Coventry last season had left a big mark on me, reinforced when he scored twice and caused us all manner of problems in the 'Game I Couldn't Forget Even Though I Wanted To' at Villa Park.

Called in Dion for a character reference and that could not have been better. George is a devout Christian and that immediately tells you something about the man. A devout Christian who kept all his fire and brimstone for the pitch.

So he was definitely in my thoughts. So was the boy at Wolves, Robbie Keane. I knew he was going to be a very good player; the entire game did. I just wasn't sure yet how good. Character reference? I know, Mick McCarthy, the boy's international manager.

'Get him – get him now. Whatever it takes. If it's £5 million, £6 million whatever. Go and get him. He is the business.' Hmmm. Not much doubt about that, then.

So Boateng or Keane. Boateng or Keane. The either-or buzzed around in my head for some time. I remember thrashing it out with the chairman, Steve and Mark one day. Running through all the permutations. Boateng – fantastic energy, boundless, does it all, runs, tackles, chases, heads it, passes it, scores the odd goal. Keane? Up front we might be caught a little light. Dublin has had his hernia operation and I wasn't sure how quickly he was going to recover. I didn't really see Merse as a front player any more – well, maybe in emergencies. JJ – could he reproduce his form and in fact go on another level? And Stan? Well, more of him later.

Yes, we might get caught up front but...

'If you had to sign one, and one only, right now, today, who would it be?' asked the chairman.

That was the $64,000 question – and boy did I wish it was that cheap – which clarified things. Yep. Boateng. 'Let's go and get Boateng'.

And we knew we could. I had originally enquired about the lad towards the end of the previous season but been given a firm 'Not interested' from Coventry. In fact, it was more than that. The Coventry chairman trotted out the same old tiresome line about our trying to poach George.

I was getting really fed up with all this. Why did we keep having these problems with Coventry? An FA enquiry cleared us of any such malpractice as they had done over the Dublin episode; but still we were being painted as the bullies from up the road.

But now Boateng was for sale. This we knew because Mr Richardson rang Stevie to tell him so. Boateng for £5 million and Darren Huckerby for £6 million. So if we were still interested in George....

Steve immediately passed the message on to me. 'Hey, you'll never guess who's just called,' sort of thing. I think it was a surprise, too, for Gordon Strachan, Coventry's manager, whom I now contacted.

'It's about Boateng,' I said when he answered.

'What about him?'

'Well, your chairman rang our place yesterday and said you're willing to sell?'

'Are we?' said Strach. 'I don't know anything about that.' Oh no, here we go again. More trouble with Coventry. But Strach was as good as gold about it all and over the course of the next few days, we began to sort out a deal with Coventry. And I was convinced that, like James before him, I was getting the right man.

But in the middle of it all, I was sat with the board again, chewing the fat. We were homing in on Boateng. Yes, I was content with that. Push Keane to one side. You can't have everything. George was the one for now. And then the chairman threw me a wonderful curve ball.

'Why don't you go and get both of them?'

I couldn't believe what I was hearing.

'Sorry?'

'Why don't you go and get both of them?' he repeated.

'What – you mean Boateng *and* Keane?'

'Yes. The two of them for £10 million. Let's get the two of them.'

Music, sweet music, to my ears. Wow! The two of them. What every manager wants to hear. I fled the room in a state of excitement. Boateng and Keane. Add that pair to what we had and it starts to look very interesting.

Now, on the day that we eventually signed George for £4.5 million, we also introduced a left back, Najwan Ghrayib, an Israeli international Ross had seen on his travels to return with glowing reports. Quick, attacking, good crosser, he would cost us £1 million and be one for the future. We were in danger of losing him to Tottenham for a while but their interest either collapsed or the deal fell through. I didn't care. I was pleased to bring him in for a position in which we have struggled to find cover. He will be ready soon as well, I predict.

But despite this extra outlay, we still had the go-ahead to get Keane. If we could.

Earlier in the summer, a bid from Middlesbrough of £6 million had been accepted by Wolves. But they knew, and I knew, that the player did not want to go there. As far as I was aware, we were the only other club to show that level of interest. So let's get the wheels in motion.

We contacted Wolves and lodged our first bid at £5 million. It was a little difficult because Colin Lee, the manager, was on holiday and the chief executive, John Richards, was in Australia. But the message came back. No. It was £6 million. That was what Middlesbrough had offered and that's what the price would be. Ah but that offer is irrelevant, I thought. Keane doesn't want to go there. Whatever Robbo is offering is neither here nor there.

It was an awful lot of money. I knew that when the bid was made by Boro it had been greeted with excitement at Molineux. Sure, they knew Robbie was a terrific prospect but he had finished the season looking a little tired and jaded, not in prime market condition. They wanted to buy new players and Keane was their last chance to raise money.

So out came the poker cards. We went to £5.5 million and still they stuck at £6 million. I felt they were adopting a very arrogant tone, I must admit. They would not consider any add-ons or whatever; it was £6 million. Or no deal.

All right then, let's check him out. Let's convince ourselves we should pay £6 million. I went with the chairman to a Wolves pre-season friendly desperately trying to read the signs. The banter with the fans was great but it also told me something.

'Come on John,' one of them was saying, 'If he plays down the road we can come and watch him at Villa every so often – and we can get some new players with your cash.' It was good, knockabout stuff, but it also told me that there was a momentum to sell Robbie.

But when we got the team sheets, Robbie was only a substitute. Now what did that mean? Was Colin trying to sort out his team without Robbie, knowing he would not be there much longer? Or did they not want us to see him play because, deep down, they didn't feel he was worth £6 million? I couldn't work it out.

Robbie came on near the end, showed a few bits and pieces, but nothing to really enthuse over. Not with a £6 million price tag on his head.

And by now I was feeling other pressures.

This could be my last cheque, I knew that. I had brought in some expensive players with the money we had raised and some of them had finished the season in less than convincing fashion. Thompson's first year had been inconclusive; Merse had spent too much of the time fighting his own demons and not the opposition; Steve Stone had yet to settle; even Watson, who had started well, had lost form near the end and struggled.

I knew James would be OK. I knew Boateng was a rock-solid acquisition. But the mentality at Villa is not one where you can splash out £6 million and stick a kid away in the reserves for a year.

But that's how I saw Robbie. He was just a good player. I had no pre-conceived notions about where I was going to play him, even. He was a good player who was going to get better and better. I saw him coming in, getting to know us, learning his trade, coming in for four or five games, then taking a breather.

People would want more than that for their £6 million. This was getting difficult to call.

Amidst all this, the last thing I needed was an inadvertent

twist of the knife from the most highly-regarded manager in the country. But reports appeared in the press that His Lordship at Old Trafford, having just pocketed a treble I had thought impossible, would invest no more than a few hundred thousand in Keane before putting him in the reserves for a year.

Fergie, I believe, had been speaking at a private dinner and did not expect to be quoted publicly. But his casual, off-the-cuff remarks piled on the pressure. Here was one of the greatest managers of all time saying the boy on whom Villa were preparing to pay nearly £6 million would warrant only a bit of loose change and a year in the stiffs at United.

Come on Robbie. I need to see something special. Something to convince not just me but the guys around me that you are worth it. So check the lad out again. Only this time, do it quietly. So on a warm summer's evening at Molineux, I hid behind a baseball cap and dark glasses, grabbed a cup of Bovril and sat behind the goal with the Wolves' fans for another friendly.

Largely, the disguise worked. One or two youngsters tried to catch me out by shouting 'Hey John', a few times but I never responded. Wolves were playing the German side Werder Bremen and Robbie got through on the keeper three times. And he fluffed every one of them.

Where is Hot Shot Keane? As a kid, one of my favourite comics had been *Scorcher* and my favourite story all about 'Billy's Boots,' an old pair the hero had handed down to him by his grandfather which, whenever he wore them, brought goals, goals, goals. And in the story, his grandad had been called Hot Shot Keane – and that's what I was looking for. 'Come on,' I kept whispering under my breath, 'show me Hot Shot Keane'.

But it never happened, nor did it in the third friendly at Molineux. I still had not seen him play well. Wolves' first League game would be at Manchester City; perhaps it will be different when the real stuff gets under way. He scored in the first couple of minutes. A well-taken goal, too. At last, that's what I need to see. And then did absolutely nothing else.

I drove away, desperately trying to convince myself that I could recommend we pay £6 million for him but knowing I couldn't. In fact, quite the opposite. Without ever making it public, we resolved to cancel our interest once and for all.

That money put aside for Robbie would have been the last of the kitty. But what if something else happened during that season? We might need someone to get us out of a mess; we might need someone to give us that extra spur as we turn the year. No, let's keep our counsel and our money. That was the decision, a decision that has since caused me a lot of trouble.

But I keep saying it. You put me through the same circumstances all over again and I would make the same choice. But a couple of days later, Coventry used the money they had raised by selling Huckerby to Leeds to buy Robbie. He was supposedly snatched from under our noses. That was not true. We were no longer interested.

In fact, had Wolves come back to us and said 'OK, we'll accept your £5 million' or even the £5.5 million, we would have said: 'No thanks, we've changed our minds'. Yep, I know. Robbie has done brilliantly for Coventry – and good luck to him and good luck to them. But remember those comments by Fergie? Remember the Wolves' fans who were happy to grab the money? That's how it was at the time and I would be lying if I told you different.

The trouble in this country is that everyone thinks that it is Manchester United who have the biggest group of players. They're wrong. No one has a bigger squad than Hindsight United. They're everywhere. On TV, in the papers, around the grounds, on the phone-ins. All those smart-alecs and failed managers who have never been wrong about a football match in their entire lives.

They never have to make the decision which carries with it any responsibility, of course. But that's the signing-on fee when you join Hindsight United. You're never wrong and it never costs you a penny.

No, I made my bed and I'll lie in it. And I'll tell you something else. A few weeks after Dion had signed, I remember having a chat with him. See how he was settling in, make sure there were no problems, that sort of thing. And what he said really surprised me; it gave me a lot to think about.

'You know, I never realized just how big this club is,' he told me. 'Yeah, I knew it was decent sized and all that but not this big. There's no escape, you know. Everywhere I go it's Villa, Villa, Villa.'

Now Dion is an experienced lad; heck, he's even played at United, even if his career there never truly got going. But that observation from such a senior player really struck home. And it set me thinking.

I don't suppose too many of you have ever stood in the centre circle with the Holte End packed and the stands, stretching back, crammed with noise and faces you can't make out. It is quite a sight. And I mean huge. Bloody huge. It takes some handling. And if you're having a bad time there's nowhere to hide. That Holte End murmur can be a killer.

I never thought about it before because I'm an arrogant sod who never doubted that Villa Park was *my* stadium. But I began to wonder after that chat with Dion if adjusting to life at Villa might be a little more difficult than I had previously imagined.

Some of the players who have arrived as big fish from smaller ponds have suddenly found themselves just one face among a big group of players. All of them good ones. They walk in to our dressing-room and there's Southgate and Ehiogu and Merson and James and Dublin. These are big guys in the game with a lot of respect, a lot of status.

The newcomer is no longer the comfortably placed star attraction. They have to show they are good enough to these new team-mates as well as conquering that intimidating stadium, crammed with out-of-pocket supporters waiting to pass judgement.

I don't know if Robbie would have handled that with us. Not the way he has at Coventry. He may have. But, clearly, some haven't. Trouble is, there's only ever one way to find out.

CHAPTER 12

Ginger Spice and Nora Batty in tights

If you asked the 1986 England World Cup squad to name their Public Enemy number one, the chap they would all have happily strung up and left to rot in the Mexican sun, I bet to a man they would have chosen Diego Maradona. Diego and his Hand of God. The chance to play in a World Cup semi-final does not come around every week and what Maradona did to them that day must have stuck in their craw.

But if you took those same England players and asked them to pick their all-time World XI, then I would again bet that the Argentinian would have been the first name on all of their team sheets. What they thought about Maradona as a man would not have come into it; in football matters, ability and performance are the only currencies.

It is the same the world over. We may hate one player or loathe another. But if they are in the team doing the job it doesn't matter; we couldn't give a stuff.

Ugo has had a few pops at me; it could be that he can't stand me. In fact, if all my players like me, then I am not doing my job properly. That, you may recall, was one of the first lessons I learnt at Portsmouth. You are not one of the lads any more, so courting friendships is a waste of time. Respect for each other's ability is all that matters. And I keep picking Ugo because he keeps playing well. And that is all I am interested in.

Archie Gemmill, the former Scottish international and Nottingham Forest and Derby player, once said that he hated Brian Clough with all the passion he could muster. But in the same breath he conceded that he would give him his last ten bob, such was the immense respect he held for him.

All this is by way of nailing one of the stories up and running by the time the players reported back for training at the beginning of the 1999-2000 season. That the supposed impasse between Stan and myself was now personal. That it no longer mattered what the player did. That it would not count if he produced the most outstanding pre-season form of his life.

My problem with him was now so entrenched, so bitter and so personal, that he would remain an outcast for as long as I remained manager. So the stories went.

Well, that is rubbish. I would never cut off my nose to spite my face. And I would never say: 'Stan has played his last game for Villa'. For a start, I would lose face if ever the time came when he did pull on the shirt again. And you never know... there might just come a time when I would need him to play.

However, with Stan there are always many different side issues which affect that decision.

And as the players returned for pre-season training, I would be lying if I said I did not have my doubts that that day would ever come.

The circus was there to greet us by the time we reported back. I think the local media were expecting me to stand at the gates of our training ground and turn Stan away.

Quite the opposite. His treatment for depression was all but completed and I was as anxious as the next man to welcome him back and see what sort of shape he was in. We had a good three or four weeks ahead of us, the first part of which would be the most painful. The physical graft. The fitness work from which everything thereafter springs. I wanted to monitor him closely during this fairly thankless stuff. To see how he coped and reacted to everything.

There was an initial confrontation that did not bode well. His boots had been tidied up and taken away at the end of the previous season and Stan was furious about it. But the way that he picked on poor Jim Paul – a more mild-mannered guy it is difficult to imagine – did not go down well with me or, I know, a lot of the other guys. So that was not a good start.

But while running he was looking fine. When he went to work with the other coaches, he was the first one I checked on. Was he putting it in? And the answer was a very positive 'Yes'.

But then the balls came out and the training ground matches started – and he looked a million miles away still. It quickly settled in my mind that Dion and Julian would be the senior partnership for the new season and it was up to Stan to break through that pecking order. That would be his test. How would he respond?

At the same time, possible transfer opportunities for Stan were cropping up. And as I doubted that he could ever again be the force he was, I was ready to pursue them. The Greek club Panathanaikos whisked him out to Athens with his agent, Paul Stretford, and spent a weekend wooing him. It seemed like a fantastic opportunity, the chance for Stan to start afresh, away from the English media glare, and put his life and career back on the rails. They even had European football on their plate for that season. We were talking about a fee in the region of £3 million, which, bearing in mind the troubles of the previous 18 months, was a good deal for Villa. But Stan rejected the idea. No complaints there; that is his right, after all.

We had phone calls from a few English clubs but all from too far down the status scale to interest Stan. Fulham, however, provided an attractive alternative. Their manager, Paul Bracewell, was prepared to take Stan on a three-month loan and have a good look-see. There could be a permanent transfer at the end of that time if all went well.

This seemed perfect to me. Stan could drop down a division, play against inferior opponents, and get his game back together. He could bang in six or seven goals, cause a stir and then thrust all the pressure on me. Fine. Would I sell him or would I put him back in our team? I would have loved to have had that decision to make. Stan's a bloody good player; I know that as well as anyone. And the thought of his coming back on a roll was something I could look forward to.

So I put Stan in the tray marked 'Pending'.

* * *

I love my music. My father had filled our house with Sinatra, and his definitive *Songs for Swinging Lovers* album from the legendary Capitol years remains an all-time favourite; I think I know every line of every fantastic song. It has always struck me as a little more than coincidence that, just as Dad's great hero came from New Jersey, so did mine – Bruce Springsteen. The Boss.

Ever since those early days, music had been the best escape, the best release for me. And since stepping into the Villa job, I had come to appreciate even more its therapeutic powers.

I've got this little room at home where I can shut the door – Michele calls it my studio and knows better than to disturb me there – and dig into my CD collection. I can go there, lock out the world, and relax. Lately, I have also been able to pick up a guitar and strum along to some of the songs.

I remember a long time ago, going round to my old Brighton team-mate Gordon Smith's house and being gobsmacked when he started strumming some Beatles tunes on a guitar. It was mesmerizing. We sang ourselves hoarse long into the night and I was hooked.

I had bought one there and then but, try as I might, failed miserably to master the damn thing, even in a rudimentary fashion. But since then I had taken that guitar around with me, a cheap £90 Yamaha, from club to club, move to move, house to house. It was like a piece of furniture. But all it did was gather dust.

Until, that is, my return to Villa as a coach with Brian. I was again inspired when Stevie had started playing at a party one night. That was it. I drove Michele mad with tortuous renditions of 'Amazing Grace' before progressing to 'Mull of Kintyre'. But I was more determined than ever to learn and now, at the grand old age of 45, I can at least pick out a few basic chords. If you want badly enough to do something, then I believe you can do it. It's what made me a professional footballer and a coach and a manager. And it's what enabled me to learn the guitar.

I recommend it to any of my peers or contemporaries. Piano, saxophone, clarinet, trumpet... whatever tickles your fancy. Music remains a wonderful way to forget all the pressures, all the madness, of the football world.

And Springsteen was always my man. There was something

about his songs that always seemed to reach me. His struggles at home, his arguments with his father about making something of his life, about putting down that stupid guitar and getting a proper job... it seemed to echo my childhood and my father telling me I would never make it as a professional footballer.

Springsteen sang of small town America and I knew where that was coming from, too. I had grown up in a small, dead-end, market town in Cambridgeshire where some people are born, reared, schooled, work, marry, have children, grandchildren... and then die. Without knowing anything else. And as an ambitious teenager in the Sixties, when Eric Burdon and the Animals sang 'We Gotta Get Out of this Place,' I knew just what they meant. I was determined to get away and make something of my life.

Anyway, that summer I would see Springsteen performing in his home town because our pre-season trip took us to New York and a prestige tournament involving Ajax of Holland, Fiorentina of Italy and – minus Stan – Panathanaikos of Greece.

Contrary to some claims, the fact that my hero would be appearing in concert just down the road was pure coincidence, something Stevie discovered long after we had agreed to take part in the tournament.

But I flew out there in high spirits – and not just because I would be seeing The Boss in action. I was delighted at having our new signings aboard and convinced that they would make us better equipped to handle the rigours of the entire season. And it was a highly useful exercise, too. Great opposition, high quality; superbly organized, excellent facilities. All the matches were staged in the stadium of the New York Giants American football team. The only disappointment were the crowds, all around the 25,000 mark. So much for the 1994 World Cup providing the game's big breakthrough across the Pond.

I think the organizers had planned on an Ajax v Fiorentina final, so it was nice to upset the apple-cart by beating Ajax in the first game, albeit on penalties. Gareth Southgate took our first that night, based on the theory that if he missed, we had four more to rectify the damage. He did. And that would be something that would come back to haunt me a few months later.

The Ajax game had been played in pitch temperatures of more

than 100°F. It took an awful lot out of us. So I was not too disturbed by a heavy defeat, 4–0, against Fiorentina in the final. They were ahead of us in terms of fitness and, in Gabriel Batistuta, they possessed one of the finest strikers in the world.

That was my first close-up view of the guy and he was sensational, the kind of player we would one day need to have at Villa if we were to be a top club. I spoke at length with Gareth after the game and he was full of admiration for the player. Gareth has played against the very best while picking up 30 England caps but, in his opinion, he had encountered nothing to surpass Batistuta that night.

His power and shooting ability were awesome. I remember his scoring a penalty in that game and I could only marvel at the way he drove it into the top corner with such concentration and velocity. If only...

All that and Springsteen too. Three and a half hours he gave us; pure, undiluted effort. I had been to concerts where the star-turn had run through their hits in an hour, picked up the cheque and gone home. Each and every time, Springsteen is determined to make the night the best of your life. It was truly inspirational and I left the arena with more than his songs buzzing around my head. There was a lesson there, too. Half measures would never be good enough; you had to give it everything, your last drop of energy, heart and soul. That's what Springsteen did; that's what the best do. That's why no matter what time I get to my office at Bodymoor Heath of a morning, I always suspect Fergie has got to his half an hour earlier.

All my heroes have this streak running through them, this relentless determination to utilize to the utmost whatever gifts God gave them. That nature blesses you with an extraordinary talent is a chance of birth; what you do with it is the true measure of any man or woman.

In the sporting world, I identified that in great champions such as snooker's Steve Davis and Stephen Hendrie, or Bjorn Borg and Nick Faldo; guys who the moment they had won one tournament, immediately began preparing for the next. I read how after one of his world championship wins, Davis was up bright and early the next day to put in four or five hours of practice. And Geoff Boycott, once dismissed for 149, went straight into the nets to eliminate the mistake which had cost him 150.

And Keegan in football. There might have been more blessed players around in Europe but none that could match his drive and desire to push himself to the limit. To tear up his 'home for life' existence at Liverpool and move to Germany, learn the language and win trophies with Hamburg. Incredible.

I have no time for one-hit wonders. The bands I love and revere are those who keep coming up with one great album after another. A team that has a great season, wins the FA Cup and spends the next six months dining out on it. That's not for me.

I have no time for the wasters and the con men. I love the tryers, the guys who give you everything, every time.

I was happy with the value of the trip. I was still sifting through various team permutations but the newcomers had settled in well and I was seeing something in Merse that was encouraging. I had not been too sure about him when we returned to training but I sensed he was getting his life in order and was at last starting to smile again. He had had a good summer, clearly enjoyed himself, and with his family life settling down once more, seemed in a pretty good frame of mind.

I was not too sure yet how or where to play him. Likewise Boateng. I wasn't convinced I could yet trust him solely in the centre of midfield. But it didn't give me any headaches. I love getting good players together and worrying about the best starting XI afterwards. That is me. And this lot were a good bunch, I was convinced of that. We were all a little older and wiser for the previous season's experiences and would show that benefit. Just you wait and see, I was silently challenging the world.

There are always massive temptations in New York, especially if you invite a bunch of fit, wealthy, heterosexual young men to take a bite from the Big Apple at any given time. We were only there for a few days and on the Saturday of our stay, we gave the squad free-time on the understanding that they should meet the 10 p.m. curfew back at the hotel. It was a big test which everyone passed.

Yes. I love my boys. They are all tryers. They will do for me.

I touched down in England to discover I was joint favourite, along with Gullit at Newcastle, for the first Premiership sacking of the season. Oh, that's nice. Gullit and Gregory followed by Gerard Houllier at Liverpool. Had I not gained anything for the advances we had made so far? Apparently not.

I think much of the bookmakers' bleak outlook for my future sprang from their image of my chairman. That old, somewhat tired, 'Deadly Doug' nonsense. I think he enjoys the mischievous element it implies; but he is a 75-year-old man now with massive experience in football; experience that has perhaps taught him that chopping and changing managers is not necessarily the way forward. That's my guess, anyway. Certainly, this portrait of him as an impatient and ruthless 'hirer and firer' did not tally with the guy I was working with.

I knew he was extremely close to Brian Little, my immediate predecessor, but that the manager before him, Big Ron, had remained distant. I would guess our relationship is pitched somewhere in between. Where Brian would see him every day and Ron not at all, the chairman and I get together a couple of times a week. And those meetings have always been worthwhile.

I have spoken to another Premiership manager who can never find his chairman. I always know that mine is just a short walk down the corridor. In fact, a lot of my contemporaries have diffi-cult relationships with their bosses but I think our working rela-tionship – which is what really matters – is pretty strong. Little did I know then how much it would be put to the test.

We have this saying we use with each other, 'Better the devil you know'. I know what he's like, he knows what I'm like. I had really felt for him during our fade-out in the previous season. He had pinned so much on winning the Championship that year and he could not understand why we were losing.

He gave me a chance for which I will be eternally grateful and there are 19 other Premiership chairmen who didn't. I would love to repay him for that, more than anything.

Before he ever got the chance to make the bookies' vision of events come true, I wanted to stick a trophy in his hand and say, 'There you are mate – that's one for you.' And then I would feel we were quits.

So, no, my low survival chances in the eyes of the bookies was of no particular concern. Neither was the noticeable shift in how

I was now seen by the media. I had become yesterday's news, last season's story. 'Interview Gregory? No, we've been there, done that, bought the wallpaper, got the duvet. Let's have something fresh. He had his year in the sun, lasted longer than we thought, but he's not the one. He's not the Messiah. Move on. Find something new.'

We were 33–1 for the championship which basically meant we were seen as nothing more than making up the numbers. Top 10, maybe a European spot if we were lucky.

All this was fine by me.

We'll bloody show you, I thought. We'll bloody show you.

And we did. Or at least I thought we did. We won at Newcastle on the opening day of the season. A fantastic result. It was our fourth opening-day away fixture on the trot and hardly the start I wanted. Gullit had changed the Newcastle team around. Anticipation was high. Have you heard the noise up there? For Goodison a year ago, read St James's Park.

I had resolved to try to relax a little more before games. The last hour before kick-off is the worst time for coaches and managers. Everything is ready. The only thing left to play with is your nerves.

I had previously opted to go out with the players and coaches and do the warm-up routines, to try to get some of the excess energy out of my system. I desperately wanted to adopt Terry Venables' approach – he could just switch off and go and have a drink in one of the executive boxes.

A stiff brandy was out of the question because the 'No Alcohol' rule was back in force but I tried to mingle around the corridors of St James's Park, chat with a few people. I hate that last hour, though. It's dead time. I just want the match to get started.

But everything went to plan. We were strong, solid, James making an impressive start behind Gareth and co. We managed to get the crowd quiet, always the first item on the agenda at Newcastle, and stifled them. But the turning point, undoubtedly, was the sending-off of Alan Shearer mid-way through the second half.

I thought he had been lucky to stay on the pitch as long as he did. Gareth got caught across the forehead a couple of times by his elbow – which I don't have any complaints about, inciden-tally. It is a physical game and as long as nothing is done in malice, well... then it's the law of the jungle as far as I'm concerned. And you have to hope you get a referee who will give you a fair shake of the dice.

The Sheffield official, Uriah Rennie, eventually red-carded Shearer for the most innocuous-looking challenge you could imagine. In fact, Ian Taylor's instant reaction, a picture of delighted disbelief, became the tell-tale image from the opening day of the season.

Perhaps Rennie was looking for Alan knowing he had missed one or two earlier in the game. Whatever. It takes a brave man to send off Shearer on his own patch and I was not complaining – especially with the mauling Alan had given us in the same fixture the previous season still fresh in my mind.

I had my own trouble with the officials that day, however. I had given Uriah stick for missing one or two things and was jumping up and down in the technical areas, calling him all the names under the sun – as most managers do amid the frenzied atmosphere of Premiership football.

Eventually, I was reported for foul language by the fourth offi-cial, Jeff Winter.

To me, that was a load of baloney. But on the opening day of the season, I always feel everybody is over-zealous, especially the game's jobsworths. Whether it's the match officials or the stew-ards or the club security guys. It is all, 'You can't do that sir' or 'I'm sorry, sir, you're not allowed in here unless you have the purple pass with two stars on.' You know?

In a few weeks it will all calm down and everything will settle into a routine. But for those opening few games, it's as if football is in the grip of the bloody civil service.

That disagreement with Winter would be the start of a series of run-ins with officialdom. But that night I did not let it spoil my satisfaction.

Shearer trooped off past me – and it was our job to cash in. Sure enough, Julian Joachim scored the winning goal a few minutes later and we ran out worthy winners.

Gullit was furious and ended up in more trouble than I did. I thought a lot of his reaction, as he tried to confront Rennie as the

referee left the pitch, was for showbusiness purposes only; maybe
he was trying to deflect from what had been a fairly flat performance by his side.

But it was a stormy afternoon and I decided to stay clear of the
press afterwards and sent up Harry to do the interviews in my
place. I knew that would upset the media folk, who were probably relishing the prospect of big-mouth Gregory spouting off
about the day's events.

Perhaps I was learning after all.

I thought it had been an excellent first day back at the office. But
when I got home to the missus – that is the city of Birmingham
– she was waiting there with a rolling pin in her hand.

The first year of our marriage had been the stuff of fantasy.
You could count the games we had lost on the fingers of one
hand. We had qualified for Europe and then led the Premiership
for three months. But now my novelty value had disappeared
and I just wasn't turning her on any more. It seemed many
people were already thinking about a divorce.

We had not spent £30 million bringing in world famous players. All we were offering punters were the same qualities we had
relied upon the season before – team spirit, hard work and
largely English abilities. The supporters just could not get
excited about this again. It was as if we had had one fantastic
party, but now I was having to do the cleaning up.

I have got a five-year-old girl and, like most children, she
always wants new toys. And that's what today's fans want. New
toys. I had been a breath of fresh air, supposedly. But now I was
just boring. They had heard it all before and seen it all before. We
want some new toys, they were screaming. And I had none to
give.

I was more than happy with the squad I was putting together;
I knew we were getting stronger. It was now going to be a long,
hard road to make up the ground on the élite. The idea of an
instant leap, an idea we had all dared to nurture the previous
year, had been exposed as unreal. To my mind, we were now
beginning a longer journey.

But to many folk, we were just anonymous. We were not only

having to tackle Premiership opponents; we were also kicking against a wall of negativity which I could not understand. All we had done on that afternoon on Tyneside was grind out another result without playing particularly well. It was clearly not going to be enough to simply win games any more.

The tabloids had already spotted it and were having great fun cranking up the pressure. It did not seem so long ago that we used to cock a snoot in this country at what we thought were the over-excitable antics that went on in Spain or Italy and South America. At the hysterical reaction and over-reaction to what, to us, was still only a game.

I don't think we can afford to be quite so arrogant any more. Our paymasters these days have umpteen channels and countless magazines and papers to fill. Inevitably, accuracy goes out the window. One national paper totted up my spending in an attempt to feed more pressure into the system – and included £6 million for Robbie Keane and £3 million for David Unsworth in their calculations.

The fact that I did not sign Keane or that we had recouped our outlay on Unsworth did not matter. No mention was made of the £26 million that had been gathered in sales, either. Or of the loss of Staunton and Bosnich on free transfers for reasons beyond my control. When this kind of feeding frenzy begins, lies get printed and half-truths get set in stone.

Suddenly, Gregory had spent over £40 million and was under the cosh. Deliver or be damned by Deadly Doug. That was the tone of their view of Villa.

I had seen this kind of treatment from a distance; Bobby Robson was probably the first to be exposed to it as England manager. Graham Taylor and, to a lesser degree perhaps, Glenn Hoddle, had also suffered. I had observed it and, at times, even smiled at it, believing it to be largely silly.

But now I was getting first hand experience of it. John Goldenballs had now been replaced by John Notgoodenough.

It was not a big problem for me. I knew what I was trying to do. I wanted a good start. I wanted to get us established again in the top six. I wanted to make sure there was no hangover from the way our season had tailed off before.

I did not take it seriously.

I'm not so sure the same could be said for the people around me.

'That was dreadful, John. Dreadful.'

The chairman was talking to me just outside the changing rooms at Villa Park. We had just beaten Middlesbrough 1–0, our sixth game of the season, to remain second in the Premiership.

'And the gate. Did you see the attendance?' he added with a heavy sigh.

It had been 28,728. Last season we had averaged 36,000, although this corresponding fixture had attracted barely 1,000 more supporters.

He was annoyed, all right. And clearly worried. Our gates for the first three home games had not got anywhere near the previous season's average.

If he was annoyed, I was furious. Bloody furious.

'Michele, come on, we're going,' I said to my wife. She must have guessed something was up. This was within half an hour of the final whistle. I would normally stay at the ground until gone 7 p.m.

But I had had enough that night. It was best to get away. I did not want to do or say something I would later regret.

It seemed to me I was getting it in the neck from all angles. I drove home, chuntering to myself. OK, we had not played well. But we had won. Again. We might have scored more goals and then, of course, everyone would be happy.

I had thrown my heart and soul into that start and we were second. We had 18 clubs beneath us. I fully understood the chairman's point of view. Income from the catering was down, the replica shirt sales were down, the bar takings were down, the season ticket sales were down; none of last season's figures had been reached.

But there were reasons. There had been a 15 per cent or more increase on ticket prices. Never mind the fact that supporters could go down the pub and, for the price of a couple pints, watch wall-to-wall football with their mates.

As you can tell, I was feeling very hurt, very unappreciated, very sorry for myself. I was finding it difficult to please the people who mattered and yet I could not see what more I could do. Everyone seemed to want jazzy, pop star names from the jazzy, international football world. I could have bought a first team player from Middlesbrough but they would rather I signed a reserve from Inter Milan.

They wanted Ginger bloody Spice in a basque and suspenders; I had given them Nora Batty in tights.

That same night, two journalists contacted me and, in time-honoured fashion, I was 'unofficially' sounded out about the Newcastle job that had been made vacant by Gullit's departure. Nothing I could do about that but the mood I was in...

When I calmed down, the John Gregory I recognized took over. The one who will never give in. Never. I would not quit. Sure, I was still angry. I knew we were not flowing. We were stuttering along. The team wasn't right yet. But, for goodness' sake, give me a break, will you? Had I not earned a break?

C'mon John, you know what you're dealing with. This is the 'want it all and want it now' society. Image is everything. Substance is secondary. Beautiful people everywhere you go with their designer labels in full view. The fact they might have no talent or might be soulless and dull is beside the point.

They look great. That's all people want. Something that looks great. Now.

But in our dressing-room we had substance, I was sure of that and it was my job to let that show. I will not give in.

And anyway, who are these people to tell me about Villa? I love the place, too. I love it as much as, if not more than, anyone. I've been here three times now. It's where I live. It feels like where I came from. And I am not turning my back on it. Those fly-by-nights, those people who just want to make a buck or two from the place, they will not drive me out. I don't care if the stadium is empty. I will still be here with MY team doing it MY way. And the day will come when you will not be able to get into the place for love nor money. You mark my words.

But I realized what hurt more than anything.

No one seemed to believe in me anymore.

The path that led to this feeling of isolation had hardly been trouble-strewn. After that victory at Newcastle on the opening day, we had beaten Everton quite comfortably and had only been denied a 100 per cent record from the first three games when West Ham scored a last minute equalizer at Villa Park.

But, nine points from 12 was fine by me. We were on our way. Our one defeat in the opening sequence came at Chelsea, a performance which did annoy me because an hour had elapsed before it seemed to occur to my players that they could win the game. There were overtones from the end of last season that day. Getting this lot to truly believe in themselves, especially on the big stages, was still the hardest trick of all to pull off.

We needed to get another signing in, I thought. George Boateng was not right, not playing as well as he could and I had Ian Taylor in a midfield holding role. Was that really suiting him? We could not get any fluency.

No the blend was wrong and I still needed to find my best team. But a solid win and performance at Watford and then that Middlesbrough victory kept the points coming in. I was thinking that second place, with so much more to come, with the team yet to click, was fine.

But then the negativity which I have referred to really kicked in when I got it horribly wrong one afternoon at Arsenal.

I picked the wrong team, played Merson out of position, asking him to do something that he could not do. I picked David James even though he was not 100 per cent fit. Our set-up was wrong, our game-plan was wrong. And Arsenal overpowered us that day. It was all my fault.

We might still have clung on to something, however, had not the referee David Elleray punished David for time-wasting over a clearance.

At 1–1, it gave Arsenal a free kick inside our area from which Davor Suker put them ahead.

We were beaten 3–1, my only positive coming from young Enckelman's performance as a substitute for David. Yes, there were no doubts that he was going to be a terrific keeper.

But Arsenal's emphatic victory, and the star-quality of their foreign contingent, cemented the view that we were now second-class citizens. It began to reach crazy proportions.

We had drawn Chester, bottom of the Third Division, for our start to the Worthington Cup and when we struggled to beat them 1–0 at their Deva Stadium, even our own supporters were mocking us. They were taking the mickey, cheering if we won a corner or had a shot at goal. It was not very nice to hear but I was now getting used to it. I couldn't help but think that it wouldn't happen at other clubs, though. Something poisonous was in the air around Villa Park and it was threatening to destroy everything I was striving for.

And I let it get to me. Not personally, but professionally. I let it mislead me into making a huge mistake.

When our season was collapsing around our ears in the previous campaign, and I had been searching fruitlessly for some kind of solution, I had changed Villa's long-established style of play. We had become stale and predictable, so the theory went; all the most successful teams in the world had long abandoned the sweeper and wing backs system in favour of the once maligned 4–4–2. That was what Villa needed to do.

Well, we tried it and drew some gains and losses. I was not convinced. But once again, people were demanding sexier football and I tried to give it to them.

The problem at our club is that our way of playing is now ingrained in the the staff. For example, we do not have any natural wingers; Steve Stone, who was trying to catch up on his form and fitness at this stage after picking up an early injury, was the only wide midfield specialist. Our centre backs, too, had all developed playing as one of three; they did not always seem so comfortable when asked to do the job in a back four.

We tried it out against Bradford and then in the return leg with Chester. We scored five against Chester and although we only got one against Bradford, we should have scored more. Undoubtedly, further chances were coming our way.

But then we took it to Leicester and endured a very difficult afternoon in more ways than one. For a start we were beaten 3–1. Even worse we had our skipper, Gareth Southgate sent off. Even worse than that, both he and I were reported to the FA on charges of misconduct. I have had better Saturday nights than 25 September 1999.

This would prove to be the start of an ugly period for me. Contrary to how it may have seemed, I did not like complaining about our game's officials. But my experiences that afternoon typified the problems both myself and many other coaches and managers were now encountering.

Gareth first of all. He was shown a red card after being booked for two scuffling, six-of-one half-dozen-of-the-other, tussles with Emile Heskey, the powerful Leicester striker. I had read before the game that Emile, a player I had first seen when I was coaching at Filbert Street and he arrived as a schoolboy, was now the most fouled player in the Premiership.

To me that could just suggest he fell over a lot and for a guy who is one of the strongest players you are ever likely to see, that is surprising.

It's all part of a striker's game. I'm not complaining about that. But you have to hope that referees are aware of what is going on.

I certainly felt that had been the case with Gareth. I was less than impressed with some of the referee's calls – it was my friend from the Newcastle match again, Jeff Winter – and felt he got conned into showing those yellow cards.

Now I imagine most people have an impression of Gareth. He's not been short of headlines over the last five years. And if your impression is of a model professional and an even-tempered, personable bloke who carries himself with great dignity then you are dead right. He had never been sent off before and he was annoyed about it. In his club blazer and tie, he waited down the players' tunnel to speak to Winter at the end of the game.

He wanted to find out why he had been sent off; he wanted to put his case across.

I think that Winter's attitude was wrong and ultimately did not help the situation which eventually landed Gareth before the FA. I lost a lot of respect for the official. I don't think it helps that he's surrounded by stewards and security guys when all Gareth wanted to do was speak to him, quietly, man-to-man. Winter should have invited Gareth into the referee's room where the pair of them could have argued the toss. I mean, this is Gareth Southgate we're talking about here; not a thug who is likely to threaten the referee's physical well-being.

But instead, it was all, 'Go away' and 'I'm the referee' or 'I'm in charge' and 'Off you go, sonny'. This to a Premiership captain and England player from the previous European Championships and

World Cup. I think he deserves a little more respect then that, don't you?

While Gareth was having his problems down the tunnel, mine came on the touch-line.

I still do not know why we have fourth officials. No idea at all. What purpose does the post serve other then give another 'jobsworth' the chance to get in the way?

All that happens is that he gets it in the neck for the referee when you feel there has been a poor decision. And, yes, Andy D'Urso, the fourth official at Leicester, got it in the neck that day. I was becoming increasingly frustrated with Jeff's performance and D'Urso kept sticking his nose in where it was not wanted or needed.

I felt his attitude was very smug. And when I said something he looked at me with a laugh on his face that suggested he was enjoying our discomfort in a 'You're getting beat, your captain's been sent off' sort of way.

I snapped. I told him that if he did not wipe the smile off his face I would punch his lights out.

I'm not proud of that, it was wrong. Hands up straight away. And that's what I was reported for.

But when I eventually appeared before the FA Commission to take my punishment, I was asked if I did not think my language was a bad example to set my players.

What century are these people from? Come on, now. My players have forgotten more bad language than I know. And they use it. Of course they do. The football pitch is our shop floor. We do not use it in public, we do not use it in TV or radio interviews or at home. But at the work-face, of course we use it, like it is down the mine or on the factory floor. If Mr D'Urso's sensitive ears can't handle it, then he is welcome to leave us all alone and take the rest of the fourth officials with him.

But this was the first of a three-match run of games which underlined to me how poorly we were being served. Our next game, for example, was at home to Liverpool. A packed house – at least the chairman would be happy – and a fixture that is always relished by our lot.

It was boiling up to a nice little game as well. There was some fantastic talent on the pitch, players nearly 40,000 fans had forked-out hard-earned money to see go head-to-head. But the most dominant figure in the game would be the referee, Rob Harris. He later acknowledged the error of his ways in sending off Steve Staunton but it was this weekend that would see the trend of confetti cautions reach its peak. How many did we have that day? Ten, 11, 12? I lost count. Many for petty offences, I know that much.

But the end result was a potentially terrific occasion reduced to a training ground exercise with players afraid to tackle. And an awful lot of fans short-changed by the whole, sorry episode.

It seemed to me by then that there had been a definite change in approach by referees. They used to work on showing the yellow card for the third wrong tackle. Now it seemed players were being booked for their first.

As a result, you would spin through the papers on Sundays and see 20 or 25 players had been sent off. Ten years ago, it was a surprise to see three or four. Is the game that much dirtier?

It was happening all over the country, not just to John Gregory, and ruining one match after another at a time when the punters had never paid more money for admission.

Of course, the frustration for those of us within the game is that we are not supposed to talk about it. Well, I'm sorry. Sod that. It was much too important to pretend we did not have a problem.

And there was no way I could keep quiet about what happened in our next match, at Sunderland. Back in the Premiership, the Stadium of Light had become one of the most difficult places to go to at this stage with Peter Reid's team rolling along without a care in the world.

We were playing well that night; 1–0 up thanks to an excellent header from Dion; keeping Sunderland relatively quiet. It looked as if we could get the three points. This was more like it. This was what we were looking for.

But then mid-way through the second half came a decision from Mr Elleray which I still do not understand today. He awarded a penalty against our young full back Mark Delaney as he tussled for possession with Niall Quinn. It seemed harsh from the touchline – Reidy looked over at me with a look which confirmed that impression – bloody harsh if you were on the pitch and incomprehensible when you saw the TV video replay. I know he doesn't have the benefit of replays. I just could not see how Elleray had been so convinced Delaney had handled. Whatever happened to 'the benefit of the doubt'?

It changed the game and gave Sunderland a big lift. They scored from the penalty and went on to beat us 2–1.

OK, let's say for the sake of argument it was a bad decision ('bad' would barely cover it) but what really angers me and annoys football folk generally is what happens next. Are we allowed to speak to this man? Are we allowed to ask for his view? Are we allowed to just vent a little of our frustration?

Are we hell.

I went into the referee's room afterwards and it appeared to be too much trouble for him to speak to me. 'Yes, yes, OK, I'll have a look at it later.' He didn't actually say, 'Now go away, don't you realize who I am' but that's the impression I got.

That decision chewed away at me for two weeks. Two bloody weeks. I couldn't let it go. No, not losing the game. That's all part of love, war and football. What I couldn't get out of my system was the fact that there had been such a poor decision and noone owned up for two weeks.

Yes, two weeks. That's how long it took me to finally get an acknowledgement from the referees' association that Elleray had, indeed, conceded his error.

I spoke to Phillip Don, the chairman of the Premiership refs, who passed Elleray's admission on to me. Not that Elleray could call me himself and say, 'Sorry John, big mistake,' which would have been fine. And God forbid that he should come out and admit it in public. No. He was unwilling to do that, said Don, because it would mean he lost face. He had been 'slaughtered' once for making the decision; to make a public admission to his error would only give him a second round of criticism. And we can't have that, can we?

Well I beg to differ. We can all accept an apology. I make mistakes over decisions every week and I have more time than Elleray and his colleagues. But you hold up your hands and say, 'Sorry, I'm only human. I cocked it up.' By putting themselves out of reach, by shutting out the people whom their decisions effect, referees are making matters so much worse for themselves.

I think it could be a generation thing. A lot of the senior referees today were brought up through an era when *Match of the Day* had a couple of cameras at a couple of games and that was it. But that has changed dramatically.

Now the technology is there and can expose every detail of every key decision and the new generation of referees needs to adapt accordingly. The old manual needs to be thrown out.

What was the point of Elleray saying nothing when the entire football community had seen the incident on television?

I think some guys have done so. Graham Poll, for example, is a referee you can always get on with because you can actually talk to him.

But we have just moved in to a new century and we have to change the way we officiate our matches. The game is three times quicker than it was even 20 years ago when it was 10 times quicker than it was when they drew up the rule book. Refs simply cannot keep up any more. They need help. I just wish they would sometimes help themselves.

But I was not winning games and my railing against authority could be seen by some as sour grapes. And I was still less than convinced we were playing to the system that suited our strengths. No, I was far from happy about many things.

We went to Manchester United, created as many chances as the champions... and got beat 3–0. They had four clear opportunities that afternoon and took three of them. That kind of clinical finishing was still beyond us.

And although I felt we were creating more openings, we were also starting to concede more. We were looking more vulnerable.

And then came the blackest weekend I can remember for a long, long time.

CHAPTER 13

'Sleep all right Mr Chairman?'

I pulled out of Villa Park and, despite the early evening darkness, my car was still recognized by one of our supporters.

'Wanker' he signalled to me, mouthing the word at the same time. I thought about running his mate over.

Horrible, bloody horrible. So it had finally come to this.

My own family turning against me.

We had just been beaten 1–0 at home by Southampton. And we had not deserved to win. We had been bloody awful. A lack of spark. And a lot of people thought that was it. We had not won for six games. The Gregory Reign was over. I was lost in a long, dark tunnel and many people were predicting I would never be seen in the Villa Park daylight again.

Saturday 6 November. The longest night. A night of massive self-analysis. The lowest point since I had returned to the club. There was now an air of disquiet around Villa Park that was being encouraged by the chairman's reputation for pulling the trigger the moment he was not happy about things.

Villa fans will always expect – no, demand – that their team beat Southampton at Villa Park. It's a status thing. And, as the Saints were having a tough time, I too had seen the game as a chance to bounce back from the setbacks of the previous weeks.

We had friends staying with us that weekend. But their timing was lousy. No one would have wanted to be in the same town as me never mind the same room. I was like a bear with a sore head.

I had to take a long hard look at myself. And the conclusion could not be avoided. I was making a pig's ear of it. I knew the players were good enough. But what was I doing wrong?

It would have been easy to come out and say the players had not performed; to blame your centre half for a goal from a set piece or blame your striker for missing a simple chance. But I had to remain loyal to them.

And I knew, I just KNEW, there was a team in there somewhere. It was a couple of weeks before our next game and it was up to me to come up with the answers before then. Balance. That was what was missing most of all. I did not have the right balance.

I tried to switch off. Pick up the guitar. But even that didn't work. I remembered a video I had, a video of Springsteen recording a song which started out as a big, thumping rock anthem and finished up as a gentle acoustic ballad. All night he worked on it with his band. He kept going until he had the sound that he wanted. He knew there was a good song in there somewhere and, although it took him until seven in the morning, he eventually found it.

That's what I needed to do. I knew there was a good team in there and I had to find it. What I was seeing on the training pitch, Monday to Friday, was not what I was seeing on match days.

Bodymoor Heath was witness to great finishing, great nine-a-sides, super football, hard-working guys. But Villa Park was seeing an all together different end-product.

It's got to be me. It's got to be me, I kept telling myself. I must be missing something and it was driving me crazy trying to find out what it was. That weekend was long and difficult. But I readied myself for work again with that stubborn streak still kicking away inside of me.

You will not get through to me, I told the world. No matter what you do. You can stand in front of my car and rant at me and make your gestures. But I will not let you get to me. I can handle anything you want to throw at me. Going through this is good; it is hardening me to a lot of things. I do not know where this comes from. But it's there. I'm going to get through this and someone is going to pay for it.

I came out of that weekend feeling like reinforced concrete. Toughened up, ready to withstand anything. I kept telling myself I was strong enough not to buckle. I WILL find the answer.

Yet again, some of Coxy's enduring advice came to me. 'We don't jump and down when we win, son, so we don't jump up and down when we lose.' He meant in the dressing-room. That has always stayed with me.

So, once again, I reminded myself not to start sermonizing or ranting and raving at the boys. 'If you lot don't listen to me you'll be getting me the sack.' I had heard it before. I knew it would just make things worse.

And the self-doubt that had invaded my thoughts in the previous season was not allowed to return. Instead there was something urging me on, something in-built. I am not going to be kicked out like a cat into the night. They will have to drag me away from here kicking and screaming.

Those were my thoughts.

All I had to worry about now was what the chairman was thinking.

My relationship with the press was now strained. On my first day as manager, I had promised to be open, honest and available. I was finding it difficult to maintain that approach now.

There were people in the media who I had known for 25 years, who I had allowed into my office, sat with them, poured them tea and coffee, waited on them hand and foot, given them stories when they could not find one. Short of a tale? Ah, ring up, 'Greg' he's good for a few paragraphs. And I always tried to oblige.

Heck, for the previous 12 months, I had given them more back-page leads then they could have dreamed of.

And now these same people were writing some very personal attacks. They were attempting to second-guess the chairman and assuming he was going to sack me.

I knew what they were thinking. They did not have to worry about upsetting Gregory any longer because he was dead in the water. There was much benefit to be gained back at their head office by getting the knife in first.

If ever you pull them up about it, the answer is the same. 'Sorry mate, but it's my gaffer, he wants me to write it that way.'

But check back at some of the articles that were being written at the time and you can reach two conclusions. Either there was an agenda to get a good old sacking story going at Villa – and that always shunts a few copies out of the newsagents – or there was some very sloppy journalism going on.

Perhaps both.

Plenty of criticisms were valid. I did not dispute that. I had brought in a collection of signings and they were hardly covering themselves in glory. Thompson was having a tough time, Stone was not yet anything like the player he could be and couldn't get in the side, Watson the same and even Boateng, a player who I was so convinced about, could not seem to settle into anything like the performance level we had seen at Coventry. They are all good players.

I had to carry the can for that. But I was still some way short of my second anniversary. Surely I would be given time – surely I had earned some time – to turn it around? And none of the 'vibes' I was receiving from the boardroom equated with what I was reading in the press.

Every game was supposed to be my last. My abilities as a manager were questioned. Yes, the same guy who, in an equally ridiculous over-reaction, they had been trying to dress up as a potential successor to Glenn Hoddle less than a year ago. I never forget that kind of double-dealing.

I knew they had jobs to do. But I knew I could not trust them any longer. I knew that when I turned it around – and that was the only outcome I thought possible – they would be all over me again. 'Good on yer, Johnny me old mate. Always knew you would pull through,' they would be saying then.

But what they did not know, as they rushed to compose John Gregory's obituary, was what had already been sorted out between the chairman and myself 48 hours after that Southampton game.

Before I drove away from the ground that night – and considered the implications of a hit-and-run attack on a Villa supporter – I had seen something that had sickened me.

I finished my press conference and left the journos gathered in the car park outside the media room. It had been a difficult session for me as, I started to sense the headlines that would greet me the next day from the questions I was being asked.

I would have driven away there and then had I not forgotten my wash-bag. My return trip took me back across the same car park.

And there they were, crawling all over the chairman's car like a pack of jackals. While I was around, they had deliberately stayed away from his car. But now I could see them in all their glory. They were after the quote, the one indiscreet sentence, on which I could be hanged, I knew that. I think all the gaffer told them was that he was 'sick as a dog'. So fair play to him.

But this was disturbing. This is the sort of thing that can drive a wedge between a chairman and his manager. He is only human. And if he's got a battery of pressmen hanging around his car effectively asking him when he is going to sack his manager, he is sure to start thinking that is what he should be doing. If it wasn't on his agenda before – and I honestly believed it wasn't – it might well be now, I thought.

And of course, I was only too aware that by now there would be other whispers in his ear attempting to influence his decision. It's at times like this that agents of the out-of-work managers start ringing up and gently sounding out their client's job prospects. Or, in one case I knew about at this time, even the wife of a former Scottish international out-of-work manager.

And suddenly old Villa players start showing their faces again, some of them with their European Cup winning medals dangling from their chest. It is the way of our world, only to be expected. I didn't blame them. But I knew they were there and I knew what they were scenting.

For me, it was as if they were eyeing my girlfriend. And inside I was churning away like a jealous boyfriend. 'Oi, mate,' I was silently shouting at them, 'Villa is my girl. You can take your eyes off her. She's out with me and she's not dancing with anyone else'.

But I had to know what the boss was thinking. If everyone was ringing up Mr Ellis trying to get a date with my girlfriend and telling him she should dump her current fella, I had to know what his intentions were. And so, driving home from training on that Monday evening, I punched the chairman's home number into the mobile phone.

'Can I come and see you?' I asked. 'We need to talk.'

'Of course. When?'

'Is now all right?'

It was time to put cards on the table. That scene in the car park had shown me that there were ways in which our relationship could be damaged and that was the last thing I wanted. I was desperate that he didn't pull the trigger because I *knew* he would be making a mistake. I was still convinced that Villa and I were good for each other; that we had many years of a successful and happy marriage ahead of us.

But I knew the easy thing to do would be the knee-jerk reaction. Sack him. Get rid of all these awkward questions. Get a new face in, a fresh face for the media to fawn over. Someone new for the fans to get excited about.

Had all this happened a year ago, I might well have gone under. The kind of run with all the pressures from around me might have been enough to bury John Gregory.

But I had been in charge 18 months now and been through the mill in that comparatively short time. That had given me the experience to cope. Maybe that run of last season did have a purpose after all, I told myself. Everything has a reason and there is a reason for everything.

And so that evening, the chairman and I sat down to get everything off our chests. And he probably had to get more off, to be fair.

'I need to know what you are thinking,' I said. 'Whatever your thoughts are, I want to hear them from you.'

Come on, let's be up front with each other, I was telling him. Say it to my face now. I do not want to be told about a quote in an article that suggested something different to how I understood the land to lie. That would be no way for us to fall out.

I knew that this was an awful period in his life, just as it was in mine. I knew that the vultures from all sides now flying around Villa Park would keep up the pressure. And I knew there must have been times when he winced at some of my comments and behaviour. The manager of Aston Villa, one of the most famous clubs in the world, a founder member of the

whole darn thing, should not be up before the 'beak' on misconduct charges.

I didn't know whether he was perhaps waiting for me to cave
in and resign. If he was he had under-estimated my willingness
for a scrap. But I am not afraid to speak the truth and I am not
afraid to hear it, either.

So let's hear it.

And we spoke. We were honest and open and blunt. He was
deeply disappointed with what he was seeing. He did not feel it
equated to the investment the club had made in the players. And
I had to acknowledge that point straight away.

We carried out a major reassessment of the squad. Was I
happy with so-and-so? What are you going to do about him? One
by one, we went through them.

And then he was looking at me pleading: 'Where do we go from
here?'

There was very little to offer him as comfort at this time other
than my determination, my certainty, that I was going to get his
ground full again and give him a team of which he would be
proud. I told him what I had been telling myself all that weekend. That I knew there was a team in there and I would not rest
until I had found it and released it.

We got everything off our chests. It had always been our policy
to talk and I was once again grateful for having a chairman who
was at least always available to do so.

And he said something that night, as he would do on other
occasions during these tough weeks, which gave me real strength
for the battle ahead. He told me that a year ago we had shared
together one of the most enjoyable and exciting periods in all his
time at Aston Villa. Now that we were going through a tough
patch, it was right that we face them together, too.

Fair enough, I thought. We've had our chat and knew where
we were.

I was confident now that, whatever did happen, I would not be
learning my fate through the newspapers.

The last thing I needed throughout all of this was the sight of the
big top and high wire back at Bodymoor Heath. But, sure
enough, the circus returned. Stan was back.

We had been monitoring his Fulham performances and, frankly, had seen little to make us think that the awkward decision I was ready to face would be presented to me.

His first Fulham game had been at Birmingham City where, predictably, he was given some terrible treatment by the home supporters. But he had worked very hard and handled all the stick very well.

But his loan to Fulham would fizzle out. The injuries which seemed to be cropping up more and more curtailed the appearances he made and although Paul Bracewell was willing to consider a deal which would have taken him there permanently, it broke down on personal terms.

Maybe in Stan's mind he had now built me up as the major barrier to his returning to our first team. Maybe he was looking at our results, reading the headlines, and putting two and two together. Get rid of Gregory and then I can make a fresh start with the next manager. The chairman, after all, still firmly believed there was a solid gold player in there. And if he sacked me, the new manager's job description would include retrieving the £7 million investment in Villa's record signing. Those thoughts must have been going through Stan's mind.

Whatever his reasons for turning down what I knew was a very attractive offer from Fulham, Stan was back with us. The big question for everyone was what I was going to do with him.

The thing about Stan is that he talks a good game. He sounds very plausible, very convincing, when you speak to him about his ambitions and his desire to play for Villa.

Some fans were now wondering if our salvation did not lie at his feet. But they were falling into the same trap that had, in my opinion, snared two of his former coaches. I was constantly picking up the papers and being advised by Barry Fry, now at Peterborough but Stan's former manager at Southend, and Chris Wright, who had handled Stan earlier in his career at Stafford Rangers, as to how to deal with him. Wright, having never operated at the higher levels, now appeared to be telling the world that Stan was being victimized by me. The players I was picking were not fit to lace his boots, he was saying.

And inevitably, there were those wanting to believe him. There we were, having a particularly tough time and here was our salvation. I almost expected Stan to ride into Bodymoor on a white charger.

But it is easy to spin dreams around Stan Collymore. His is such a sumptuous talent that we all want to believe that it is going to explode into a flurry of thrilling, goal-laden football. I wanted to still believe that. I would be stupid not to. I was in trouble and I was again looking for answers. I had never closed the door on Stan.

It is just that he refused to open it.

I judge everything on merit. If ever I change the team, and leave someone out, I might well stick him in the reserves at, say, Scunthorpe on a wet Wednesday night just to see how he reacts. He might give me the 'hump' or he might get stuck in.

Now 95 per cent of my squad have, at various times, passed the test. They have all had these moments. Steve Watson, Steve Stone, Paul Merson; they've all found themselves back on the Old Kent Road when they felt they should be on Mayfair or Park Lane. But one by one, they had all rolled up their sleeves and battled.

Paul particularly. Stan's return coincided with the rebirth of Merse, who should have provided a template for what was required. With his talent and his reputation, he might have felt he should have been guaranteed a first-team starting place. Instead, he was having to fight his way back through the reserves and by impressing us in training.

No special favours. No hand-outs. But he came through it all. And he came through it a better person, of that I am convinced; someone who was more aware of his position at the club, his responsibilities; a far more understanding professional than he had been a year ago. And he is much the better for it all.

So there was Stan's role model. But when I looked at him, all I saw was a guy still kidding himself that he did not have to put the slog in; that a couple of hours' work-out in the gym was all that he needed to be ready for the Premiership again.

Stan simply had not passed the test and I could not begin to consider him until he did. In fact, he grew ever more reluctant even to take the exam. I write these notes at the end of January and the board in my office shows that Stan's last game for the club was a reserves match in the first week of November.

We've had just a few too many flu bugs and groin strains. Well, I can't judge him on the training pitch. I've got to judge him in the reserves. Not once, or twice. But five or six games. Show me Stan, show me how bad you want it.

Don't keep telling Villa fans how desperate you are to play for the club. Show them. With Stan, I was used to hearing a lot of words but I was desperately short of seeing the action to back them up.

'Yeah,' as Big Ron used to say, 'don't tell me pal, show me'.

But there was something else and there was no point avoiding it.

I knew that the moment I brought Stan back into the dressing-room, I would 'lose' six or seven of his team-mates. My dressing-room had gone through the ringer with our results and they had not deserted me. I had drawn a lot of strength from that. We were in it together.

So the very least they would expect is that this player earn the right to pick up a first team shirt again. And not have it handed to him by a couple of old mates who have never worked at this level and managed a very different Collymore to the guy who continued to bewilder and baffle me.

'Here you are pal,' said a Coventry fan, handing me a pen. 'You'll need that to sign on with in the morning.'

I chucked it back at him as he turned away but, a few seconds later, still managed a smile. I knew where he was coming from. That was the sort of stunt I would have pulled.

I suppose it had to get worse before it got better and it just had done. Beaten 2–1 at Coventry. And the winning goal would be scored by the player we baulked at signing in the summer.

Ignorant of my meeting with the chairman, I prepared the players for this match against a background of intensifying media speculation about my future.

If Villa lost, it was assumed, I would be sacked. Such was the personal rivalry between my gaffer and Mr Richardson at Coventry, that the theory went that defeat would see Mr Ellis lose so much face someone would have to pay. And that someone would have to be me.

By now, Robbie Keane, the player we had nearly signed in the summer, had established himself in the Premiership with some terrific performances for our neighbours. And with George still not a convincing figure in our team, the sub-plots of the game were barely hidden.

In the build-up, I had a fatalistic view of Keane scoring against us. There had been so much wisdom with the aid of hindsight about our missing him, especially in a season when we were struggling to score enough goals, that this particular chicken had to come home to roost. It's just football's way. I had already defied one unwritten rule, that the Manager of the Month loses his next game; I couldn't hope to get away with another, could I?

By then, I had opted to take on the gifted Italian front player Benito Carbone from Sheffield Wednesday in an effort to find fresh craftsmanship in the opposition penalty area.

For me, the big 'miss' for the team was still Yorke. We had acquired Dion's assured goal-taking, presence and leadership; in Joachim we had a player of truly outstanding pace and in young Darius Vassell, a truly exciting prospect.

But we had no one who could accept the ball under pressure and control and set up play as well as Dwight. Among Yorkey's many attributes, that was the quality we still lacked. Beni was perhaps as close as we had come so far to finding a replacement.

I was initially sceptical of taking him on for a couple of reasons. He had a row with Wednesday's manager Danny Wilson about not being in the side, and on one occasion had flown home to Italy in disgust at being left out. But all the checks that I made suggested that he was not difficult to handle; just very passionate about his football.

A second quandary for me concerned his motivation. With Wednesday ready to offload him, we had tried to do a permanent deal but that had fallen down on personal terms. I had taken a shine to Beni when we got together. We went for a drive around the area and a tour of the ground and talked football. I got a good 'spark' from him; he seemed desperately keen to play for Villa.

But then the personal terms proved a stumbling block and left me wondering if I had been mistaken in my reading of the guy. Did he want to play for us? Or was he just interested in the pay cheque?

Happily, he answered that for me when we struck a kind of

'loan' deal, with Beni agreeing to stay until the summer on a substantially reduced contract. He could have a good look at us, and vice versa.

And he had made a stunning debut, too. Against Wimbledon who, somehow, managed to sneak off with a point from a 1–1 draw, Beni gave a virtuoso display; it seemed as if we had found the key to everything. But he should have had a hat-trick and that raised my one concern about the guy – his reputation was a scorer of great goals but not a great goal scorer.

The kind of finishing I wanted to find was what United had shown us that day at Old Trafford when they beat us 3–0. I was quite happy to keep the 4–4–2 formation even if it meant we were shipping goals – providing we were scoring more at the other end.

But two things struck me from that Coventry game. The first was the need to get back to our old system. Coventry's first goal, created by Keane, would not have arisen against our more familiar back line.

The second was the beginning of the recovery. I saw it amidst all the baiting and mickey-taking I endured at Highfield Road that evening. I think the chairman did too. As I say, throughout this difficult period, the dressing room had remained tight and together. And I was proud of that and it was starting to pay dividends.

I tried as hard as I could not to let the pressure get to the players. After all, I was not the one who had to go out and perform on match days. They did and I didn't want anything to get to them. I could not stop them reading the papers but I wanted to protect them as much as I could and certainly not blame them. They could not be working any harder.

I could cope with all the crap as long as I still believed in them. And I did. I had great faith that these were good players. We did change some things that night, notably pairing George and Ian Taylor in midfield as a central partnership. And 'partnership' is the word. They struck up an immediate understanding and, most importantly, a natural balance.

Behind the scenes, Merson was getting back to full fitness and I was becoming more encouraged by what I was seeing from him. Being beaten by Coventry hurt, but... here we go, I thought, here we go. Now we're getting somewhere.

All the media saw was the score-line. They didn't know the chairman had been down to our dressing-room afterwards, offering words of comfort to my staff – I was upstairs doing my press interviews at the time – and telling them to make sure I knew everything was on an even keel. It was still 'Gregory for the Axe' stuff the next day.

But I remembered some years ago reading a story about my chairman in which he was quoted as saying he was never able to sleep the night before issuing a P45 to one of his managers.

So I called him the next morning.

'Sleep all right Mr Chairman?' I asked.

'Fine, thanks John. Fine,' he replied.

CHAPTER 14

'Stay close to your players, son.'

Playing at Villa Park throughout that slump was difficult for us, no question. At that stage we did not have anyone to take the game by the scruff of the neck. As results and form deteriorated so did the patience of the crowd. It used to be moans and groans on the third or fourth pass that went astray. Suddenly it was the first.

It is at times like that you need a Souness, a Robson, even a Gascoigne, to say, 'Give me that fuckin' ball, I'll show you.' Shearer or Keegan, they are another pair with that same special quality. Guys who are not afraid to make a mistake. I had an honest and talented bunch of footballers. In fact, they're too bloody nice at times. But at that stage I wanted someone who had Souness' devil to grab hold of it and make them play.

But at least now I was clearing things in my mind; the Coventry match had shown me a good deal. It had confirmed that in the weeks before, I hadn't set the team up properly.

You know, preparing for matches at this level can be extremely specific. It's not just set pieces and concentrating especially hard just after we had scored. It's more like, what shape should you take up when, for example, the opposition left back has got the ball? Or when the wing backs swap sides during an attack? What I want is for the players to follow instructions and then, within that framework, express themselves. It's a fine balance, but when you get it right, and you get it right with good players, then the team starts to flow. But there had been a breakdown in communication. I wanted my players to win the second ball in midfield, and they didn't. I wanted them to shoot when they got into shooting positions, and they didn't. They were not doing what I had instructed them to do.

But, of course, players are as fallible as the rest of us. There's a famous story from the last World Cup, when the Bulgarian team manager sat his squad down to watch a video of their next opponents and then asked each of his players to write down what formation they had played. He got 16 different answers. It wasn't that they were not paying attention. It is just that there is nothing like football to promote different opinions, even from the professionals.

David James came to us with five or six years of Anfield coaching telling him to throw the ball to his back-four. But I didn't necessarily want that. 'No David, we don't do that here.' I could not allow him to do as he pleased.

George Boateng – he was another who found the adjustment difficult. When to go, when to stay, when to get into the box, when to hold back… the players cannot make it up as they go along. The manager has got to be precise and clear about how he wants you to play. And I realized now that lines had got crossed, communications had suffered from interference.

I remember after that Coventry game thinking about some pals who work on the Formula One motor racing circuit who told me how all the cars have roughly the same amount of power, same four wheels, same steering wheel and a seat. Not only were Alain Prost and Ayrton Senna outstanding drivers, but they could also set up a car like no others. That's what made the difference. The parallel was clear.

I still felt I had an outstanding car at my disposal; I just had not set it up right.

So that was one thing. Sort that out. Some fine-tuning. Make sure once again that everyone is very aware of what they are supposed to be doing.

And it all pivoted around the way we played. I am never afraid to seek the opinions of the players, especially the seniors; let them have their say, frankly, fiercely, at the right time. Privately, when there are no other ears around. I enjoy talking to them like that – no holds barred. Merse – he is always terrific value for a heart-to-heart session – Ian Taylor, Dublin, Alan Wright and, of course, the captain Gareth Southgate. 'Come on, get it off your chest. What do you *really* think?' I like to say.

The skip, particularly. I had spoken to Gareth about changing to a back-four and he had been positive. But the system had not been doing Gareth or the team any favours. He was trying to hold them together but, by changing his usual game, I had made his individual job much more difficult. I had ignored the golden rule: strikers win matches; defenders win championships. Now I wanted to revert to five at the back. It would be like slipping into a comfy old armchair. Reliable, secure. The cracks were starting to show. So it was time to go back to him and say, 'What do you think, skip?' 'Yeah,' he said, 'let's go back to the "five".' Southgate was all for it.

I was angry, bloody angry, about what was going on around me. What had started as distaste had become contempt for the media for feeding on the carcass of Aston Villa. I saw them taking cheap, easy shots and I was bloody furious about what I was reading.

I could not believe that I could have misread these guys so completely. I could not believe how disappointed I was in them either. Yes, I knew they were just trying to earn a living, or steal a living as I preferred to think of it. But had all the goodwill, all the fun of my first months counted for nothing? Clearly not.

All their moves were so predictable. Turning to players out of the side, getting them to air grievances, trying to set up a 'Me-versus-Them' scenario. Pathetic. I could do their jobs standing on my head with my eyes closed. The difference is they would not know where to start with mine. They had been so eager to sup at my table; now they were even more enthusiastic to condemn me. Bastards.

But what could I do? I had to be hospitable and polite; the job demanded that. But I would not let them get to me. No way. Not even when our defeat at Coventry was greeted with a kind of disbelief that I could survive the week.

I am sitting here, reliving all this now while looking at newspapers suggesting David O'Leary is 'losing it' at Leeds and that Bryan Robson cannot survive at Middlesbrough. They are, supposedly, struggling to handle the pressure. In reality

Bryan's sheer presence has helped transform Middlesbrough into a fashionable alternative to Merseyside or London or Manchester. And, as I write, David's lot are still second in the table and in the UEFA Cup. I bet I know precisely what they are thinking.

I was not cracking – far from it – but pictures from our next game were used to suggest otherwise. With our old, three centre-back defensive system reinstalled, we claimed a goalless draw at Everton, a performance that proved to me I had not been mistaken when I thought I saw improvements in the defeat at Coventry.

But, as far as the outside world was concerned, I was a stressed-out, tension-riddled, tightrope-walking mess of a manager.

At the tail end of that Goodison afternoon, our defenders were 'fannying' around with the ball on the edge of our area, the result of which was an Everton goal-attempt which might have been costly. In sheer frustration, I kicked out at our physio's kit-bag.

Actually, it was a great strike, a left-foot volley which took off in the wind and sent the bag cartwheeling towards the pitch before spilling its contents around the touch-line. I felt slightly silly the moment I did it and quickly picked up my dummy and put it back in my mouth. But the pictures in the tabloids confirmed the popular image of me at that time. 'He's definitely losing it out now,' they said. 'How much more of this can Doug put up with?' they asked. 'The idiot should get out now while he's still got his sanity'.

But quite the opposite was true. That Everton result had been another big step forward. The game might have been quickly forgotten by supporters but for me, there was plenty to remember and savour. And when we then whacked four goals past Southampton in a Worthington Cup tie four days later – this against the opposition who had dared to beat us just a few weeks earlier – I knew we were really getting somewhere.

We were comfortable at the back, so comfortable, I could not believe I had allowed myself to be distracted in the first place and change our way of playing. Sod Ginger Spice, I was quite happy to wear Nora Batty's tights again. They were going to keep me warm this winter.

I don't believe in any single turning point. It is a popular myth. 'Turning points' are generally a combination of many different things. But this result, taking us into the quarter-finals, felt like it brought me some breathing space.

Bobby Robson had given me my England breakthrough as a player and he sat me down before our next match for a quiet word, this time as a manager.

It is one of the paradoxes of management. We are all there desperately trying to beat the other guy, even if it means dropping him in the shit. It has to be done. But beyond that, there is a tremendous camaraderie. There is a tangible bond between the guy at the top of the Premiership which runs through to the poor geezer struggling to put a team out at the foot of the Third Division. It says, 'I know what it's like mate, and if I can help, I will.'

And that was Bobby, an hour before our next game against a Newcastle team he had steered away from the relegation zone since succeeding Gullit. He came and sat in my office just down the corridor from the changing rooms and asked me how I was coping. He had been there, seen it, survived it. He had been the poor guy on which the tabloids had sharpened their teeth when he was England manager. He had been hounded in a way which has established the tone of football coverage in the media that we now regard as the norm.

And he had come through it with his dignity and his reputation intact. Once the headlines had screamed for his sacking as England manager; in between the Hoddle and Keegan regime, the headlines had demanded he be reappointed. He knew what it was like and I listened intently to what he was saying. Happily, what he told me reinforced my own view.

'Stay close to your players, son,' he said. 'You need them and they need you. And you don't need anyone else.' And that is what I felt I still had – a solid dressing-room, all pulling the same way, all pulling in their direction, in *my* direction.

It was a nice touch by Bobby and I appreciated it, although I could have done without his team then beating us by a single Duncan Ferguson goal! It was their only real chance in a game short of goal-scoring opportunities. We fluffed ours; they didn't.

George Boateng celebrates his second goal – unfortunately while he was still playing for Coventry and, even more unfortunately, scored against his next employers.

It's the Lollipop Kid at a time when life was far from sweet.

I tried to be open and honest with the press at Bodymoor Heath but felt my attitude was eventually abused.

The men behind the man behind the team. Lining up before the start of the 1998-99 season with (back, from left) Malcolm Beard, Terry Standring, Alan Miller, Bryan Jones, Jim Walker, Steve Burns; (front from left) Kevin MacDonald, Paul Barron, Steve Harrison and Gordon Cowans.

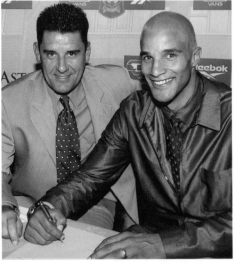

I like my goalkeepers big, loud and commanding. Mark Bosnich (left) followed the Yorke trail but I had a hunch David James would be a fantastic replacement. I was right.

The deal that never was. Juninho sat in my office ready and willing to sign. But the figures could not match up.

Having signed Paul Merson, could I dare to go for the country's top striker? Gareth closed down Alan Shearer.

Given the same set of circumstances I would make the same decision. Robbie Keane ended up in the sky blue of Coventry.

©Allsport

I look at the kid and wonder if he realises how good he is and what's ahead of him. Gareth Barry in action.

©Malcolm Cousins / West Midlands Soccer

The eventful Worthington Cup quarter-final with West Ham. Both games went to extra time before Ian Taylor, in the middle of a hot patch, settled it with the last goal of a 3-1 win (below).

©Allsport

©Allsport

'Get yourself over to Leicester and ram those words down my throat.' A farewell to Stan.

The comeback against Leeds that put us through to the sixth round of the FA Cup. Benito Carbone celebrates one of the goals from his memorable hat-trick.

My favourite picture (below) as the boys are caught up in the seconds that follow our FA Cup semi-final victory at Wembley. We owed a lot to big Dave's saves in the penalty shoot-out, including the last one (above).

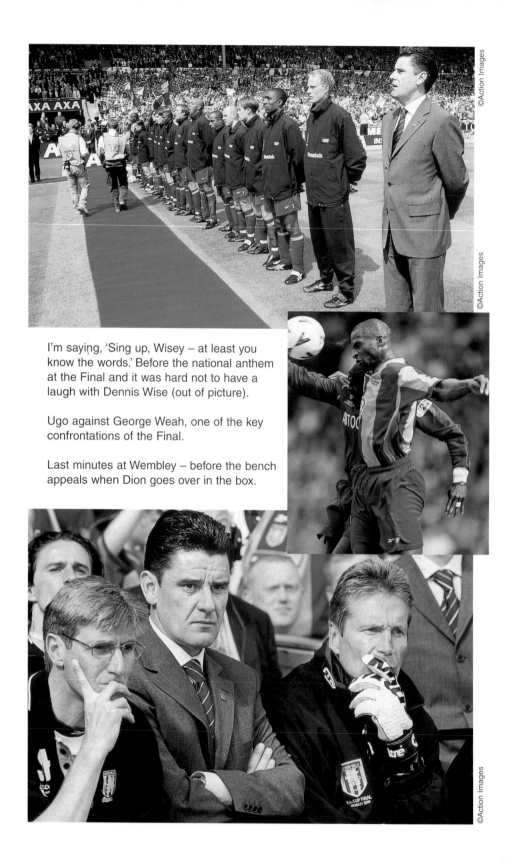

I'm saying, 'Sing up, Wisey – at least you know the words.' Before the national anthem at the Final and it was hard not to have a laugh with Dennis Wise (out of picture).

Ugo against George Weah, one of the key confrontations of the Final.

Last minutes at Wembley – before the bench appeals when Dion goes over in the box.

End of story. But, amid the disappointment of the result, I still felt we were coming out of our slump.

What I needed, though, was a run. Not win a couple, draw one, lose one; I needed a run of four, five, six games undefeated. Until I had that, I knew I could not shake the hounds off my tail.

We had stopped the rot at Everton and reached the Worthington Cup quarter-finals. But it was now 11 December, and we had not won a Premiership match since 18 September. For the bulk of that period, we had been without Ugo. Now he was about to return in time for the start of our FA Cup campaign.

In the disappointment of defeat at Highfield Road, I had made a few cracks which were interpreted as my believing Ugo was dodging the muck and bullets when we needed him most. I had thought that he was going to be back for that match. My comments were meant to be light-hearted; but I had forgotten that I was not being given any latitude by the press any more. Everything I said was being taken literally.

As you might imagine, I soon had an angry Ugo knocking at my door, wanting to know what on earth I was suggesting. The headlines were unpleasant and Ugo was deeply upset. He admitted that he, too, thought he would be fit for the Coventry match but then, when his injury still had not totally cleared, felt he had to pull out.

We had words. It was something I could have done without in the middle of this bad sequence even if I do feel he can be a little over-sensitive at times. But we cleared the air and settled our differences. We don't go out to dinner together, but I still think the working relationship is good. And that is what matters.

I was just desperate to have him back and at last he was. It can be no coincidence that we have barely looked back since.

Home to Third Division Darlington, already knocked out but allowed back in under the season's unique 'lucky losers' scheme, employed to cover the absence of Manchester United. No complaints from me. Darlington were having a good season – but were three divisions down. We could not ask for more.

Except, of course, that this was the Cup. This was the land of calamities. Other than the next round, victory would mean nothing to Villa; defeat would mean everything.

By the time that tie came along, I still felt insecure enough to wonder what might be going on above me. The chairman had steadfastly refused to speak about me in public. Yes, our clear-the-air session was still fresh in my mind. But I still wondered – was that good or bad? I still didn't really know. I did know that if we cocked this one up, they might well be expecting me to walk away.

But what do you do? My credibility, my career, was on the line here. I couldn't run away. That's how it is in these situations. No one is going to help you but the players. I had been through hell and I hoped I would never have to do so again. But the man who never made a mistake never made anything. Now I had to make sure I won this bloody game.

We did win, 2–1. It doesn't sound too convincing does it? But I felt it was. Darlington did well, very well in fact, but I felt we were always in control. I said so after the game and upset a few people. I think I was supposed to shower praise and admiration on the 'plucky losers'. When I didn't I seemed to further upset their manager, the former Middlesbrough and Liverpool player David Hodgson.

He had openly declared his dislike of me before the tie; now he unleashed another barrel of vitriol. Worrying about him kept me awake for, oooh, at least a couple of minutes . . . nah, not that long.

But one by one, we were overcoming the hurdles. We were fighting our way through. We were getting there. Next was our Worthington Cup quarter-final a few days later. It was going to be tough. West Ham away. And they were hot at that time, particularly at home. But if we could just get through this one, then...

We got through all right. But how is another story.

CHAPTER 15

'Stay where you are Gaff, just stay where you are.'

The guy I feel sorry for these days is Stevie. Stevie Stride. For 20, maybe 25 years, he has taken his seat at games to watch his beloved Villa in comparative peace and quiet. Now he has a raving lunatic sitting next to him.

The poor lad gets prodded in the ribs at regular intervals while this babbling fool shouts things at him like, 'Did you see that run?' or 'Why hasn't he passed it there?' or 'Why do I keep picking him?'

The babbling fool is, of course, me.

On 25 November, in between the Coventry and Everton games and with my neck still in the tabloids' noose, my verbal exchange with Andy D'Urso at Leicester brought me a touch-line ban for a month.

I didn't bother attending the FA hearing in Birmingham as there would have been little point. The die was cast.

When the verdict was announced it was hardly a shock. I knew it was coming. But I thought it was going to be the end for me. I thought I wouldn't be able to cope. I loved the involvement the touch-line still gave me. It was as close as I could get without playing. That touch-line was still a drug to me. And now they were telling me to go 'cold turkey'.

That's it, I thought. I would lose my grip on the job to which I had fought so hard to cling... and I would be stuck in the directors' box, powerless to prevent it happening.

Just to make sure I got the message, the FA threw in a fine of £5,000 and ordered me to pay costs of £2,000.

And it proved to be the best £7,000 I have spent in my life.

If my job was under threat, that 'punishment' saved it. If I was hanging on by my fingertips, then without knowing it at the time, the FA reached down and plucked me from the cliff-face.

Yes, it was the best thing that ever happened to me.

I look back now and realize that my ranting and raving on the line was proving counter-productive. I was telling players where to run, who to pass to, where not to pass, how to pass and with which part of the foot; everything short of where they were going for dinner that evening.

For most it probably did not have a major impact other than to crank up the pressure a touch. But for the touch-line players, like Alan Wright and Steve Watson and Mark Delaney, it was probably a pain in the backside.

By removing me from the equation, they were suddenly able to relax. Now they could play their own game. And it showed. No question.

But that's looking back. When the ban itself arrived, it felt like it might be one kick in the privates too many.

I still felt we needed another voice down there in the dug-out and so I brought in our reserve coach Kevin MacDonald – and if you think I can shout, you should listen to him. I also set up a mobile phone link with Harry. It was not great, I thought, but it's the best we can do.

And so the first match of my sentence arrived – that all-important Worthington Cup tie against the Hammers. Great timing.

Five minutes. That's how long we were playing before I made my first call. I don't remember what it was about – possibly a minor adjustment, probably nothing. But I needed to get it out of my system. The noise of the crowd made the phone calls impossible at times. On occasions, I had to make my way to the tunnel and beckon Harry or Kevin to get an instruction across.

But as the game wore on, I realized it was concentrating my mind. I knew I would get 10 minutes at best with the team at half-time. I had to make it count. I was getting a more expansive view; a wider, broader image of the game. I saw that Frankie –

Lampard Jnr that is – was not tracking back with Ian Taylor. Fine for us at times but it was enabling him to get into more dangerous areas ahead of Ian when West Ham got forward.

Must make sure that 'Tayls' goes man-to-man for the second half, I told myself. Little things like that were much clearer and when half-time arrived, every second of the team-talk counted.

So that was a positive.

The flip-side of the coin was that I had lost my release. There was no physio's kit-bag to kick any more; no more running down the touch-line; no more screaming and shouting. There was no way to get rid of my frustrations.

I returned to the directors' box and began talking Stevie through the tactical nuances of the game. 'Yes, John,' he would say. 'No John,' he would add. And then the occasional, 'Really, John? How fascinating.' What he wanted to say, of course, was, 'For God's sake – just shut up and let me watch in peace will you?'

But he's a nice guy, Stevie. He put up with me.

Still, this was no good. Now I knew how a caged tiger felt. I had to do something. I went down to our dressing-room, poured myself a cup of coffee, and strolled back to the directors' box. It's a rabbit warren at Upton Park with a narrow set of stairs which require you to stop and wait for people to pass by.

I was amazed at the amount of work being done behind the scenes while the match was going on. The catering staff gave me some quizzical looks as much as to say, 'Shouldn't you be out there?' For my part, I'll always wonder whether the Ron Greenwood suite got that extra order of sandwiches. I felt like taking them myself. Anything to keep myself occupied.

But we played bloody well that night. Ian Taylor had put us in front only for Frank to equalize in the second half. Stevie keeps a stopwatch and at 90 minutes, extra time was beckoning. It was time once again to leave Stevie's side and get down to the play- ers' tunnel. I knew my ban would now be redundant; the pitch would become an extension of our dressing-room and I would be allowed to speak to the players at the final whistle.

But as I arrived at the bottom of the tunnel, West Ham's manager, Harry Redknapp, was coming the other way, his face like thunder and muttering various obscenities along the lines of, 'I don't fuckin' believe that'. As he passed me, he shook my hand and said, 'Well done John – all the best in the semis'.

What on earth was he going on about? 'But it's extra time isn't it?' I asked.

Dion Dublin, he told me, had just scored.

What? Fuckin' Brilliant! Yes! Yes! Yes! I thought, desperately trying to mask my excitement.

But the joy lasted for only a few seconds. Suddenly, an almighty roar went up. There was pandemonium out on the touch-line where I still could not tread. That was a home crowd roar, I thought. Harry turned and went rushing back past me.

'Now what the… ?'

West Ham had been awarded a penalty.

'Fuck it, fuck it, fuck it!'

I dashed upstairs to the directors' box just in time to see Paolo di Canio stick it away. It was 2–2. Extra time after all. And back down those bloody stairs.

'Listen boys, you've got to go and win it again – and you can do.' I tried to remind my lot of their fitness, their running power. And I do not believe there can be too many fitter teams in the country than Villa. 'Come on. You are playing well.' And they had been. This was a strong West Ham side who were a real handful on their own patch. But we had matched them. Again I sensed the improvement in my team.

'You can do it, fellas. You can do it. Come on.'

But a third goal would not come. And that meant penalties.

We had been thorough in our preparation; we knew penalties were a possibility and we had sorted out our takers. But, like they always say, the training ground is not the battlefield.

The 120 minutes had been very draining; some of the boys were now carrying knocks and bruises. If anyone did not feel confident about taking a penalty, I had to find out. I remember asking young Darius Vassell, one of our promising rookie strikers, if he fancied it and he suddenly made out he was from Peru and did not have a clue what the hell I was talking about!

I couldn't blame him.

Anyway, it didn't look as if it was going to matter. If Wrighty stuck away our fifth penalty, we were through. No problem. He had won the penalty shoot-out for us against Ajax in New York. He's good from the spot. C'mon Wrighty…

Tonight of all nights, he slammed his penalty against the bar.
Shit.

And we all know what happened next.

You don't have to ask the captain a second time. He is always
ready to stick his neck above the parapet. We had Gareth down
for Penalty No. 6 and he would not even think of dodging the
moment. Anyway, I felt this was a good opportunity for him to
wipe the slate clean from Euro '96 and his famous miss against
the Germans.

I reckon he would have done, too, had he been taking his
penalty to win the game. I have no doubt that in those circumstances he would have smacked it away without a problem. But
it was sudden death now and he needed to score to keep us in.

The pressure was suffocating; the noise, the derision from the
West Ham fans, was packed with hopeful anticipation.
'Southgate's gonna miss, Southgate's gonna miss.' They piled it
on the lad.

And here's a point that still riles me – why is it that the police
have the say-so as to which end the penalties are taken? They
insist that they must go ahead in front of the home fans for
'safety' reasons. Why? It's a hell of an advantage to give to the
home side.

Anyway, I am only delaying the inevitable, the horrible.

Sure enough, Gareth stepped up and Shaka Hislop, the West
Ham keeper, guessed correctly, took off to his left, and saved it.

We were out.

And Southgate was getting slaughtered.

Shit.

Will fuckin' nothing go fuckin' right this fuckin' season?!!

Talk about things coming back to haunt you. On the coach journey
home, I watched a rerun of the incident which brought West Ham
that penalty and the goal that took it into extra-time. I felt – no, I
knew – their striker, Paul Kitson, had really kidded the referee.

But I couldn't complain. When he was playing at Leicester, I
remember my coaching sessions with him, teaching him, telling
him to take advantage of everything that comes your way in the
box.

Apart from feeling sorry for myself, I felt for Gareth. What he must be going through. If football is the new rock 'n' roll, our skip was about to get the Gary Barlow treatment. Ridicule and mockery. He does not deserve that.

But he is a positive man, one of the most positive I know, and excellent at getting things in perspective. He knows what he is good at. He knows that every time that England squad is announced he's in there. Because he should be. One of the best defenders in the country. A penalty miss? I knew he would have it in perspective before too long. Come Saturday, and we go again. A clean sheet. No, he'll be all right. I didn't worry about Gareth.

And God knows we cannot afford a hangover. It was Sheffield Wednesday, the bottom club, at home on Saturday. The team was picking up but that run I needed was still eluding me. I was not out of the woods yet. Lose this one and those bastards will have a field day. Even more worrying, we will start getting dragged into the relegation fight. No thank you. Another must-win game was ahead; no time for feeling sorry for ourselves.

That was Wednesday night. On Friday morning, the phone rang in my office at Bodymoor Heath. It was Stridey.

'Have you heard about West Ham?' he asked.

'What about them?'

'The substitute the other night,' said Stevie.

'What substitute? What do you mean?'

Stevie began to explain in a little more detail.

'The lad they brought on in extra time, Omoyinmi I think his name is. Well, apparently, he had played for Gillingham in a previous round while he was on loan.'

I still was not quite sure what Stevie was telling me.

'So? Isn't he cup-tied then? What does that mean?' I asked.

'Well, it means we can either have the tie awarded to us or we will have to replay it.'

'Where?'

'Well, in all fairness, probably down there,' said Stevie.

Now hang on, this is creepy. Something I never, ever expected. This had to be an omen. Omoyinmi? Oh yeah, the little lad who came on in extra time. Never seen him play before. He hardly got a kick. Bloody 'ell. What a cock-up. What were they playing at down there? This kind of thing does not happen. Someone is trying to tell us something here. Yeah, maybe, just maybe, just at-long-last-soddin' maybe, the worm was about to turn. Thank you Lord – and not before time.

The day rumbled on and the story began to break. I didn't say anything to the players. Not until I had more information. I got to Villa Park after training as quickly as I could. The phone calls started coming in. The messages were going backwards and forwards.

The chairman was playing hard ball. He wanted the tie awarded to us. Secretly, I imagine he was making sure that at the very least, it would be replayed. West Ham, of course, were furious. But the 'old man' was just looking after his club's interests. All kinds of ramifications were possible. But by the time I drove home, I knew we were heading for a replay. Yeah, this is a sign all right. This is the little shove from up above we have been waiting for.

There was time to make one call. The skipper lives just down the road from me and I could not resist swinging the car into his drive and knocking at his door.

Gareth answered.

'Hello Gaff, what is it?'

'Well, you know that penalty you missed the other night?'

Like he needed reminding.

'What about it?' he said, possibly suspecting he was about to be the victim of a cruel wind-up.

'Well, it won't count mate. It won't count.'

I told him the story.

'Well,' he said. 'It will be easier to wipe it from the records than it will from my memory'.

But, do you know, I think he was quite pleased...

Down at West Ham, Harry is one of the best. A great guy and a great manager who has done a terrific job for his club. Their Premiership profile had improved significantly under his control. I felt for him over this episode but I could not feel sorry for his club. Someone, somewhere, had not done their job.

When Benito Carbone had signed for us, we asked if he had played in the Worthington Cup for Sheffield Wednesday.

'No Meester Gaffer,' he said. 'Me no play'. Well, something like that anyway.

But between myself and Steve, we got on to the League to check. And, sure enough, we found out that Beni had come on as a substitute for Wednesday in the last five minutes of their tie against Stoke.

We had done our homework and someone at the Hammers should have done the same. Sorry, but it's true. Somebody down there messed up, big time. Of course it was unintentional. But they should have checked. We heard that the boy himself, Emmanuel Omoyinmi, had been asked the same question and, like Beni, said no. Like us, someone at the Hammers should have checked.

It was a costly error. Only Harry will be able to tell you how much the whole episode affected them but they had a tough run for a spell after that. It is understandable. One minute they were in a semi-final; the next they had it taken from them.

Not surprisingly, there was a little bit of resentment in the air when we went back. I think West Ham might have been angered by some of our chairman's comments but the players were fine with each other. They knew the replayed game sprang from circumstances beyond their control and got on with it. But by the time we returned a month later, we were hot. And we won another absorbing tie in some style, 3–1, again after extra time.

It was ironic that while the original game had marked the start of my touch-line ban, that second game on 11 January, marked the first match in which I would be allowed back in the dug-out.

Should I go back to the touch-line? Or should I leave things as they were? I wondered.

I spoke to Ian Taylor when we arrived at Upton Park.

'Tayls,' I said. 'Where do you want me tonight? Shall I stay upstairs or... '

I never got to finish the question.

'Stay where you are, Gaff. Just stay where you are.'

You couldn't blame him. What had happened during my absence from the touch-line made it a very easy question to answer. The team was playing again, starting to flow, and getting results. It had to be more than coincidence. It had to have something to do with the players' relaxation and the change in ME, my method of operation, especially come match days.

If ever I thought I was having any kind of influence on the team from the touch-line, I knew now that I wasn't. Instead, I was spending more time on detail before games. My preparations had to be more thorough because I couldn't really change things tactically until half-time. Now I had to be certain, absolutely certain, that everyone knew what they had to do before each game.

More than at any time as a manager, I was going into real detail. I studied the report sheets about the opposition more thoroughly; I was scouting them myself whenever possible. I was spending more time on my 'homework', trying to make sure that there were no stones left unturned. This wasn't basketball. When the team went over the white line, I was stuffed until half-time. I couldn't call a time-out.

And, as I say, I began to treasure, to covet my half-times.

It was a fantastic lesson, one the FA could not have dreamed it was giving me. I suspect one or two of them were more interested in clipping my wings. Instead my team started to fly again. And so did I.

We had Ugo back. We had our back-three restored. We had Boateng and Taylor providing a telling partnership in midfield. And we had Merse. Yeah, a big welcome back to Merse.

Paul Merson is an alcoholic. No one, least of all Paul, tries to run from that fact. In his life, he has known incredible highs and unbelievable lows. But he has a daily problem coping if things are going against him. Every day that he gets through without a drink is a triumph for him. Whenever he has problems, the temptation to leave them in the bottom of a bottle chatters away in his ear.

No question, then, that his biggest ally at times like that is his football. I thought I had lost him after his one aberration with us the season before. I wondered if Paul would ever again be the player we have seen since.

But he had put it behind him again. I mentioned how there were encouraging signs in our pre-season training. And now he started to re-emerge in our first-team plans at about the same time as Ugo. His would prove to be an equally significant impact.

He realized that a reputation and big price tag were not good enough to get him into the team. It was what he was doing today that mattered. And I now saw him working exceptionally hard.

He now had a home in Birmingham, which certainly helped. Living on the doorstep, 10 minutes from work. He needs company; he is not at his best alone. And he was getting a fresh lifestyle together with friends around him. He was not stuck on his own, morose and hearing old voices from the past tempting him with a drink or a flutter. If he did have problems, he was leaving them behind at the gates of our training ground.

Whatever challenges we put in front of him, he was getting on with it. His fitness particularly. He was working hard again and it was coming together. Bit by bit, he was lasting longer in games. It had to be that way. I remembered the crowd slaughtering me in that home defeat by Southampton because I had substituted Merse. Couldn't they see the guy was knackered? If you are not fit enough, you cannot execute your skills. Not even if you are a player of Merse's ability.

Thankfully, he had taken a long hard look at himself and realized it was Villa or oblivion. He realized he needed to be doing well with his football. The training ground, the games, became his escape again. Just relax, enjoy what you are doing, what you are SO good at, and enjoy the company of the players and the coaching staff. You could see it all running through his mind.

During his spell out of the side, we had our discussions. He let me know about his worries. Did he still figure in my plans? Did I still want him? Of course. But it was up to him. There can be no preferential treatment. When he got back into the side, it had to be solely on merit and with the respect of the entire dressing-room behind him.

And that's what began to happen.

Paul began to turn in the performances which told us he was the Merson we had signed. He was getting back, making tackles, getting around the pitch in the last 15 minutes.

And sure enough, it came. That moment when we saw all his slog, all his lonely hours, all his sacrifices, all his battles with God-knows-what demons that threaten him... we saw it all pay off. In one moment. One glorious footballing moment.

It was the next game, in fact, the one against Wednesday. I felt that the really crucial period for my job and my team had come and gone and I had survived. I watched them playing on the back of that first West Ham performance and everything was looking so much healthier. The blend, the balance… it was all so much better.

But it was still a tortuous afternoon. We still had to win to confirm we were on the 'up'. Wednesday had taken the lead with a penalty. And, as the match wore on and we tore at them, knowing defeat was unthinkable, their goalkeeper Pavel Srnicek saved not one but two of ours. The first from Dion, the second from Merse. They were good penalties; they were even better saves. Pav was having an inspired afternoon.

Into the last 20 minutes, and still we were losing 1–0. At least the Holte were still with us. They could see what was happening, too. We were playing all right. It was better, so much better. But we needed that win; a win to take the pressure off everyone. And we needed a goal. Somehow, somewhere…

And then Merse produced a special, a run and shot from outside the area that bent its way into the top corner. It was a goal he would not have scored a few months, maybe even a few weeks, earlier. He would not have had the running power left to get there. Now he was still going, still going deep into this match.

And it was an inspiring moment, one which pushed us on and saw 'Tayls' finish off the job with a winner. Merse – still fresh, still thinking, still crafting – provided the killer ball in the build-up.

Merse has been a revelation since those early weeks back in the team. I made sure I let him know how well he was doing; how much progress he was making. And that he could not let it slip. He could not go back to the depths of the previous year. He was ahead in the game now – and that's where he had to stay.

Sure, it's tough getting there but even harder staying there. An old cliché but, in Paul's case, one that is particularly relevant.

This is how it had to be. For our part, we had to be watchful, careful. Especially as on current form, I am forever passing him in the corridor after games when he is clutching magnums of champagne as Villa's Man of the Match.

'Do you want me to look after that for you son?' I keep saying.

I feel like I am taking a loaded gun off a child.

Long may I be able to do so.

But victory over Wednesday was not without cost. A freak accident just after our winning goal would hurt us. They brought on a substitute just before the re-start, Gerald Sibon, who was startled by the sight of big Dion haring after the ball on a direct collision course with him.

Sibon stood there like a rabbit dazzled in the headlights; Dion reacted too late. *Crunch!* At the time we all thought it was just a nasty bump and nothing more. How wrong can you be?

Dion had crushed a vertebra. An inch either side and he would have been in a wheelchair for the rest of his life.

Full marks here go to our doc, Dr Barry Smith, for ensuring the right medical treatment from the pitch to the hospital, where our No. 9 underwent surgery that night.

Jim, our physio, sat in on the operation. He watched spellbound as the surgeons removed the damaged bone, the size of a fingernail, and then extracted an identical 'substitute' from Dion's hip and slotted that into the same area. Amazing.

When I went to see him the next day, Dion was fretting over whether he would be fit for our next game. The fact was he might not have been fit to go for a walk. Knowing what had taken place, I would just be happy if he could play again one day.

But losing the big man was a major, major problem. He is a popular bloke, a key figure in the dressing-room. A real gent, a real leader. There are so many arseholes in the game but Dion is one of the nicest guys in the business.

And he had scored 50 per cent of our goals. If you stopped DD scoring, you stopped Villa. That was the accepted view.

There has since been a lot of claptrap that Dion's absence worked for us; that it forced us to play a more precise game, a shorter game. We no longer threw it into the box and hoped he would get on the end of it. So the theory went.

It's crap.

We started to play better because we were starting to play better. And that was before Dion's injury. End of story. I recalled Carbone's opening game alongside Dion, for example, and they hit it off immediately. Good players on the same wavelength.

When we got Carbone fully fit and settled, I wanted to have some more of that. No chance now. No Dion for the foreseeable future.

But it wasn't important.

Football isn't when you realize what might have been confronting our No. 9.

CHAPTER 16

'Go and ram those words down my throat.'

I finally lost my rag with Stan at a meeting early in the new year. He now had new advisors, having parted company with his long-time agent Paul Stretford. His barrister, Jonathan Crystal, was there now, with another gentleman with whom I was not familiar: his lawyer, Robert Davies. Fairly high-powered stuff.

New faces. Same old story. And I had had enough.

Stan had been given time over the Christmas programme to go to Montpellier and discuss a loan until the end of the season. The French club abruptly ended the negotiations, however, when he refused to play in a trial match.

And so another summit meeting was called with the board, myself and Stan and his people. They soon got to the point.

Stan was still not training with the first-team squad and was being denied the opportunity of playing in the team. All he wanted was the chance to do what he came here to do. Play for Villa.

I countered by telling him the reserves gave him precisely that opportunity. But so far, he had played in two reserves games. Sorry, not good enough.

And off we went. For two hours. Two more hours of my life wasted talking about the same thing.

I could see that Stan's new team of advisors had been charmed by their client. Stan is articulate and, when he wants to, can state his case convincingly.

They wanted me to put Stan back in the team. See how he got on. I had spent the last 20 months talking over this same crap time and time again. I snapped that afternoon. I got bloody angry.

I had guys in my first team on a fraction of Stan's money, working 10 times as hard. They had no idea of the players' charter. You know? The one about the jerseys hanging together. You get in that team only because you have earned the right. The dressing-room is where you find your greatest allies AND your biggest critics. If you are not doing it, they let you know. In different ways, sometimes via me, 'Sorry Gaff, but I can't play with this bloke.'

And now here's this pair of lawyers telling me what team to pick? Well, excuse me. If Alex Ferguson wants to tell me how to do my job, boy, I will sit down and listen to every single word he says to me. But this lot? Do me a favour.

Still they chip away. Stan's lawyer tells me that Stan has got the best goal-scoring record in the club. But all I was hearing about was the past. In fact, the saddest thing was to hear Stan resort to that as well. He started talking about all the great goals he scored for Forest and Liverpool. Three, four years ago.

I think it may have been this meeting that finally snapped the chairman's patience, too. There had been times when, short of giving me a direct command, he made it clear he would have liked Stan to at least make the bench.

But I asked him on one occasion, 'Does it make you feel better if he plays because of all the money we've got tied up in him?'

'Yes,' he admitted.

'In that case, I would be putting him in the team for the wrong reason.'

Now the chairman, realizing that he had been down this road so many times before, began to see the waste of all this talk, talk, talk.

Stan made a final plea. He wanted to train with the first team. Sure, I could understand that. But I wanted to see it. Come on then, Stan, show me. Show me how much you want to train with the first team.

He still had not played since November. Now there were two reserve games coming up against Sheffield Wednesday and then

Sunderland. Two days before the first of them, Stan called the training ground, said he had flu and wouldn't be in for training. The following week, the day before the next match, he complained of a pulled groin and missed that one too. Coincidence? Legitimate injuries? Make up your own mind.

My argument had not changed. I mean, look at Merson. At one stage, this England player, this fuckin' World Cup England player for goodness' sake, had the indignity of going over to Loughborough to play against the university students. With a bunch of our youngsters. And Stan.

He had gone about his job in the right manner. In fact it was the test that proved he was ready to come back. Stan, uninterested, had been hauled off at half-time. That was the difference. And I was not going to bend the rules for him.

I knew it was difficult for Stan but if he could have just shown me something, something to prove how hungry he was... a good performance in a reserve game, a goal or two, or even the threat of a goal. Anything.

There were times in that bad run when I was under enormous pressure to play him. From the board, from some sections of supporters. And there were times when we were at our lowest ebb, when we could not score for love nor money, when we were so desperate, so bloody desperate for a goal from someone, anyone. Do you honestly think I would not have picked Stan if I thought he provided a solution?

Fortunately, by the time that meeting came around, I was in a stronger position. We had had a good Christmas. Another important game against a team directly beneath us, Derby, had followed the Sheffield Wednesday match. It was Boxing Day.

We had an outstanding performance that day from George Boeteng while Ian Taylor was continuing in a hot run of scoring goals, and a 2–0 win reinforced my view that the team was coming round.

In Dion's absence, we were having to cope with Julian Joachim and Beni as a spearhead – the Premiership's lightest front line I imagine – but these early signs were encouraging.

And young Darius came on and produced something that day that we saw from him on the training ground and in the reserves but had not yet seen in the Premiership. Until then. Darius was potentially a big, big talent. But the step up to first-team level had been proving difficult for him.

It was a bit like a player moving up to England – he starts concentrating on not making mistakes instead of doing the things that took him there in the first place.

As a raw talent, Darius has the precious ability to beat people easily. And he has frightening pace to go with it. They came together that day when he set up both of our goals. The big question mark for Darius now is whether or not he has the mental toughness to go with it. But what a talent.

My touch-line ban was not only proving a success, it was providing a few laughs on the way. That day, with the clock ticking down, I was trying to get through to Harry on the mobile as I made my way down from the directors' box for the last time.

He couldn't hear what I was saying.

'Hang on Gaff, I can't hear you. Say again?'

In truth I can't remember what it was I was trying to tell him. But I kept trying.

Now I had reached the tunnel and Harry, with his back towards me, had moved to the mouth of the tunnel to try to cut out the noise of the crowd. In the end, I was standing barely a yard behind him, but Harry, the phone welded to his ear, was oblivious to my being there.

I tapped him on the shoulder.

He barely looked round but said, 'Not now, I'm on the phone to me gaffer'.

'Harry, I'm right behind you, you idiot'.

Yes, it was nice to be able to laugh again.

We continued to play on that upward curve; we were getting better and better. Tottenham got away with a draw at Villa Park in the next game before we headed off for the first game of the new Millennium. Leeds, away, top of the table and laying waste to all who ventured near Elland Road. This was the acid test.

I had watched them at Arsenal the week before and was reminded just how big an influence on the team was exerted by Lucas Radebe. And I knew he would be missing from our match. So would their midfield player, Lee Bowyer, who I regarded as one of the best in the country at that time. We would be missing

Dion of course and Ian Taylor was suspended but... I still thought we could do well. Elland Road was heaving, intimidating, 12 games in a row had been won here.

But they looked vulnerable at set pieces and, with Merse capable of putting the ball on a pinhead, that would be one area to exploit. Lo and behold, we went there and dominated the game, winning with two goals from set pieces by the skip. Remarkable.

I was now in the habit of missing goals by the bucket-load because I always seemed to be making my way either to or from the directors' box when they went in. I missed an absolute stunner by Harry Kewell that day which brought Leeds back to 1–1 straight after half-time.

But we were no mugs now. The back-three were awesome and we had another bonus in the re-emergence of Steve Stone. He was playing in a different midfield role to the wide position in which he had forged his reputation. But he was proving he could handle it. And Watson did a good job on Kewell – sometimes I ask more of my wing backs than maybe I should but I set high standards – and David James had relatively little to do.

This was a day, though, when I really missed not being down there able to release some of the tension and pressure building inside me. Yeah, that day was tough. Holding on to our 2–1 lead I could barely stand it. I got up, sat down, shuffled, got up, walked around... at one stage, I wandered down one of the corridors and started looking at all the old pictures on the wall, feigning interest.

'Well, look at that, the Leeds team from 1957. How fascinating... Crowd still quiet. That's good... Oh, and this one, the Revie team. Now did I end up playing against any of them?' I don't know whether I was fooling anyone. I certainly wasn't fooling myself. Back to my seat. Still 2–1. Come on boys, nearly there.

And then my mobile rang. It had to be Harry wanting to tell me something. What's up now? What have I missed? I wondered.

'Hello Dad?' It was my boy, Stewart. Great dopey sod. 'You all right, Dad, what you up to?'

'Stewart, do the words "eff off" mean anything to you right now?'

'What's the matter?' he asked, oblivious to where I was, what I was doing, and what I was going through.

'I'm in the middle of a bloody game.'

'Are you? I thought it was 5.30 kick-offs today. The Sky game is Everton v Coventry. I just thought ... '

'Stewart – can we talk later?'

I can laugh now. At the time, well...

But we hung on. Deserved to as well. The new year felt good already, it was 3 January, 2000 – the 10th anniversary to the day of my sacking from Portsmouth.

OK, I admit it. There was a smug look on my face when our coach pulled out of Leeds that night.

I must admit I had my doubts about Martin O'Neill's intentions. Leicester City's manager had contacted me shortly before we were due to play his team in a two-leg semi-final of the Worthington Cup, our reward for beating West Ham at the second time of asking.

He wanted to know about Stan.

Or did he? What was going on here? Was he genuinely interested in signing Stan or was he just trying a little gamesmanship in the build-up to our cup-tie?

Wembley is important, always important. I had been there as a coach with Brian. But that was still reflected glory. The triumph was Brian's. Rightly so. So this was massive for me. It meant everything. IF we could get there and *if* we could win, it meant European football next season. And winning trophies is the ultimate currency for any manager.

I was so close now, with my team playing well, feeling good, players relaxing, enjoying their game. Yes, we had a problem for this competition. We had lost Dion and we now lost Vassell, also to injury. I was getting worried about that lad. This was his third injury of the season. Was he physically up to this level of football? And, of course, Carbone was ineligible. It left me with Julian alone as a striker of any experience.

But my attitude was positive. If you want to make a problem worse, fret about it. If you want to find a solution, look to the positives. Don't give the players the chance to find excuses.

We had enjoyed a fairly charmed passage in this competition so far and it was easy to imagine, to hope, our fortune would carry us all the way. We had drawn the League's bottom club,

Chester, in our first round. We drew Manchester United next – and Fergie kindly sent down his third team. Southampton we had beaten comfortably and, of course, we had that amazing second chance against West Ham.

But we knew Leicester would be a different kettle of fish. They had become that month's favourite whipping boys in the press because they had had the temerity to beat some of the more fashionable clubs in penalty shoot-outs.

Martin found himself defending his team but he used the opportunity to build-up the 'underdogs' tag that serves Leicester so well. Some were comparing them to Wimbledon, with all that that implies. That irritated Leicester even more, although they can be pretty direct and do rely a lot on set pieces. They have got guys who can deliver outstanding free kicks and corners and some big players, strong in the air, who can attack them. But Martin is clever with the blarney. He was whipping up his players and their supporters into an 'us against the world' frenzy. The reality is he's got a bloody good side packed with internationals.

But keep our nerve and we can do it. We can beat Leicester. I was convinced of it. And if we could... well, it was only human that I thought about the satisfaction I would gain at the expense of those who had been tormenting me just a couple of months earlier.

Now here was Martin asking about Stan knowing, I am sure, that he was still a vulnerable point on the Villa agenda. A record buy who had never come off for the club and who I was now refusing to consider for the first team. A managerial pal rang me and, raising my suspicions even further, said, 'Oi, watch that Martin down the road. He's a clever sod. He could be having you on.'

Was Martin trying to unsettle us before the two games?

I was not sure. But Martin asked me, straight up, for a no-holds-barred assessment of Collymore. He wanted to know everything I could tell him. Good or bad. I didn't try to kid him. I said yes, it's true, there's a bloody good player in there somewhere. But I couldn't find him, no matter what I tried. Martin had done a fantastic job digging out forgotten riches from players such as Tony Cottee; maybe he had the answer. I didn't know. I didn't hold anything back.

Martin was given the all-clear to further pursue his interest.

And we left it at that for the moment, agreeing that the issue would be put to one side until after we had resolved our semi-final. But when I put the phone down, I couldn't stop thinking, 'What's he up to?'

We failed. We failed miserably against Leicester. Miserably. I was not too unhappy with the fact that the first leg, at our ground, was goalless. It was a dull, negative game. But a clean sheet was the prime requisite. Leicester played it largely on the back foot but that was understandable. We had a couple of great chances to prise a goal out of the tie but it eluded us. Still, we could score in the second leg and if we did, a draw would be good enough. That was my thinking.

But we choked at Filbert Street. We bottled it. We had too many players willing to take a back seat, too many players looking at Merse and saying, 'Go on, Merse, give us one of your specials.' Everyone was leaving it to everyone else. We did not get going until the middle of the second half.

That second, decisive match, was settled by one goal and we just could not break them down. It was a horrible, horrible experience. Had we gone out after giving it everything but being outplayed by the opposition, it would have been a comfort. I would not have had any complaints. But we had not done ourselves justice. It was a tame surrender.

Our dressing-room was how it should be. Quiet. If you lose a League match, within a few days you have the chance to put it right. But with a Cup game, the finality of it all is chilling.

It's gone. We've blown it. And above us and all around us we can hear their crowd. And we can hear their dressing-room. And you get the bangs on the door accompanied by comments like, 'See you some time, Villa. We'll give you a wave when we're walking out at Wembley.' Rubbing it in. You're numb. Utterly numb. It is a killer. The only way we could make any sense of that evening was to learn from it. To absorb the gut-wrenching punch it delivered and make sure it didn't happen again.

The chance to do so was looming fast.

'Oi,' I said to Stan as he stood at the door of my office at Bodymoor Heath. 'You get yourself over there and make sure you ram my words down my throat'.

He looked back at me. I hoped he realized that, despite all our battles and differences, I was being genuine. I think he did.

'Yeah,' he replied. 'And you make sure you win the FA Cup.' He turned and left my office for the last time.

It was Friday, 4 February, two days after we had left Filbert Street, shattered and broken, and two years to the month since I had watched him launch my reign so brilliantly against Liverpool.

Now the circus was leaving town. For the last time.

Martin had been genuine after all. Stan was going to Leicester. The deal was not the best for us financially, but I believe it was the best deal for us as a football team.

Aston Villa had paid £7 million for Stan and invested another £2.5 million in wages. That was £9.5 million of the £11 million total package involved in the Collymore transfer. But I saw it as a saving of £1.5 million because I had long been convinced that Stan was never going to do it at Villa. A new club, a fresh start was his only chance.

And the best of luck to him.

Football is probably the most talked-about pastime in the country. But the paying public, the administration staffs, the media, even the boards who run the clubs, none have a clue about what really goes on behind those dressing-room doors. It is a unique environment that has to be experienced to be truly understood. The respect. The camaraderie. How you earn your spurs.

All the time there had been that pressure to pick Stan. The chairman had wanted me, requested me, to put him on the bench at Derby for that Boxing Day match. But I still don't think that he truly understood the consequences of such an action. Sure, it might mean that we put a coat of paint over Villa's multi-million pound investment and retrieve a few bob on Stan's eventual sale. But the cost to the dressing-room, in my opinion, would have been catastrophic.

I had worked hard to make everyone aware that there were no favours, no favourites. Every shirt was claimed on merit. And sorry, but Stan had not merited that shirt. And I was not going to break that code. Not for Stan, not for the chairman, not for anyone. My decision. And nothing will ever persuade me I should have done otherwise.

Martin was welcome to the circus. But I genuinely hoped Stan could make a success of it. You might find that strange. But it's the truth. I've said before – you have your rows, say your piece, get it off your chest, and then start afresh the next day. Life is too short to wish ill of anyone.

And there was no joy in my heart because Stan was leaving. Quite the opposite. There was a sadness, a strange kind of sadness. And a sense of failure. I thought back to that first game against Liverpool. Why could he not repeat that? Why had I not been able to get that from him ever again?

So many times, so many, many times, I felt I had cracked it with him. But it never lasted long. It was up to him now.

I will always look at myself and wonder if I could have done anything else. But I am not sure I will ever find an answer. Ultimately, people who go around thinking certain players do it for certain managers are kidding themselves. First and foremost, players do it for themselves, their family and their friends. Their loved ones. Isn't that what we all do?

I know he will have his moments. He will have those days when the whole of football looks at Stan Collymore and thinks about the great stages he could have dominated. I know the threat is there. I know we might look back and say, 'Well, didn't he make Gregory look silly.' But I could only handle it as I saw it.

I had lost count of the amount of times I had told him that, had I been given his talent, I would not be messing around in England with a couple of international caps. I would have been playing for Barcelona or Inter Milan or Juventus or the like and winning European Championships and World Cups.

But now it was all over and the sadness lingered. Stan had failed at Villa. So had I.

He came in early that morning, shook hands with those who were there, a kiss for the girls in the kitchen.

And I forgot to do something which, when I next get the opportunity, I must remedy. You see, at home I've still got his shirt. His shirt from that first game against Liverpool. It was the game, the victory, that got me off to a flyer. And I will always be grateful to

Stan for that. Always. Next time I see him, I hope he will sign it for me, so I can get it framed and hung on the wall next to my other souvenirs.

Yeah, the circus was leaving town and that side of it Martin was welcome to.

But go on Stan, you ram those fuckin' words down my throat...

Now, what to do with Carbone? Beni had come to us as we slithered into our trough of October and November. His debut, against Wimbledon, had been outstanding. Truly outstanding.

But I had not seen that from him for a while. It was partly understandable. He had missed a lot of football during his dispute with Sheffield Wednesday. His match-fitness was down. And we demand a lot of hard work from our strikers. There had to be a period of adjustment. He certainly gave us craft. And he was a delight to the eye, a wonderful player to watch.

But the goals, his chance-taking, was still not convincing. There was no hurry. We had what I considered a perfect deal in that he was with us until the end of the season and that gave us both a chance to look at each other.

I was a different guy, now, too. I was not quite so trusting of anyone any more. Not automatically at any rate. I had now been at the helm of a big club long enough to know there were a lot of liars and cheats out there. I wanted to make sure that wasn't the case here.

I was thinking, 'Be careful, don't rush.' As a Bosman transfer at the end of the season, Beni would be after a fortune. There was no real fee involved. That money would go to the player. But the club had got its fingers burned on big contracts before. I wanted to be sure.

There were agents trying to put the frighteners on us too. There were clubs in his native Italy who were interested – according to his representatives. I think it was partly genuine. But I still suspected the idea was to prod us into action and give Beni, and them, their pot of gold.

But he was becoming far more of a team player and striking up a good rapport with those around him. He was beginning to feel at home and wanted to stay.

And then came the clincher.

I still wanted us to make headway in the Premiership. I still felt we could reclaim a place in the top six. But in terms of glory and silverware, we now had only one road to salvation.

The FA Cup.

And in between the two Leicester games we were presented with our second collision of the season with Leeds, just 27 days after we had rattled their chain at Elland Road. It was a fifth round tie. This time we would be at home. People, our own people, were looking at us as if they still needed convincing. This was another major opportunity to silence a few more of the critics.

And I was really excited by this match. I knew it would be a sharp contrast to the first game against Leicester, which we had staged a few days earlier. I had travelled up to Sunderland the previous weekend to see Leeds win at the Stadium of Light. They were 2–1 up with 25 minutes to go and still trying to make it 3–1 or 4–1.

They were a very open attacking side and I knew that no matter what happened, our forthcoming game was never going to be dead.

That thought was with me at half-time, when we were 2–1 down and yet to 'get in their boots'. We were letting Leeds play; maybe a little bit fearful. But I knew there were more goals in the game and I felt they could be ours. It was whether we would have the ability to take our chances.

Merse and Beni performed to the very highest level that afternoon but the tie will be forever remembered for Carbone's hat-trick. Yeah, we won 3–2, with Beni's second goal the outstanding, memorable highlight – a cleverly disguised chip from 35 or maybe 40 yards which caught Nigel Martyn, Leeds' England goalkeeper, off his line.

It was breathtaking. And as it flew in and Villa Park erupted, I nipped down the seven or eight steps in the directors' box to where the chairman was standing, still applauding the effort.

'What do you think, chairman?' I whispered in his ear. 'Shall we send him back now?'

His response was instant.

'Don't you dare let him out of your sight'.

Merse finished that afternoon getting a huge cut over one eye after a terrible clash of heads with Leeds defender Michael Duberry. The match ended for both of them in that moment with Michael in just as bad a state as Merse.

But our man's discomfort was worthwhile. Some superb individual skills had set up the winning goal for Carbone, with the clash of heads coming at the final, decisive moment when Merse flicked the ball across goal just as Michael tried to head it clear.

Both players had to leave the pitch but, as Merse was taken away to the hospital, it was down to our club doctor Phil Bickley to attend to Michael's stitches for a nasty cut on his head. That was bad enough. The poor lad was blissfully unaware as the doc got to work of an even more painful surprise awaiting him.

'Ah well, at least it was worth it,' said Michael as the doc began cleaning him up.

'What do you mean?' asked the doc.

'These stitches. They're worth it. Heading the ball out for a corner.'

Oh dear. Ah well, he would have to find out sooner or later.

'Sorry Michael, but Merson got the ball across to Carbone. And he scored.'

'You mean it's not 2–2 any more?'

'No – you're losing 3–2.'

Ouch! It wasn't just the stitches that hurt, then?

CHAPTER 17

'Winner'

I have the same ritual for each match. Just before my team goes out, I stand at the dressing-room door and roll the armband up the captain's sleeve. And tell him to keep a clean sheet. It was something I used to do with Andy Townsend when I was coach. Now I am manager and Gareth is my captain. It is symbolic. I am handing *my* team over to him. 'Here, they're yours for the next 90 minutes. Look after them, will you?' And I'm very choosy about who I give that armband to.

That ritual is something the players see. What they don't know is what always goes through my mind, what I visualize next, as each and every one files past me. I always imagine I have a rubber stamp with 'Winner' moulded on to it. And as each player passes, I stamp the back of their shirts, 'Winner', in indelible red ink. So there's no doubting it.

I used to think twice about one or two. But when, as manager, I can stamp 'Winner' on the back of every Villa shirt that passes me… then I know I am getting somewhere. And that was how it was starting to feel now.

Gareth Southgate: 'Winner'. Georgey Boateng: 'Winner'. Ian Taylor: 'Winner'. David James: 'Winner'. Big Ugo; 'Winner'. And so on. One by one they go past me and one by one they get stamped. It is the prime requirement. We have all seen the great upsets over the years, the triumph of underdog over superior ability. It can only happen because of the kind of qualities I am referring to now. Stevenage would never have pushed Newcastle

213

to the limit a season or two back had it not been for that passion, that desire, that hunger.

And don't be fooled into thinking it is the sole property of the game's journeymen; their only way of competing with the best. It is the quality that keeps the cream at the top, too. Today's great players, from Beckham to Bergkamp; they all have it. They don't need the money. They don't need the kudos. They don't need the admiration. They need to win. That's why Fergie stays at the top of his profession. He doesn't need to polish his ego any more or improve his bank account. He is just a born winner.

And it's not about kicking people on the pitch. It's about not going missing when you are 2–0 down at Anfield and you can't get a touch. It's about working your socks off in training on Monday morning after you've been beaten on Saturday. It's about being part of the dressing-room, too. It's knowing that when your team-mates look round the dressing-room, they gaze at you and think, 'Yep, I'm glad he's on my side today. He'll look after me.'

It's about all sorts of qualities, all sorts of measures of a man. It's even about being humble enough to stop your car and get out when there are 20 or 30 kids waiting in the pouring rain for your autograph.

Winner. Winner. Winner.

Now I look at my team and I am able to think, 'Yes. I fancy this lot against anybody'. We've got the right types. We've got a chance now. And if that defeat at Leicester had jolted my confidence, what happened next soon repaired it.

By beating Leeds, we had earned an FA Cup quarter-final at Everton. Before that we had Premiership games against Watford and Middlesbrough and both were won with outstanding team performances and 4–0 scorelines. Merse scored two brilliant goals against Watford, really establishing himself as the darling of the fans.

But when we went to the Riverside and did the same on a difficult night for 'Boro there was a tinge of regret clouding my satisfaction. The sad part was seeing the finest English player of the last 15 years getting carried off towards... towards, who knows what?

I did not have a problem with Paul Gascoigne's much-publicized challenge on George. I never castigate the opposition for their tackling. I was more annoyed that the referee missed it. We all try to win the game and there is physical contact in English football we should never, never, lose. But you rely on the referees to keep it under control.

As Paul was stretchered away that night I could not help but wonder if that would be the last we would see of him at this level. I had played against Paul in my last season at Derby when he was a mere sprog. I 'did' him up at Newcastle and he turned to his big centre-half, Paul Jackson, and said 'Hey Jacko, make sure you do him'. That was a response I recognized. I loved that. And I've loved Paul ever since that moment.

I think as a nation we have been very selfish about Gazza. We wanted him to cut out the antics, become a fitness fanatic, become a slave to his ability. And have no personality. But then the world would have been a much duller place.

He may not have reached the heights we all thought he would. But he still leaves us with some fantastic memories and our game is a better place for the bits of Gascoigne we have enjoyed. I am not so sure it would have been the same had he become the man he could not be, as so many of us demanded.

I always think that for every player there is a three-year peak when everything fits into place and they can do no wrong. Gazza's came very early. Tottenham had the best of him; I'm not so sure Middlesbrough have. But he is still the best English midfield player we have seen in the last 15 years. I certainly never saw anyone to rival him. Gazza would always have had my stamp on his back even though he has never been associated with the outstanding teams of his era.

But it was team success I was chasing now. And it was time for Everton at Goodison. It was a tie I felt we were more than capable of winning. But there was an important reminder to be issued to the players before we got down to our final preparations.

On the Thursday before the Sunday of the match, 20 February, we called the boys together and for just a few moments, took them back to that night at Filbert Street. 'Remember it? Remember how it hurt? Remember how it hurt even more because we never got started? Because we didn't close down that cross or allowed that header or missed that tackle?'

Because we were not quite at it. That could not happen again. If it did, then we would have to go through that same miserable experience all over again. We tried to make sure that the players knew we could forgive them anything except not performing. That made defeat unbearable.

I love Goodison. It's a fantastic old stage where you can still close your eyes and imagine Everton's great players of the past. There's no shiny new plastic or concrete blocks obscuring the view of their history. And Everton's supporters are some of the most fiercely loyal and noisiest on the planet. Even 10,000 there can sound like 40,000. Throughout their relegation struggles of the previous seasons they had still turned up in huge numbers.

And the atmosphere that day did not disappoint me. It was Everton's last chance of silverware, too. They were as hungry as we were. We could win it. I was still confident of that. But it was a daunting task and we were going to have to be good. Very good.

Five minutes before we go out and it's time to check: 'Is that everything? Does everyone know what they are doing?' No, there was one final thing. One final hangover from the Leicester match that was nagging at me.

A piece of scrap paper in my pocket. I've got loads of them, never forgetting Terry Venables' advice to make notes. Jot down ideas. Whenever. Wherever. I still have pocketfuls of them. And there was one I wanted to dig out now.

In Merson, we had one of the best deliverers of a free-kick or corner in the game. Paul can put it on the proverbial sixpence. But Leicester had dealt with all of our crosses, all of our set pieces. They had height and power at the back – and so did Everton.

If we wanted to get some joy from any corners or free kicks, we had to do something just a little different.

Defenders are always well set for corners. They know where the ball is going to be delivered from. It's always the same. As a result, they only have to keep half an eye on the corner flag. They can concentrate on their opponents' movements.

But if you work a short corner and change the angle and the time of the delivery, then it is a little more disconcerting. Then they have to look at where the cross is coming from. It distracts them. And, hopefully, that can give your bodies in the box the chance to find space.

Just before we go out, then, I call Merse, Beni, Gareth and Ugo
together and I pull out a scrap of paper on which I had scrawled
a different routine. I transfer the idea to the magnetic board in
the Goodison dressing-room.

'If we're static at corners, they will head them away all day.
We've got to move them around. Beni, you come short and give it
back to Merse for a different angle. And Ugo, you peel round to
the back post, see what you can pick up there.'

And what a dividend. First corner we get, we catch Everton a
little off guard with this variation and it works like a dream.
Merse picks out Ugo at the far post and his header back across
the face of goal is met by Steve Stone, 1–0. Thanks Tel boy,
thanks. I later catch a snatch of comment from Trevor Francis on
the Sky broadcasting team talking about the hours spent on the
training ground perfecting such moves. Sorry Trev, not this time.

One-up and we're in control. We have handled Everton's early
fire. So far so good. Come on boys, stay tight now.

But then a mistake by young Barry. When we had come up to
Goodison for that precious goalless draw on a day many were
predicting the axe would fall on my neck, Gareth had been
magnificent. But in this match, his golden touch would not come.
He was getting caught in possession and, just as I think we are
starting to get on top, he makes one error too many.

Joe-Max Moore pounces, 1–1. And it has cost us control.
Everton are fired up. They had paid us a compliment by changing their team to counter our set-up and now it is working for
them; their three midfield players are having more of the ball.

Merse, particularly, is getting by-passed. It's furious out there.
No space. No time. The board goes up for a minute's extra time at
the end of the first half. I leave my seat and reach the dressing-
room, having made my decision. Merse is going to have to come
off, Ian Taylor can come on.

I wait for the players to return and Kevin Mac eventually
leads them in.

'Kev, I'm going to make a change. I'm taking Merse off for
Tayls,' I tell him.

'Aye, OK – but he did great for the goal didn't he?' says my
coach.

'What goal? What are you talking about?'

I had missed yet another one. Kevin tells me about it, how Merse had cut through and forced a parried save that Beni tucked away on the rebound, 2–1. Now that's a bonus. But it doesn't change my mind.

'That's good – but he's still coming off,' I say.

I sit down with Merse.

'Listen son, I'm bringing Tayls on for you. You've done your bit. Fantastic. You've made your contribution. This is a team decision. You've stuck one foot in the semi-finals. Now I want Tayls to make sure it's two feet.' Words to that effect anyway. Merse takes it well. He understands the reasoning. Brilliant.

And that's what happens. In Tayls, George and Steve Stone I've got a midfield three who can out-run and out-fight any other combination in the country. I mean that. From a purely defensive, shackling point of view, I would back them against anyone.

We get Tayls to play in John Collins' boots to stop him creating. They can't get through us or behind us. Instead, Everton have to bomb it into our box from out wide and we deal with that well. Barry simplifies and tightens his game. Now, let's win it and get out.

Before the match I would have been content with a replay but now the seconds are ticking away and we can go through at the first time of asking. The tension is thick in my stomach. And yet again I curse the absence of any release. I wish I had Jim's bag to kick again. Time for more of those walks. More fake interest in the pictures on the walls. And they've got a few at Everton. But we get there. The FA Cup semi-finals. At Wembley. We're one step away from the Big One.

That game, and the way that we won it, taught me a lot about my team. They were growing up. We are forever telling them 2–1 is a good enough score-line. It doesn't have to be 3–1 or 4–1. That brings you no extra prizes, especially in the Cup.

Now instead of the staff having to scream it from the touch-line, the players were doing it themselves. You don't have to cross it with five minutes left. Their keeper catches it and two seconds later the ball is in your box. And in an effort to make it 3–1 it's suddenly 2–2. Don't make 50-50 passes when you are winning with five minutes left. Frustrate the opposition. Deny them possession.

When I could bear to look, the boys were doing it themselves. They wound the clock down superbly that day and as they trooped back into the dressing-room, I had my rubber stamp ready for each of them.

'Winner.'

So why didn't it feel great? Why wasn't I elated? No Villa team had reached the FA Cup final for more than 40 years and now we were 90 minutes away. Why did it feel hollow? I knew the answer; I just didn't like to think about it.

It was a day like that at Goodison, a victory everyone connected with Villa could savour, which reminded me just how badly I had been hurt a couple of months earlier. I'll try to explain. Imagine falling in love. Hopelessly, completely. So much so that you give your heart and your body and your soul to the object of your affection. You live for them, eat, breathe and sleep for them. Everything you do is geared towards their happiness. You burn all your bridges, you give up everything you have. And then she turns around one day and says, 'Sorry mate, I don't like you as much I thought. In fact, I'm starting to get the hots for somebody else.'

Imagine that scale of hurt. Imagine how you would never give your heart away quite so easily again in the future. Imagine how you would close down a little inside and keep your emotions in check.

And that's precisely how I was feeling.

I had been hurt, seriously hurt, by what had gone on, by the threat of my mistress' rejection. Villa's rejection. Scarred, just as I had been at Portsmouth. But there, my reaction had been a determination to prove the them wrong. This was different. Here, it was a case of self-preservation.

The club I loved, the club to which I was totally devoted, had dared to think about getting rid of me. I had allowed them to think about getting shot of me. In fact, I practically handed them the gun. And they actually thought about pulling the trigger. And, what's more, if they could do that once, they could do it again.

'Come on son,' I kept saying to myself at Goodison, 'don't be such a misery. You've reached the FA Cup semi-finals. That's got to be worth something. Enjoy it. Celebrate.'

But this new voice inside was telling me different. 'No. Don't get carried away. Don't let it in. They won't thank you for any of this, you know. There will be something else not to their liking one day. Something else for which you will cop the blame. So don't let it show.'

And there, right there, is the biggest change in me. That victory at Everton was followed by the second anniversary of my appointment and I realized how much I had grown up, more wise to the ways of this world into which I had been pitched.

The little boy who chased after Bobby Moore's autograph was still there, still in love with the game, still a serious football romantic. A short while later, for example, I attended a reserves match and was introduced to Brian Clough.

Cloughie for goodness' sake.

He shook my hand and gave me what I think was a nod of approval. He knew what I had been through. And it was a fantastic, lump-in-the-throat moment for me.

As was the day the phone rang and it was Geoff Hurst – sorry, Sir Geoff Hurst – wanting to speak to me. Me. Geoff Hurst for me? I'm not quite sure about the conversation because as he spoke, I was 12 years old again, glued to the black and white TV set on that hot afternoon in the summer of 1966, and my dad was jumping about the lounge because Weber had just equalized. 'Those German bastards,' he was shouting, 'they killed my sister'.

And now here was Sir Geoff, scorer of the most famous hat-trick in English football, asking to speak to *me* on the phone.

No, the soppy old romantic is still in here. But I won't let him out quite so easily in the future.

I would be surprised if you expected us – the managers that is – to feel differently. The hysteria surrounding the game these days is an out-of-control monster. That Sunderland v Leeds match, for example – the one I went to before we played David O'Leary's side in the FA Cup. Okay, Sunderland had a tough time that day. Leeds were flying. But they were actually booed off the pitch at half-time.

I could not believe what I was hearing. This obviously could not be the same Sunderland who had won the First Division by a landslide and then tore into the Premiership when even their own fans thought they would be in for one long survival fight. They had been brilliant. Absolutely brilliant. And now they were being booed... Incredible.

What did these people want, for goodness' sake?

And the public seem so easily swayed by what they read or hear from the media when so much of it does not stand up to scrutiny.

Take my case. After my first year at the club, they were talking about me as an England manager. All these glowing tributes. I was flavour of the month. A year later, I was an incompetent buffoon. The same people have written those things within a year of each other. To me, that makes *them* stupid and incompetent, not me. They wrote the nonsense in the first place. I didn't. It has no logic, no intelligence, no sense. How can I have gone from one extreme to the other in so short a time?

Unfortunately, the punters don't see it that way. They get swept up and carried along with it all. The upshot for me, though, is that I cannot relax any more at press conferences. I have become a little sour about it all. I cannot deny that.

It's not that I expect the game, the job, to be a pristine virgin. God knows I have been around long enough to have seen just how dirty a whore she can be at times. But I always thought she was the whore with a heart of gold.

Not always true.

As I write, we're doing OK; we're winning a few games and preparing for the semi-final, a big Wembley day for the club. And when I meet people after the matches, they are all back-slapping and smiling and telling me how well we're doing. The journos, the media, the hangers-on, the people who feed off Villa, the people who are on the outside and want to be on the inside; the Guest Lounge lizards. 'Well done Johnny Boy, always backed you mate; always knew you would pull through,' they say.

I know that if and when we have another bad trot, they will be fawning all over the chairman again. And I know precisely what they will be saying.

Being able to see through all of that crap has been the biggest lesson of the last two years. Being able to tell the difference between the genuine and the sycophants; identifying those who have always tried to befriend the manager when things are going well – and that might be me, or Brian or Big Ron – but during the tough times, have beaten a hasty retreat. Generally to the chairman's office.

I haven't quite got it back yet. There is a streak of bitterness in me that won't go away. I am finding that hard to get over. Maybe the summer will change things; soften me a little.

But of one thing I am sure.

I will never let them get to me.

CHAPTER 18

'I know, I'll try not to think about the match.'

Bang! Wide awake. Sunday, 2 April, 6.55 a.m. Not a drowsy, foggy, where-am-I-who-am-I-what-day-is-it? kind of awake. This was an instant, switched-on, plugged-in surface from sleep. I knew why as well.

Eyes wide open, arms folded behind my head, staring up at the hotel room ceiling. It was here. Sunday, 2 April. FA Cup semi-final day. Me, little Johnny Greg, taking Villa to Wembley. Think of it. Me. And 36,000 of our lot are following us down here. I wonder if they're up and about yet? Course they are. Fantastic. We haven't been to the final since 1957. The world was in black and white then, wasn't it? They're up and about all right.

Five to seven and I wished it was five to three. The waiting is a killer. It was always like this as a player. Every Saturday 7 a.m., wake up, instant tension, instant excitement. Match day was here. Best feeling in the world. Kick a few, maybe score; definitely win. Who am I playing against? Oh, he's a good player. Got to be sharp today, Johnny boy. It was always 7 a.m. too, the body-clock took care of that. And I always wished it was five to three. I've seen players totally knackered by kick-off time because the waiting for the game, the excitement of their anticipation, had drained them. There were occasions when I would be on the snooker table by 8 a.m., desperate for something to do to pass the dead time stretching ahead. Yes, that was what it was always like as a player. But you get older and a little immune to it, I suppose. Rarely do you get the intensity of that electric charge when you wake on the morning of a match as a coach or manager.

But this was clearly an exception. This was the moment it really began to sink in. The moment my eyes opened I knew it was *that* Sunday and my thoughts were racing away with me. What's it going to be like? What will I do if we win? Will I be able to contain myself? Never forget Sam Allardyce. (We were playing Bolton, I should point out, and Sam was their manager.) I remembered Leicester's play-off final against Swindon in 1993. I was there as a coach with Brian Little's Leicester team. Great game and a dramatic game which, painfully, Swindon won. At the final whistle, Swindon's No. 2 John Gorman ignored our bench and ran straight for Glenn Hoddle on the pitch to celebrate with him. Lack of respect, that, in my book. We've all been guilty of breaking the codes of courtesy in the heat of the moment. But this is Wembley. So no matter what, no matter how it turns out, if you do win, don't forget Sam. You know what it feels like.

I don't really know Sam. Our paths have crossed on a couple of coaching courses at most. Hang on. Didn't he captain Bolton that day when you were captaining Villa? League match, 1978-79 season if I'm not mistaken. We won 3-0. I marked Frank Worthington. Didn't give him a kick. Is that a good omen?

I don't know.

But Sam seems a nice guy and he's done a good job at Bolton, no question about that. What's more he's a big bugger, so best not to cross him. If we score a spectacular winning goal in the last minute and all you want to do is sprint on the pitch and scream to the heavens... don't! No, at the finish, don't forget Sam. What time is it now? Only seven o'clock? God, another five or six hours of this. What am I going to think about for the next five minutes?

I know, I'll try not to think about the match...

No, that's not worked. Try again...

No, still not working.

Back it came, thoughts flying. For a fleeting moment, even the nightmare scenario slipped through my guard.

What if we lose?

Get rid of that idea straight away. No thank you. No negativity here. Ban that immediately.

Penalties?

Yes, it could go to penalties. We've got that covered haven't we? Yes, all sorted. Wouldn't it be great if it went to penalties and up steps the captain to score the one to take us to the final? Now that would be sweet.

You can stop that nonsense. Now you are being a romantic. We're not playing this for Gareth to banish some ghosts from the past. Get it into context. This is an FA Cup semi-final for goodness sake. Villa haven't been to the final for 43 years. And that reminds me, I must get Hendrie on if we are to go to the wire because he takes a good spot-kick. Now what time is it?

Oh, great. Five past seven.

Time's really going to fly this morning, isn't it?

I had slept well, though, and why not? For a start, worrying is pointless. I know colleagues who aren't happy unless they have got something to worry about. If they do not have a problem, they will nag away at things until they find one.

But I went to bed on the eve of that semi-final quite content. It would take care of itself now, I thought. I can't get them any fitter. I can't make them any better in the next 12 hours. We had prepared as best we could. There was nothing I could do between now and kick-off to change them. Yes, it would take care of itself.

And I thought we would win.

That quarter-final against Everton had barely been five minutes old when both Walter Smith and I knew whoever won that day would be facing Bolton, the only surviving club from outside the Premiership, in the semi-final.

The information was irrelevant at that moment but, after our Goodison success, I was asked if Sam's First Division team was the draw I would have preferred. It was a loaded question because the journos were waiting to dig out some anti-Bolton comments from me. But, me being me, I said, 'Yeah, bloody right it's the draw I would have chosen'. Because it was. It was either Bolton, Chelsea or Newcastle. What did they want me to say? 'Actually, I was hoping for Chelsea please because they're the toughest pick of the lot.' I knew Bobby Robson and Luca Vialli would be thinking the same.

But I also knew that we still had a tough hurdle to get over.

Bolton were not unknown to me, although I wondered about how much my players knew about them. I always speak to them about other games and sometimes they haven't seen any of the goals from the previous weekend.

Later on in the build-up to the semi, it became clear that quite a few of our lads had not heard of the men blocking their path to the final. 'Who's he again?' 'He's from where?' 'Well, what position does he play?' Managers are into it because it is their job to know about the opposition. But I wonder whether the players are in love with the game as much as the coaches. Then again, who am I kidding? It was like that when I was a player and I guess it always will be.

But Bolton were a good footballing team, I knew that. Sam, as I say, had done an impressive job since being appointed earlier in the season and they were in the thick of a very good run as our meeting approached.

I went to see them play Sheffield United – a match Bolton won 2-0 – and they were very neat. In some ways, very old-fashioned. Out and out 4-4-2. Two wide men, two front men who receive the ball well with their back to goal. They play a lot to feet. Play out of the back and try to build it. Not a lot of height, true, but Wembley would suit them. And they were going there as total underdogs. All the pressure would be on my lot. And yet, I felt if we were 'at it' we would have enough to win the day. And I had no real complaints about the intervening weeks. Our form had stayed pretty solid, with just one blemish when we had been beaten at Southampton. But we were ticking over nicely. Merse was getting better, if anything, and the boys at the back even more commanding.

We had lost David James for all but the last game before the semi-final but he was back now along with a bonus I could scarcely believe. In the last 10 minutes of the 2-0 victory over Derby a week before the Bolton match, Dion had returned. A guy who had been written out of the script by everyone except, crucially, the player himself, was fit again.

About a month before Wembley, I had started to see him at Bodymoor Heath, jogging and then kicking a ball about and then, horror of horrors, even heading the darn thing.

I kept thinking to myself, 'Should he really be doing that?' But all the time, our advice was that he could do anything as long as it didn't hurt. Which sounds pretty basic but also pretty logical. After all, no one knew how Dion felt better than the lad himself.

His progress was testament, really, to his tremendous conditioning as an athlete and also that fierce desire. The best have it, and DD was – is – one of the best.

Anyway, the semi got closer and closer and suddenly there was Dion, joining in the five-a-sides and then the nine-a-sides. And every time he tumbled over, all of us winced and held our breath. And each time, he picked himself up, no problem at all.

The acid test, though, was going to be against less friendly opponents. Our boys were never going to give Dion the kind of bone-jarring challenge he needed to prove to himself, as much as anything, that he was finally back.

He had to get out there amongst the muck and nettles.

On the morning of the Derby game, he was given the final 'all-clear' by the specialist. A short while later, he discovered he was on the bench for that afternoon. With the game safely wrapped up, it was ideal to send him on and watch him win his first header.

Such is Dion's competitive spirit, the spur of getting fit in time for the semi-final must have driven him on. Just how much it meant to him became clear to me when, on the Wednesday before the semi-final, I pulled everyone together for the reading of the team I had selected for Wembley.

'... and up front, we'll have Julian and Beni,' I finished. And I saw in Dion's eyes, just for a few seconds, the unmistakable mark of a penetrating disappointment. He had had no real match practice and, for me, that made the prospect of his starting at Wembley unfair. He had already worked one miracle getting fit so quickly; but that would be asking too much even of him.

It was truly a bonus to have him among the substitutes. He quickly masked his disappointment. 'Well, I never expected to play. I am just lucky to have got this far.' But he had clearly dreamed of starting. Never mind. His moment would come.

The weeks between the quarter-final and semi-final had also enabled me to cast a glance towards next season. Luc Nilis was a player I had admired for some time, from the moment I had watched him play for PSV Eindhoven in a pre-season friendly against Everton at Goodison. As the season unfolded, I got word that he would be available on a Bosman free transfer and was looking to come to England. We started to check on his progress on a regular basis as he established this devastating goal-scoring partnership with a certain Ruud van Nistelrooy.

In all we watched him 10 times and I watched him three times myself. And I liked what I saw more and more. Van Nistelrooy was the player the whole of Europe coveted and with good reason. It was not an exaggeration to compare him to the great Marco van Basten and there was absolutely no doubt that he was a magnificent goalscorer. But the figures being quoted for van Nistelrooy were very heavy indeed.

Luc, though, was free and I could not see how we could turn that business down. Shortly after doing the deal to bring him in, I met Bobby Robson – who had worked with Luc at PSV – at the England v Argentina friendly international and he confirmed my own conclusions. Luc was 32 but his fitness levels were superb and his qualities undoubted. I felt our fans would take to him because, like Beni, he is a delight to the eye. Three games a week might be beyond him, we both agreed, but he had all the right ingredients to make a big impact.

Yes, a combination of Nilis, Dublin, JJ and Carbone for next season was already an exciting prospect.

But would Beni still be here? That was the one nagging distraction in the build-up to our trip to Wembley. Much had been made of our failure to agree a deal with Carbone and his people before the English transfer deadline passed, an impasse caused by the wage demands presented to us. When the figures landed on the chairman's desk, they quickly sobered him up after all the excitement that Beni's hat-trick against Leeds had stirred.

It meant that this mutual trial would continue all the way into the summer. But I was still not too worried by that. When you stripped everything away, his staying at Villa was a perfect solution for everyone. Beni knew there would be an attractive deal for him at the end of the season if he carried on making the kind of progress we had seen since just before Christmas.

Our gamble was that our offer would be his most appealing prospect of employment. Beni could not lose. Neither could I. If he wants this bad enough, I thought, then we would see more fireworks before this campaign is over.

No, I could live with the Carbone Affair. This was the biggest single most obvious test of my nerve and of my aptitude for management so far and I was absolutely determined to keep it under firm control. People were watching and wondering how Villa and John Gregory would cope. I knew that. So although it could have been a distraction, I was anxious it wouldn't be.

In the gap between the Everton and Bolton ties, the emphasis from the coaching staff and myself was always on 'the next game'. The FA Cup still has the power and mystique to take over a club's entire focus. But you can't afford to let that happen. We could not afford to let our Premiership results slip away again. So while I knew this semi-final was there at the back of everyone's minds, it was pushed back as far as it would go.

By now, though, the players were a self-functioning unit. Yes, the boys were great; a pleasure to be with. They had grown tighter through adversity and through the way they had started to turn their season around. Maybe they were getting a little bit of overdue credit, too. I had sensed their dismay when the press reports did not match what they felt was the quality of their performances. Remember that victory at Leeds at the turn of the year? All they read about after that was how David O'Leary's team had had a tough season, how they were such a young side and sure to run into hiccups, how key players were missing. As an afterthought, it seemed, it was mentioned that a team called Aston Villa from somewhere in central England had beaten them 2-1 with both goals scored by a Mr G Southgate.

Well, that's what it felt like and it needled them, I am sure. It needled me, because they had played bloody well that day. But there is a feeling at Villa that we have to do a little more than some to get any acclaim. We might be pretty much the top dogs on our own patch, but alongside the elite in the Premiership, we are not a glamorous club. I don't know why that is. Maybe our players just aren't pretty enough!

But we went into the semi-final with a little bit of credit starting to roll our way and I sensed the boys were a little more at ease with themselves. They were certainly making my job a delight once again. They were running their own dressing-room with minimal interference from me. Any sorting out to be done was cleared up before anyone had to come to the manager.

Poor Neil Cutler, a goalkeeper who had joined us from Chester, had the temerity to come in late one morning. The boys ripped into him.

'Oh I see, big time now is it?' followed by 'Couldn't you manage a shave?'

'But I was stuck in traff...'

'Oh don't give me that'.

I heard them slaughter him. He wouldn't be late again.

Gustavo Bartelt, a striker who joined us from Roma for a trial period, turned up for one match with sunglasses perched on top of his hat.'Oi, get them off – it's not sunny and this isn't a cat-walk.' Same treatment.

On away games, we eat at 6.30 p.m. on the Friday night. At 6.20 p.m., everyone is there. No chasing up. No phone calls to rooms to get them down there. We all sit down together. The boys know what is expected of them. Very few reminders required. Yes, everything was ticking over smoothly now.

And I had long resolved that this semi-final would be treated as a normal Premiership away game. The temptation to make it special, a day trip to Wembley, was obvious. We got word that Bolton, perhaps not surprisingly, were going down that road with new suits and a get-away-from-it-all break beforehand.

But I didn't want our focus disturbed by meetings with Gareth Southgate to sort out suits or track suits, or special motifs on shirts, or players' 'pools', or breaks at a health club or whatever. No. The one concession we would make to the fact that this was Wembley and an FA Cup semi-final was to get away from Brum a night earlier. Get away from the phones. Otherwise, it was business as usual.

I had known pretty much what team I wanted and got it. Dion was the only wild card as I had not expected him to be able to play. But he would be perfect to come on to try to either save the game or win it. But Friday morning came and our last training session before leaving for our hotel, Hanbury Manor in Ware. And Merse nicks a hamstring.

I had the team set up and Paul was its inspiration, a key element in the starting line-up. He felt it tighten and pull a little and stopped instantly. Ah well, nothing we can do about it now. As I say, a problem does not get solved by fretting and cursing. It's happened; deal with it. Wrap him up, get him on the coach – with a masseur providing constant attention – and let's get down there.

I sensed a little bit of tension starting to build but that's good. Leicester and that Worthington Cup semi-final was still there in everyone's mind and had taught us much. Especially about ourselves. Let's keep that fresh. It remains the perfect motivation.

On the Friday night, a fax arrived at the hotel from someone I'd never heard of. One Damian Dugdale. What does he want? 'Dear John, we've never met, but I am throwing myself at your mercy. I am desperate...' I don't believe it. Cheeky bugger wants a ticket! I couldn't help but smile. We'd managed to get away from all the fuss and attention and here he was telling me how it had taken him four hours to track us down, how he lives in Lavender Hill, couldn't get up to Villa Park to queue for a ticket and how he would pay anything, do anything, for two tickets.

One of the best parts of this job is the opportunity it provides to give someone a moment they will treasure for ever. I remember that in the thick of those awful results back before Christmas, I agreed to go to a little local junior school and be interviewed by a group of youngsters to help with a literacy project. They would interview me and then write their stories. We managed to keep the visit a secret and the picture on their faces when I walked in to the classroom will stay with me forever. As will the comment from one little terror who promptly told me, 'My dad says Villa are crap at the moment'. Out of the mouths of the innocent...

Anyway, here was another chance.

I happened to have two spare complimentary tickets. He'd left his telephone number; in fact, he'd left about 32 telephone numbers in the ridiculous hope that I would call him. So I did.

'Hello?'

'Yeah, Damian?' I asked.

'Yes it is. Who is this?'

'It's John Gregory.'

'Who?'

'John Gregory. You faxed me.'

'Yeah, right. Who is this?'

'No, it's me. John Gregory.'

'This is a wind-up. Who is it really? Who's put you up to this?'

'No one. It's John Gregory.'

'Yeah, sure. Come on, who is this really?'

'Look, it's John Gregory here. I've got your fax and you're a very lucky boy. Get yourself to the tunnel entrance at 2 p.m. on Sunday and there'll be two tickets for you. Access All Areas. OK?'

I could hear his spluttering astonishment crackle down the phone line. But, like those kids, I wished I could have seen his face. Saturday morning and a training session at Borehamwood Football Club – thanks lads – and all eyes were on Merse. He looked fine. In fact they all did. More than ever, I was convinced that we were going to win. It was one of those sessions we had to stop because it was so good. Whoooaaa. Easy, tigers, I thought. Big game tomorrow. Let's keep it in the locker until then shall we?

I could still feel that edge, that touch of tension. But it was good. Because the tension was underpinned by confidence. Not arrogance. Everything was pretty relaxed. They were thinking 'Winning, winning, winning'. This lot are going to give everything, I thought. Whatever else they would lack, it would not be effort. They were not going to sell themselves short again. I was sure of that.

Back at the hotel for dinner with my staff, and I noticed they were unusually distracted. I soon saw why. A fellow guest was enjoying a candle-lit dinner with what we took to be his partner. And she was a stunner. They couldn't take their eyes off her.

Later that evening, I bumped into the guy while I was away from our table. 'Hello John,' he said, asking for an autograph before cutting to the chase.

'I hope you don't mind but well... it's just that... well, I'm a Villa fan and I haven't got a ticket and I was wondering...'

Another lucky bugger. I gave him a couple of tickets and returned to my seat.

A few moments later, I was back at our table when I noticed the jaws of all the staff had dropped into their sweets. I felt a tap on my shoulder and a lovely voice said, 'Mr Gregory?'

I stood up and turned around to be confronted by the drop-dead vision from the nearby table.

'Do you mind if I give you a big, big hug?' she says. 'Thank you, thank you so much. You have no idea how much this means to me.'

'That's all right, love. Any time,' I say, cool as I could be. I sat back down and revelled in the faces of the entire Villa coaching staff wondering, 'How on earth did he do that...?' Great fun. Great times.

So here we are. Match day. And one thing that has not changed since my playing days. The match day breakfast ritual. Always fresh strawberries. And truckloads of toast and buckets of tea. Brilliant. Except for the fact that they have forgotten my strawberries and sent a kind of yogurt concoction instead.

Oh no. Can't go any further without my strawberries, thank you very much. But an apologetic staff sort that out and everything seems fine. A morning walk with the boys, half a mile there, half a mile back, just to get some fresh air, and start to get focused. Yes, everything is fine. The banter is good, the mood is still good. I can do no more, I think. They are as ready as they will ever be. Come on clock, start ticking a little faster? I don't know how much longer I can keep a lid on these boys.

It is a half-hour coach journey to Wembley from the hotel and I reasoned that that should be good. Not too long to get bored and stiff and anxious; long enough to feel the occasion gathering momentum. That way, the build-up can take care of itself without any input from me.

Bit by bit, the number of banners and flags and scarves increases and the buzz on the coach picks up. Those who have not done this journey before, such as George Boateng, Benito and young Mark Delaney, are relishing every second. But then even the 'old hands' are getting swept up. Merse, the captain, David James. They have played at Wembley on countless occasions, but these moments still make the spine tingle. And it was special. Because it was *now*.

I asked the steward at the tunnel entrance to tell me when Mr Dugdale arrived to pick up his tickets. Sure enough the arrival of Wembley's luckiest supporter was brought to my attention and at last I got the chance to see the look of wonderment on his face.

'Do you want to come and have a quick 'pic' with some of the lads before we get ready?' I ask him. It's like asking a kid if he wants an ice cream, and Damian struggles to blabber a few 'thank yous'. But I knew what this would mean to him. Through my football connections, I once got the chance to meet one of my heroes, Neil Finn, the chief songwriter and lead singer with the band Crowded House. I could barely speak when actually introduced to him. This was my chance to do a little of the same. I love this job. And I know that this chap and his partner are never going to forget these moments for the rest of their lives. In fact, they are going to be telling folk in a pub years from now about the weekend they were in the Wembley tunnel having their picture taken with the Villa lads and no one is going to believe them. 'If we win, I'll see you back here afterwards,' I tell him. But it was time to go now. The clock had ticked round, as it always does, and the waiting was over.

It was time to get serious. Leicester. Leicester. Leicester. Once again, that achingly-painful failure was the centre of our team talk. Remember those bangs on the dressing-room door? Remember their supporters crowing? Remember how *you* felt because you had not performed?

The dressing-room door shuts an hour, sometimes 90 minutes before kick-off and minds begin to concentrate. In those final moments of preparation before you lose your players to the occasion, instructions are reissued, reminders are dealt out, fresh advice is offered. But I know for most of the boys it goes in one ear and out the other. By then, they are disappearing into their own tunnels of focus. Nothing I or the rest of my staff say now is going to make that much difference. We have done our work. They are slipping from our direct control now. So, stand at the dressing-room doorway and go through that ritual.'Here's the armband, Skip,' I say to Gareth. 'On you go, son. Clean sheet. Clean sheet.' Not for the first time, I am struck by the knowledge that I couldn't be handing on *my* team to a better man, a better pro.When I had first arrived at Wembley that afternoon, my immediate thoughts were how shabby it all was. Just one little thing summed it all up – a hook on the wall with one screw missing meant that it spun round and upside-down when I tried to hang up a bag.

But then they are knocking the place down aren't they? What's the point of lavishing money on it now?

I am struck, always struck, by the enormity of this stadium. Not so much in size, but in status. But those feelings of neglect strike me again when I leave the dressing-room a few moments after the team.

The Bolton fans are gathered at the tunnel end and I did not want to walk around the perimeter and give them an easy target to boo. So I cut across the pitch and discover what a few of my boys had been moaning about earlier.

It's terrible. Like a sponge. When I played here, it was tidy and neat and short and crisp and... well, you knew the ball would just fizz across it. But this pitch was dreadful. It was going to have an impact, no doubt about it. Passes were going to hold up.

Our game plan was simple. We expected, we knew, that Bolton's best period would be in the opening 20 minutes. So, as ever, the reminder had been that 0-0 is a perfectly acceptable half-time score. We are a good second half team. Our fitness can match anyone's. If it has to be that way, then we'll do it that way.

And Bolton fulfilled those expectations by starting superbly. We gave them a couple of early chances which I did not expect and, having taken my regular seat up near the Royal Box behind the pitch-side benches, I can see the pressure gradually engulfing my players. They know they are favourites. They know they are playing a team from a lower division and they are so worried about losing they are forgetting how to win it. Despite all that quiet confidence, all that eagerness I had sensed in the 48 hours beforehand, that apprehension was weighing us down.

Big Ugo was struggling to cope, first with Eidur Gudjohnsen and then Dean Holdsworth; we were not flowing and Bolton's fans were getting excited, giving their team tremendous backing. We lost Ian Taylor early in the game because of injury but I was quite confident about Steve Stone going on – he had been within a whisker of starting anyway. But it was a worrying first 20 minutes. Bolton were a good enough team to get everything right on the day and beat us. It's the hole-in-one scenario. Every so often you get everything right and pull off the perfect shot. The best just do it more regularly.

Sometimes players influence games with dramatic input. Sometimes it is a little less obvious, a little more subtle. And so it was that afternoon with Merson. He began to influence our game, to settle us down, to get us passing. Yes, that's more like it. Come on boys, relax. You can win this. Relax.

And then two chances. Bang, bang. And both missed. By poor Julian. Each time, as he was played clear, 36,000 Villa fans had roared their anticipation. Despite the din, I could hear his mind clicking over. 'Oh my God, I hate these,' he was thinking to himself. Then it was, 'I can't afford to miss this one.' Followed by, 'I've got so much to lose here if I don't score.' And finally: 'Oh shit – I've missed!' Julian was always thinking about what was going to happen when he missed.

But what can you do? You can't freeze frame and put the stunt man on, can you? Julian is the only one who can get those chances because of his pace and he just has to come through it. (Later on, I would see TV pictures of myself pretty much kicking the Wembley wall in anger and frustration at the misses. The truth is I was going to, only I pulled out at the last second because I noticed that I would have been kicking solid concrete. And I didn't want a broken foot.)

At half-time I thought, I've got my 0-0 and I'm happy. Lots of areas where we can tidy up, improve. Although we got some movement in the middle of the half, by half-time it had stopped. Still, I felt we had smothered Bolton and ridden out their storm. I felt we would now control them and could not see them troubling us big time. The question was whether we could step it up.

But we didn't. Truth is, it was a pretty dull affair. They cancelled us out as effectively as we did them. The game was drifting. Time to do something.

Beni had been struggling with a bit of a thigh strain, a kick on the ankle and a large cut above his left knee. He was not flowing. And he had those bloody stupid golden boots on. He suddenly produced them in the dressing-room before kick-off and told me his sponsors insisted he wear them. But I was not too happy about that mainly because of the signals it sent out. But I also felt JJ could still earn himself a chance somewhere with that pace. No, Beni can come off and let's get Dion in there. We need his presence now. They are looking much too comfortable at the back; we need him to upset them a bit. Much was made of what happened next. The truth is that I did not know about Beni's display of bucket-kicking petulance until afterwards. I was too busy on the line giving instructions to Dion.

I think Beni went to walk straight out of the ground. I think he expected to find the dressing-rooms behind the dug-outs. When he realized he was staring at a car park, he turned around and came back and sat down. Good. Because, no matter what, it is important we all stay together. Had he gone off in a sulk, I would have sent someone to bring him back. But the decision did not bother me, despite howls of protests from the fans. Beni was struggling and not having any impact and these are the decisions I get paid to make. Over the course of a month, if you get enough right, you win more than you lose. I knew those jeers would be coming when I made my choice but my skin is as thick as a rhino's now. Someone has to say, 'That's it. That's what we're doing.' And not fret about a few boos. The other option is to concede to the mob and take off one of the team's milder characters. A non-complainer. I've seen it done many times.

But that's the chicken's way out.

And anyway, I was more struck by Dion's last words to me as I waved him on, blissfully unaware of Beni's struggle behind me to turn the removal of his hairband into an act of defiance.

'I'll score the winner for you, Gaff,' he said.

But the goal would not come and extra-time was inevitable long before it actually arrived.

Still, I fancied us more than ever now. Our power and endurance was good. Legs would tire, space would open up. We would finish the stronger, I was sure of that.

But at the same time, I had sensed throughout that we were not getting too much from the referee, David Elleray. I felt Bolton were enjoying what I call the sympathy factor. I do not think it was premeditated in any way; but from what I could see, Elleray appeared to be giving Bolton the benefit of the doubt. Especially when he started the extra period by sending off Mark Delaney for a second booking. Mark had been the player Elleray had penalized for handball in that infamous incident at Sunderland. Now here he was getting the rough end of a decision at Wembley. The lad must be thinking Elleray has got it in for him.

But the curious thing was that, reduced to 10 men, we enjoyed our best spell of the match. Only after enjoying a remarkable escape, though. As anyone who watched the game will know, Holdsworth should have scored after being set up by Gudjohnsen. That was Bolton's big chance. And they blew it. David James did particularly well to stop Gudjohnsen scoring by forcing him wide and, at the same time, by not giving him a contact which could have resulted in a penalty and or David's dismissal.

But Holdsworth had us at his mercy from the pull-back. I don't believe in names being on trophies but when he lifted his shot over the bar, I know quite a few Villa fans who became convinced it would be our year.

These things happen in football. Ask Bayern Munich and Manchester United. We had been taken to the wire but survived. Now it was our turn to win it. The dreaded penalty shoot-out was with us.

We had spent an hour in the week sorting out our order. Stone was always going to start. And I had no worries about Lee Hendrie and Gareth Barry going next. As the end of extra time neared, young Lee was supposed to replace Julian, who we knew would not be up for a spot-kick. But by then George Boateng was injured so Lee had to come on for George, and he had been down for one of our penalties. But Lee would be fine, so would Gareth. I do not know if that lad ever gets nervous. I can't tell. I sometimes look into his eyes wondering what is going on behind them. Does he realize how good he is? And what's ahead of him? And he is probably thinking, I wish the old fool would stop looking at me like that.

After those three, there would be Dion and then Merse. Then little Wrighty. I think I even had James down for seven or eight, ahead of the captain. I hoped this would be one shoot-out Gareth Southgate could watch from the sidelines even though I knew that if I asked him, he would take that long walk forward.

But I felt my trump card in all this was James. And as we waited for the 'fun' to begin, there was time for a last word with him.

When we had sorted out our list at Bodymoor four days earlier, we had used Cutler as the keeper during the trial runs. We dared not risk putting James in goal because he would have saved too many and ruined some of his team-mates' confidence.

It was time to make sure David realized just how imposing a figure he would be for the Bolton players.

'Look at the size of you,' I told him. 'You know when you stand between the posts, we can't see any of the goal from the penalty spot. Honest, Dave. We can't see it. Maybe a little bit of netting in the top corners but that's your lot.'

Bozzy was very good with penalties and we had got ourselves another one in David. They are both big guys – but agile. They fill up that goal and can get to the top corner if needs be. And I was being serious. When you put that ball down on the spot and look up, you can barely see any of the goal if David is between the posts.

Last words issued, last encouragement handed out. There was nothing else for it now. It would take care of itself. Back to my seat in the stands and watch it unfold. It would be down to nerve. A little bit of skill but mainly nerve. If not, then we would never have seen players of the stature of Socrates and Platini and Baggio miss big, big penalties. If the nerve goes, you've had it. So come on boys, keep it together now.

They did. They all did. In fact it all flew by. After all that build-up, all that tension, our release to elation was swift. While Stoney, Lee and the impossibly-cool Barry – with the best penalty of the lot, of course – plonked ours away no problem, David saved Bolton's second and third from Allan Johnston and Michael Johansen. From the moment he saved the first, I thought to myself, that's it. Game over.

At 3-1, our fourth spot-kick would take us to the final. For the briefest, briefest moment, I thought about rushing down to the pitch and getting the captain to step forward to take it. Give him the chance to exorcise 1996 and all that.

But then it was back to reality.

Dion was walking forward. And his words came rushing back. 'I'll score the winner for you,' he had promised. I remembered that flicker of disappointment in his eyes when I read out the team. Now, here was Dion's reward for that long, lonely, gutsy struggle to get fit. He was strolling forward to finish off the job. Well, well, well. He's going to do it. I don't believe this. Good as his word. He's going to get me my winner. And he did.

I never got the chance to see Sam until we were both down the tunnel. The Bolton staff had been busy commiserating with their players while I was still hugging and kissing staff and wives up near the Royal Box. When I did catch up with him, I realized there was very little I could say. As he sucked on his cigarette, all I could do was congratulate him – genuinely – on his team's performance and wish him all the best. But just as at Goodison in the quarter-final, the elation flooded through me only briefly. This time, I sensed, it was the same for the players too. By the time we reconvened in the dressing-room – and Cheeky-Fax Damian had rammed his camera full of the photographs that will in future prove he was not lying – the reaction was what I would have wanted.

OK, we're through. But we haven't done anything yet. The Cup now is as far away as it was when we kicked off against Darlington. What would United be doing now? They wouldn't be throwing their shirts into the crowd, would they? So come on, cup of tea, warm down, another game on Wednesday at Hillsborough. I was already beginning to think about what team I would play there.

But I still felt we deserved our place in the Big One. We were the first Premiership team Bolton had had to face. We had had to get past three Premiership teams to reach this semi-final. Two of them, Leeds at home and Everton at Goodison, represented particularly formidable barriers. We had earned the right to get to the FA Cup final.

I was pretty proud as a player. All my shirts from various opponents are tucked away in a box in the loft. But I am even prouder of my management career. I don't think I can explain why, particularly. It just is that way.

So before we left the dressing-room with the dodgy hook, there was time to make sure I had another souvenir for my wall, another memento to be signed and framed and mused over in the years to come.

'Hey big man,' I shouted to David James, 'your shirt, please.'

CHAPTER 19

'The Pantomime Horse did it in four'

I am a sucker for a challenge. I love setting myself an improbable task, staring it in the face, taking it on... and winning through. I am a firm believer that you can do whatever you want in life *if* you work for it and believe in yourself enough. That's why I had started 1999 accepting Ian Wright's challenge to strap on my guitar and sing live on his Friday night TV show – without, I hope, making too much of a fool of myself. Don't be daft, John. You can't do that. Well, yes I bloody can and I bloody well will. This is my life and no one tells me what I can and cannot do. It was great fun and a good release. Which was all I wanted from it.

And that's why, on the Sunday morning of 16 April 2000, I found myself in the company of 32,000 other souls on the streets of our capital ready to run the London Marathon.

When I look back now, I realize I was, to say the least, a little foolish taking on such an enormous physical and mental challenge with such limited preparation. As a player, I had a good 'engine'. In my twenties, fit as a butcher's dog, I had run the length of Brighton beach and back again – a virtual marathon distance – to raise money for a local school. But what the heck, I thought, I still kept in reasonable shape. A marathon in middle age? No problem.

I love tackling these extra-curricular projects. They carry what I firmly believe is a very positive side-effect – they keep me

241

fresh for my real labour. Routine can lead to staleness and that is the real enemy of the training ground. Keeping my mind alert, having challenging distractions, is essential. But never, absolutely never, at the expense of the day job. And that meant preparing properly for a 26-mile run was out of the question.

It would be too time consuming. It wasn't the two-hour training run that was the problem. It was the half hour beforehand to get the massage and warm-up routines right, not to mention the hour afterwards to get over it. It would take three or four hours out of my day to train properly. That was not possible.

So, as the race neared, I had to be content with the odd run around Sutton Coldfield after dark. Stupid really. I take no chances with the stresses of football management and have my ticker regularly checked. I make sure everything is as it should be. And so far, everything is. But guys younger than me have dropped dead playing squash.

The marathon training manual says that, ideally, you build up to a 15-mile blast and then ease down. I soon reasoned that a 15-miler would provide one of three outcomes. It would either:

A: kill me;

B: kill me;

or C: be fatal.

And why practise dying?

But the London Marathon has consistently enthralled and inspired me. All those folk, from all age groups and all levels of well-being, pushing themselves through absolute hell to raise £250 for this or £400 for that. Amazing. Well, I had a dressing room packed with young millionaires and just a few weeks earlier had watched Michele's mum, Pearl, succumb to the ravages of Alzheimer's disease. If I could do this, I could raise perhaps as much as £10,000 to help the fight against the disease. That had to be worthwhile.

So the challenge was there. And I was soon using the FA Cup final as another source of motivation. 'You want to win the Cup, Johnny Boy?' I was telling myself, 'then you have got to do this.' I ask my players to do the equivalent of two marathons every weekend in terms of the demands I place on them against the quality of opposition they face. I need to stand before them and say: 'There you go. I've done my bit. If I can do that, then you can go out and beat Chelsea'. I could not face the other scenario. 'Well Gaff, not so tough after all then?' or the unthinkable: 'So, tell us Gaff – why exactly did you quit?'

That was simply not an option.

Within half an hour of Dion's conclusive penalty at Wembley, the echoes of a previous FA Cup final were filling my head. As a player, I had experienced this very English annual showpiece with QPR, then from the old Second Division, against Tottenham in 1982.

All I heard as the match neared was how I should make sure I enjoyed the day, soak up the occasion, revel in the unique atmosphere and take everything in. It was *the* day out for the fans, everyone was telling me; and for the staff, for the administrators, the club's caterers and for the business folk. It is a day you will tell the grandchildren about, I was told by pros, ex-pros, uncle Tom Cobbly and all. Well, forgive my bluntness, but I can't think of another word.

It's bollocks.

We lost that final after a replay by which time I had worked out that if I wanted a day out in the future, I would take the kids to the zoo. For me and for the current Villa players, the FA Cup final is another day at the office. Same rules, same challenge. Making sure you stick it to the other guys, because, by God, they want to stick it to you. Our semi-final strip was still strewn across the dressing-room floor and I was already consumed with the idea of winning one more time at Wembley.

At that stage, I did not know who we would be facing. The second semi was to follow a week later. It would be Chelsea or Newcastle but, as far as I was concerned, it did not matter who came through. It would be bloody difficult.

Deep down, I was convinced that Bobby Robson and Shearer would prevail. Remember that opening game of the season? The glance that England's captain had flicked in my direction as he was sent off left me convinced we had unfinished business; that we were destined to meet again in what I was sure would be a huge game. I would spend the intervening week convinced that the script for this year's final had been written at St James' Park nine months earlier. Sadly for my old England manager, Bobby

Robson, I was wrong. It would be Chelsea. Fair enough. Their victory changed little of the scale of the task we would be facing on 20 May.

Well, perhaps Chelsea's progress did carry one niggling worry for me. In my very first Premiership away game as Villa's manager, we had won at Stamford Bridge. But since then, they had moved on and beaten us four times out of five. I was determined that these results wouldn't get the players believing that Chelsea were our bogey team. There could be no place for such thoughts in the final and my antennae were immediately tuned in to seek out and destroy any fresh evidence of negativity in the camp.

But that was seven weeks away. We had an important period to get through and on the Monday after our Bolton game, I held a short team meeting to spell out my objectives. No slacking, no easing off. Seven games meant 21 points and I want them all please, gentlemen, thank you very much. I had the ultimate carrot to dangle in front of them – a Cup final place – and resolved to give as many of them as much chance as possible to be in the side. When we walked out to meet Luca and his all-star team, I did not want any grumbles from players claiming they had not had a chance.

'Well, sir, I trust you won't be going quite so fast this afternoon'. The young policeman's sense of humour was not appreciated. He had just pulled me over for speeding down the M1. Ten to eight on the Sunday morning of the London Marathon with the motorway deserted. But he had nicked me for speeding and telling him I was on my way to the Marathon's starting line cut no ice. Not the best start to the day, then. But in terms of discomfort, there was much, much worse to come.

I had read my Marathon 2000 Handbook and adopted their advice. Every nook and cranny was smothered in Vaseline as I started, nice and steady, aware that the first four or five miles of the course rolled gently downhill; runners had a tendency to push along too quickly and pay the price later.

So, nice and easy does it. First mile completed. There, that wasn't too bad. Only another 25 to go now. But I didn't really know what to expect. I had been too busy running Aston Villa

FC. It occurred to me in those opening strides that the only time I had focused on what now lay before me had been that morning.

Still, lots of banter... and lots of people going past me. In fact, everybody was going past me. I was tootling along, not wanting to be noticed, but everybody was going past me: young girls, old girls, young blokes, and old blokes. Wombles, clowns, Fred Flintstones, Dalmatians, waiters in grass skirts, blokes with plastic breasts. All carrying excess weight.

And all going past me.

Surely there could not be anybody left to pass me? A glance over my shoulder and there are bloody thousands still to come. Mind you, at the seven-mile mark, I distinctly remember passing someone for the first time. 'See you sucker,' I thought in mock celebration. Not for long, though. I had to move out of the way to allow two blind runners, helped by assistants, to breeze by. Followed by a pantomime horse. Pull that cap down and hope no one recognizes you, son.

Plenty of fun, though. At least for those opening few miles. One fella, wearing this season's Villa shirt, joined the throng leaving me behind. 'Up the Villa,' I shouted to him. He looked back briefly and yelled: 'Yeah, cheers mate,' not realizing I was the manager of the subject of his obvious devotion. Wonderful.

But the banter and good humour started to give way to the slog. There comes a point when you begin looking for the mile signs; when you tell yourself if you can just get round that bend, it will be there and you will have chalked another one off. I suddenly found myself looking for the nine-mile marker, and when it arrived, realized I had to do the same again and another eight miles besides. Crushing.

One yard past the 10-mile sign, I was looking for the 11-mile board. But then I forgot what was next. Was it 11, or perhaps it could be 12? And when it was only 11... oh, you have no idea what that did to me. Soul destroying; absolutely soul destroying.

It started to hurt, really hurt. The course heads out towards the Isle of Dogs and plays a particularly cruel trick on the strugglers. On the other side of the road, those who have completed 21 miles are sprinting along in the opposite direction without a care in the world. For a moment, the thought flashes by. Nip under that strip of red and white tape and I've only got five miles to run. But you can't, can you? Maybe? Go on, no one will see you. Shut up. Don't be stupid and get on with it. You got yourself into this; you can get yourself out of it. Come on. It's the Cup final. To win that, you've got to do this.

I looked forward with relish to the halfway mark. When it came, I was half-dead. And I didn't have to be a genius to work out how I would feel at the end. But at 17 miles, the longest, loneliest stretch began. I remembered the handbook advice was to walk through the water stations. I had desperately been trying to avoid dropping to a walk.

'The idea is to finish it, John, not set any records,' I told myself. And I slowed to a walk for the first time. Oh, it felt great. Absolute bliss. And it hurt like crazy to start running again. But after that, any excuse I could find for a walk and I was on to it. But that 17 to 21 mile stage would prove the worse. Marking Souness had been one thing; now the only guy trying desperately to beat me... was me. And I am an even tougher opponent. 'Am I mad or what?' I kept asking myself.

Up ahead, a TV crew. Please stop me and ask for an interview. Anything to take the pain away. Hey, we can have a chat for an hour or two if you like. Never before have I been so happy to have a microphone thrust into my face.

But with three miles left, I had cracked it. That's three or four laps of the training ground, Johnny Boy; come on, you can do that in your sleep.

I even repaired a little of my pride by passing a lot of people over those last few miles. That surge of impending achievement filled me. Up ahead, a shaven-headed geezer came into view. The Cup final returned. 'Come on, that's Luca Vialli and if you want to win the final, you have got to pass him.' I did. I kept giving myself silly little targets like that.

And I got there. Five hours and eight minutes – but I got there. I had completed the London Marathon. I felt elated, relieved, hell I was even still alive.

But it was not long before I was also annoyed with myself. Normally, when I take something on, I like to do it to the best of my ability. But I had broken that rule. I had not prepared for the race. I had not done it as well as I could.

But that's the trouble as the years pass by. You still feel 21 inside. I knew as I plodded over the finishing line, that I could do it much better. Five hours? The bloody pantomime horse did it in four. Michele, Stewart and Bella were there to greet me at the end. And as they helped away their paralyzed husband-father, he already knew he would have to come back and do it all over again. Properly.

And I will.

On Tuesday, 2 May, I signed the contract of a lifetime. Ten years after Jim Gregory had fired me; 10 years after working on the butchers' markets in Windsor and Guildford, handing out chicken legs and sirloins to the old dears and getting £40 a day for it; 10 years after wondering if the Portsmouth debacle had ended my career in football for good; and 27 months after Doug Ellis had taken such a huge gamble on me. And, as every journalist has reminded me in every interview I have done since, just five months after that Coventry fan had offered me the use of his pen for the P45 so many assumed was coming my way the next day.

I know that the rewards for those involved in top-class football these days are obscene. But I didn't start that particular fire. And I had paid my dues. I had worked hard, bloody hard, to get this far and I was not going to apologize for it.

Briefly – and it would be patronizing if I suggested it was longer than briefly – guilt muddied my thoughts. Two nights after shaking hands with the chairman as we put our signatures on the contract, I drove home from the Villa Park press conference mulling over the front and back pages of that night's Birmingham newspaper. They made uneasy bedfellows.

The back page told how John Gregory had become the best-paid manager in Villa's history. The front was dominated by a 'Good Luck' message to the negotiators of the Phoenix bid to buy the stricken Longbridge Rover plant. Villa reaching the FA Cup final for the first time since 1957 was a big story in our region. But the crisis that afflicted Longbridge, and the thousands of families it affected, was even bigger.

But what could I do? Beat myself up over my good fortune and pretend that helped? Would it make me and everyone else feel better? I had been there; getting the sack had scared me. It still terrifies me. More than anything, that's what motivates me. And the fact that this new deal gave me greater security did not change anything.

No one has ever handed me anything on a plate. I have had to work hard for everything I've earned and I suspect that will always be the case. My talents were not that of a Gascoigne or a Platini or a Cruyff. I had to grind away at my game. Work, work, work, to better myself to the point where I shared the same stage as the top players of my generation. I did not have a glitzy, glittering playing career, competing in World Cups and becoming a celebrity at the age of 21 and then walking into one of the top managerial jobs in Europe. I had to prove myself over and over and over again. It has been a long haul and it still hasn't finished.

As I signed that deal I thought about getting the sack, about the summer of 1990 filling in on a radio station and on the market, about the days at Leicester on £15,000 a year, driving up to watch Grimsby reserves play Lincoln reserves on the Tuesday night before travelling to Torquay v Rotherham in an Auto Windscreen Shield first round, first leg after training the following day. It wasn't just the engine of the five-year-old Volvo 343DL that got me through the slog of those miles. It was my determination to prove myself. All over again. It had not come easy.

So no, sorry. I could not apologize for getting this far and for landing a deal which I knew some folk would, naturally enough, resent when their evening paper landed on the doormat that night. I had bloody well earned it.

And I knew that the chairman, Steve Stride and Mark Ansell had made a major commitment of faith in me. For my previous contract improvements, I had had to go knocking on the chairman's door. But the subject of a new deal came up in our first get-together after the semi-final victory and the negotiations were swift, easy and painless. I could have absolutely no complaints about that.

The contract is a good one, loaded with success-related incentives. Fine by me. If, in the final year I win the Champions League, Wimbledon, and the British Open and have a No. 1 album, I could even retire to the Bahamas. But, seriously, the challenge the board have thrown at me is only the one I would have wanted.

It was all a sharp contrast to the final months of 1999 when, who knows, maybe only the absence of a strong rival suitor stopped someone running off with the 'missus'. I knew I had walked precariously close to the edge; I knew she, Villa, had nearly dumped me. And I was determined never to give her that opportunity again. Yes, there was strong sense of personal satisfaction that she was once more so enamoured with me she gave me this contract. But when I awoke the next morning, it was the fear of being ditched which had me springing from my bed. Nothing had changed.

The FA Cup final was now a little over a fortnight away. And more than ever, I wanted to walk into the 'old man's' office on the Monday after the game, slap that famous old trophy on his desk and say: 'There you are, mate. That's for you. How could you ever doubt me? Told you I would prove them all wrong.'

But to do that, we had to beat one of the best teams in the country. And our record against the cream of the English crop was not good. Our season finished with a defeat by Manchester United, a team we have not beaten since 1995. We should have beaten Arsenal at home but didn't. Chelsea had drawn at Villa Park but had the chances to do better.

Only against Leeds had we really enjoyed success, completing the double in the League and also winning that fabulous FA Cup tie. That would be something to concentrate upon as the day neared. My players had to know that they could overcome the best teams in the country. They were good enough. I was convinced of that.

They had responded to my challenge as well as I had the right to expect. After the Bolton game, they reeled off three wins against Sheffield Wednesday, Leeds and Tottenham. That last game, a 4-2 victory at Tottenham on the eve of the Marathon, had been remarkable for the quality of our goals. Three of them, from Dion, Benito and Alan Wright, were all contenders for Goal of the Season.

We had finished the match on a high, with Merse, thrilled by victory from 2-0 down at the home of his old North London rivals, brimming with enthusiasm. 'They couldn't keep up with us at the death, could they?' he was saying in a noisy, buoyant dressing-room afterwards. He had finished the same fixture a year earlier in tears, fearful that he couldn't 'do it' at that level any more, disgusted with the shadow of a player that he had become. The contrast could not have been more vivid, his personal triumph more impressive.

Yes, the boys were on a high and at that point, I would have backed them to go on and complete my mission impossible to win all of our remaining games.

But the final weeks of the season would underline our great weakness, something which the events at White Hart Lane had temporarily obscured. Dion had been out of the side for four months and yet when he returned, he was still our top goalscorer. Goals, or the lack of them, remained our major short-coming and checked our progress over the final three or four weeks of the Premiership season. We drew with Leicester, Sunderland and Wimbledon, but had the play and the chances to have won each game. We had lost fewer matches than Leeds and yet they had finished 11 points and three places ahead of us. Without trying, I could think of a dozen points tossed away in games we should have won. The absence of a clinical, predatory goal-scorer had cost us those points and I knew that we had to fill this yawning gap in our make-up.

But that was in the future. Right now, our FA Cup fate was in the hands of these guys and I could not be more proud of the way they were handling themselves in the build-up. Their attention to duty did not waver, leaving me to concentrate upon our only other problem – injuries.

Suspensions and injuries had interrupted the development of the partnership between Ian Taylor and George Boateng – so crucial to our improvement since the turn of the year – and when Taylor tore a hamstring in the first exchanges of the semi-final against Bolton, I wondered whether we had seen the last of him for the season.

The problem was magnified within a few days when the next cab off the rank, so to speak, was also crocked. Steve Stone damaged a medial knee ligament against Sheffield Wednesday and he, too, was unable to play a full game before the final. In Lee Hendrie and Alan Thompson I had alternatives, but the blend would be different without Taylor or Stone. I wanted one last momentous performance from the 'bulldogs' that could play a big role in toppling Chelsea.

Taylor, though, was having none of it. Miss the final? Me? No chance. We had already benefited from one unexpected comeback with Dion's return. Now Taylor was hell bent on another. I had already seen him do it, back in 1996. He overcame a thigh problem to play in the League Cup final victory at Wembley when he had no right to be fit in time.

We had been happy to agree to play a couple of testimonial matches in late April and May in the knowledge that they might be useful if Dion had any hope of getting fit. His incredible recovery had made that issue redundant. Now a benefit game at Swansea for their old central defender Keith Walker 10 days before the final gave Taylor a priceless chance for a run-out.

He came through well enough and then he played another 30 minutes in the last match against United. Thank God, he would be ready. Stone, too, managed his first, meaningful practice match on the Monday before the final. He might be OK for the bench if nothing else. We will see.

We had Chelsea watched in every match after their defeat of Newcastle but there was little new to be learned. We were only too aware of their qualities, their extravagant depth of talent.

However, there was pressure on Chelsea, too. Despite their promise in so many tournaments, the trophy cupboard was so far bare for the season at Stamford Bridge. Sure, that could breed extra determination among Luca's players; it might also breed the kind of unease, the same pressure of expectation that had made my players stumble against Bolton.

No, I wasn't complaining about our preparations. Our injuries were clearing up. Our form had been solid enough. We were even attracting lots of goodwill from around the country, largely because of the heavy influence of foreign players at Chelsea. Even the great man himself, Fergie, was rooting for us because of his admiration and affection for Dion.

After that final game, Fergie came into my office for a drink and it was clear he had been deeply concerned by Dion's injury and then hugely impressed by his recovery. A broken leg had wrecked Dion's stay at Old Trafford earlier in his career, but that had not prevented Sir Alex forming a warm opinion of the man. He made it clear that nothing would give him greater pleasure than to see Dion walk away from this season with an FA Cup winners' medal.

And who was I to disagree with Fergie?

CHAPTER 20

'Sing up Wisey'

One sentence, one simple, soft, soppy sentence brought home the enormity of it all. Cup final morning, team hotel, everyone up and about, everyone getting a sense of what the next few hours would bring.

My son Stewart called, just to wish me luck, I guess, and in the middle of our conversation, he said it.

'Dad, I'm so proud of you'.

Floods of tears. Try as I might, I couldn't stop them. I was determined to stay focused, stay on the case and not let emotions get the better of me. But those words blew a hole in the dam I had so carefully constructed to keep all the sentiment stored away until such time as it could be safely released.

It hit me now with a force that took me by surprise. It may be that today's kids are growing up with a diminishing sense of the sheer... what's the word?... glory?... of the FA Cup final. But for my generation, the memories will never leave us.

I can still recall flickering images of my first final, 1960, Wolves v Blackburn. I think it was 3-0 to Wolves. Five, six years old, my dad glued to the black-and-white TV, and me nipping in and out of the lounge, watching for a few moments and then out to play again.

By the time the next one came along, Spurs v Leicester, I was hooked. And I saw every one after that. I can name them all, in order, especially through the Sixties. The next year, 1961, was Spurs 2 Leicester 0, then Spurs again, 3-1 against Burnley, then

Man U 3 Leicester 1. Dad was really glued to the set for the next one – his beloved West Ham came from 2-0 down to beat Preston 3-2. Howard Kendall, the youngest FA Cup finalist, was centre forward for Preston. And what was his name? Yeah, that's it, Alex Dawson, big and brawny, and Ronnie Boyce hit the winner, and Hurst, Peters and Moore.

At half-time, dad always got up and made a pot of tea. And at the end, I was straight out onto the street to re-enact the match, with Wolstenhome-style commentary, of course. It's all there. Nothing else came remotely close. The Cup final was *the* event of the year.

And now it was my turn.

I was going to be leading out *my* team for an FA Cup final. All those Saturdays spent transfixed by events at this place they called Wembley, which I knew, just knew, had to be a palace. And now I would be right there, right in the middle of it.

Without realizing, Stewart had bridged the gap, completed the circle. I knew what this would have meant to his grandad and Stewart's words now told me what it meant to him. 'Dad, I'm so proud of you,' he had said. And as I cried my eyes out, I also knew, clearly, for the first time, what it meant to me. Another day at the office? Who was I trying to kid...?

It had been a relief to get away after training on Thursday. For all of us. I asked the captain how he was feeling and he said, 'Fine – but I just want to get away from all this lot.'

We had spent the previous day dealing with all the media requests and were desperate to escape from the microphones and the photographers and the endless faxes from radio stations in the Philippines or the Caribbean wondering if they could just have a minute of your time. This is out of control. Take a memo, Miss Jones. We really do need to get a press department to cope with this in the future.

A couple of days after the semi-final, Paul Barron and Jim Walker had gone hotel hunting and we had struck lucky with the Grims Dyke Hotel in Harrow. Up on the hill, you could walk to the end of the drive and see the twin towers in the distance. Great setting. Just what we needed. Nice and relaxed. Friends and families would be welcome. Pop in, have a cup of tea, have a chat after training.

Yes. Let's keep it nice and relaxed.

The boys already knew the team. I had told them the starting eleven after training on Wednesday. I felt the guys who would shoulder the pressure, the responsibility, should have the chance to settle down, get focused, be relaxed and sleep a little easier. There were 10 other guys from whom I had to select five substitutes. That one had to wait. But I was not looking forward to it.

Ian Taylor had known he was playing before any of them. I watched him anxiously through the final 10 days of the season. Hamstrings are a bloody curse. You are always walking a thin line and I was waiting for him to break down again. But, thank God, he hadn't. And I called him on the Tuesday.

'How are you Son?'

'Fine, Gaff, fine'.

'Ready to play Saturday?'

'Yeah'. I heard the relief in his voice and that's when I knew I had to tell the boys the team early.

And the training in this final week had been bright. Once again, Harry and I found ourselves having to rein them in. Easy fellas – leave something in the locker for Saturday. Bit of a game coming up, you know?

The final sessions, once again at Borehamwood, were fine-tuning. Set pieces, ours' and theirs', how we would set up for corners from left, right, and how we expected Chelsea to line up. We were told to be ready for a switch from Luca. Di Matteo would move to the other side with Poyet swapping to their right, where they would try to utilize his aerial ability against Alan Wright. We knew how adept Poyet was at becoming the third striker but this did not overly concern me. Wrighty could handle that challenge.

And then, finally, the regular 'what if' sessions. That's when we get the players to pose the questions. What if Poyet goes there? What if Zola switches out there? What if Di Matteo drifts in here? Where do I go? Chelsea's strength is their movement. What if, what if, what if?

The key thing is not to get too bamboozled, too distracted. The old Arsenal centre-half, Bill Dodgin, was my manager at Northampton and I have never forgotten one piece of advice he passed on to me.

255

He told of the days when he used to play against, ironically, Chelsea, just at the time when new coaching strategies, particularly for forwards, were becoming fashionable in England. And he would be marking Barry Bridges, who would peel away on these wonderful, arcing 50-yard runs towards the corners intended to create space and drag defenders out of position.

But Bill always reasoned, quite sensibly, that to score a goal, you have to be somewhere around the penalty area, you know, fairly close to those white posts. And he used to watch Bridges take off on these marvellous, energetic decoy runs, admire them, applaud them even... and then wait for him to come back again. 'Well, he couldn't score from out there, could he son?' he would say.

A simplification, I know, but not without a grain of truth. The danger areas were always those in and around the penalty area. Facing a team as adept as Chelsea at movement off the ball, you had to keep your wits about you. And remember Dodgin's First Law: they've got to get near the goal to score.

I couldn't help but have a chuckle on Friday night. Sky TV's coverage of the build-up was certainly thorough – we even had to watch the referee, Graham Poll, having his hair cut and eyebrows combed.

Graham had called me on the Monday before, clearly concerned about a story in one of the Sunday newspapers claiming that, as a youngster, he had always been a keen Chelsea fan. He was at pains to point out that this was not the case and that I should have no worries about his impartiality come the final. Truth was, as I told him, I didn't have any worries on that score. Graham is, as I have already stated, one of the best refs on the circuit. All the same, I watched the Sky feature through to the finish. Just to make sure he was not having a blue rinse and 'CFC' shaved in to the back of his head.

I was right. The worst part of this whole period was telling five of the guys they would not be figuring. Saturday morning, and a stroll around the hotel grounds, just to get everyone together, and I realized I had to put them out of their misery.

I got them together: Steve Watson, Alan Thompson, Najwan Ghrayib, Neil Cutler and Richard Walker. Sorry guys, but there's no easy way to say this...

I knew how I would have felt. Not making the starting eleven is bad enough. But at least on the bench you get stripped, you warm-up, you get a player's 'feel' of the occasion and the chance to go on and make a name for yourself. But these five guys I was now speaking to would not even have to change out of their suits. They would be strangers, outsiders, at a party they had helped to arrange.

I decided to tell them that morning to give them a couple of hours to come to terms with the disappointment. I knew it was a kick in the balls. I knew they would take it badly. One of the guys, I later learned, sobbed his heart out in the privacy of his room.

'Go away now and try to get over your disappointment because we are still in this together,' was the best I could say. 'Come two o'clock, we need you in the dressing-room, geeing the boys up. I can't have any long faces around there.' They did not let me down.

The hours were ticking down now and I knew we could not have asked for much more from our preparation. Whenever I heard the boys rallying one another, talking about what was to come, it was clear they felt the same. When a boxer steps into the ring, he has to know that everything and everyone important to him is there, in his corner. That's how we felt. We couldn't have done any more than this. We had come so far. Been through so much. Even the media were recognizing that this gave us something that, perhaps, might provide an edge. Chelsea had to be the favourites. Common sense told you that. But this desire... this willpower we had shown to come this far, the way we had pulled ourselves up by our boot straps...

And then the day gathers its own impetus. Suddenly, the game that you have been thinking about for six weeks, having tried and failed miserably to shut out, is galloping towards you. Suddenly we're on the bus, and the traffic is starting to thicken and clog up Wembley.

It feels good. It's Cup final day, so that obviously means the sun is shining. And the occasion already feels good. This has not been a happy week for English football's PR around Europe. The crowd trouble at the UEFA Cup final a few days earlier had taken care of that. But as I look out the window on the half-hour drive to the Twin Towers, I see our lot and Chelsea fans mingling quite happily. In the same pubs, walking down the street together. Yes, this is good. This is how it should be.

And then another powerful, emotional 'whoosh'. Villa fans had been allocated the Tunnel End and that meant that when we turned the corner to travel the final few hundred yards to the stadium, we were greeted by a mass of claret and blue. It took us all by surprise. It was magnificent. Inspiring. Tingling. Oh my Lord. This means so much to so many. We can't let them down. We simply can't. And I start to well-up again. God, amongst many other things, this is going to be a difficult day.

The walk.

I suppose it is *the* moment. The single most stirring image from every Cup final there has ever been. As a supporter, you will know how you have felt if you have been fortunate enough to see your team come out of that tunnel and walk into the Cup final arena.

Well, take that feeling, multiply by 120, add a few thousand and you will get an idea of how it is for us. On the inside looking out, so to speak.

I'll try, but I doubt I will be able to find the words to do it justice. I know, though, that whenever I want, I will be able to close my eyes and remember every second, every sound, even the smell of it.

My heart and mind were locked in their own private war. My mind was saying, 'Get a grip of yourself for Christ's sake – there's a game to be won'. But for the minute or so that it took to walk from the tunnel to that red carpet stretched out before the Royal Box, my mind was fighting a losing battle. My heart was winning hands down.

In front of me was Matthew Stride, 10 years old, son of Steve and mascot for the day. I knew where Steve and Matthew's mum, Carolyn, would be sitting. Ruffle Matthew's hair and point out mum and dad, 'Can you see 'em, Matthew? Up there. Look.' And, I knew, just knew, they were sobbing their hearts out, bless 'em. And I realized that Matthew, at his tender age, could not comprehend that the rest of his life would be a struggle to come up with something as good as this.

And those fans. God, those fans.

You have no idea what you looked like from where I was. But you were beautiful. Just beautiful. Such a sea of colour, of claret and blue. I remember, half way out, I was overwhelmed by the desire to break ranks, rush to the perimeters and hug every last one of them. Beautiful. It's the only word I can think of.

But this has to stop. Come on son, stop it. Get a grip for God's sake. You're falling in to that 'day out' rubbish. Come on, game time.

Break the mood with a laugh. Yeah. Let's have a laugh. I see Graham has lined up for the presentations alongside the Chelsea boys. Hmmm, can someone check the back of his hair please?

We're lined up, Chelsea opposite. And I remember thinking what a fantastic country England must be. It has to be for all that lot over there to come here.

The drum roll before the national anthem and I attract the Chelsea captain's attention.

'Sing up Wisey – you're the only bugger who knows the words,' I shout across to him. Wisey has a laugh. Great player. Great lad.

They are all there, though: Zola, Weah, Poyet, Desailly, Deschamps… the whole bloody lot of them. But are they as tight as my lot? As if to partly answer my question, I took my seat up in the Royal Box just before kick-off with Gareth pulling the team together in a huddle he had called for beforehand.

Wham! George Boateng got us rolling. That's what we needed. We had played Manchester United the previous week and Ugo made a tackle that had everyone out of their seats. 'Yeah, get in there Ugo'. Trouble was, it was after 35 minutes. The previous half-hour had been like a testimonial. That was no good to us. That should have happened after a minute.

But after barely a minute of this game, George cleaned out Wisey with a fantastic challenge. Took the ball and knocked the Chelsea captain off his feet in the process. No complaints from Wisey and just what we needed to set the tone. I jumped out of my seat. And suddenly all the jokes about Poll being a Chelsea fan were not so funny.

A free-kick? Are you sure? I wondered if he was telling George,

'You're not allowed to kick Dennis Wise – you might hurt him. He's my captain.' Just joking, Graham.

But it didn't matter. George had set the tone. We were off and running. In rugby, you cannot win unless you win your tackles. It's the same in football. Sure, you have to intimidate your opposition. In rugby, you have to keep getting up... and then get hit again. And it's the same in football. And I knew that if George and Ian Taylor could keep dumping Deschamps and Wise on their backsides they would eventually get fed up with it.

No, I was thrilled with our start. Poyet was getting no joy on our left; Di Matteo was out of the game on the other side. And we were starting to get a few punches in. Little moments which suggested that Chelsea's defence could be breached. No this was good. In fact, so good, that it was 25 minutes before I felt I needed to make my first phone call from the Box down to Harry on the bench. I wanted Merse to play closer to Dion and Beni.

Punch in the number. Please ring first time. It does.

'Welcome to the OnetoOne answering service. The person you are trying to reach is not available at the moment. They may be if you try again later.' Why didn't the voice add ' ...when we've all finished watching the FA Cup final.' I should point out that we are having to drag Harry kicking and screaming into the technological age. He had forgotten to turn the darn thing on.

Poyet and Di Matteo switched back over and in the 10 minutes before half-time, Mark Delaney was sitting back and not going with Poyet into the midfield areas. They were suddenly playing three against two in there and that was giving them too much time on the ball. Poyet was able to turn and come at us and Mark was doing nothing. Adjustment needed. Chelsea do get good movement.

But I was comfortable and relaxed. I felt we had done everything we set out to do in that opening half. In fact, I was more relaxed than I had been in the semi-final. There had been times in that game when I had been on the edge of my seat, angry, annoyed at all the things we were doing wrong and feeling that Bolton could score.

Chelsea, in contrast, were not breaking us down. We had had a good match-up. And Desailly and Frank Lebeouf were probably seeing more of the ball than anyone, which I took as a good sign.

It meant Chelsea were having to go back to their central defenders.

Walking back to the dressing-room, I was content. We had got through the first five or six rounds of sparring, and we had no cuts. No one had hit us in the face yet; no one had chinned us. We had protected ourselves very well. And we had got in a couple of right hooks from corners and free-kicks. Taylor and Dublin had been within a whisker of decisive headers. I felt we were unmarked and Chelsea had a couple of red patches above the eyebrows.

So half-time. The guys are very upbeat. They know they have done well. They don't need me to tell them. A few things to sort out. A couple of 'what ifs' to settle. But we've done well. And now we can step it up. Now a few chinks will start to appear. Now we can look to Merse and Beni to get that little extra space. You will make mistakes. So will they. But now we have to try to win it. You have to play with courage.

And then a final word.

'Forty-five minutes guys. That's the difference between you being FA Cup winners and FA Cup finalists. Forty-five minutes to show you are the best team today. Everything you have worked for. Everything. It has come to this.'

My walk back to my seat took me past our fans. 'In forty-five minutes,' I kept thinking. 'I've got walk back past this lot.' There is an overwhelming sense of responsibility. We carry it all. All their hopes and dreams for that day. Villa had waited so long for this and there would be no easy escape at the finish if it doesn't work out. It's not like our fans were at the other end and I could slink away unnoticed.

And I thought about all the times that I had imagined Gareth picking up the trophy and turning to raise it to the supporters; all the times I had imagined winning goals and even holding the trophy myself.

The next time I see you lot, I muttered to myself, I hope, I pray I have got that Cup to show you...

I waited as long as I could before the press conference. This was going to be difficult, the most difficult question-and-answer session of my career, and I knew I needed to be in control of myself. If I walk in and the first question is, 'Well, John, how do you feel?' there had to be a very good chance I would step down from the podium, walk up and chin the guy.

In fact that was, pretty much, the first question. So I was grateful I had gathered my senses as much as possible. The second question took me by surprise, however.

'Will you be happy when Luc Nilis comes to the club,' someone said.

What? Is she serious?

'You're not from Belgium are you?' I asked.

'Yes, how did you guess?'

Oh, just a hunch. Well, here I am. I've just lost an FA Cup final and my second question is… well, bizarre, surreal. I expected to see John Cleese, Eric Idle and Michael Palin begin a debate about what the Belgians had ever done for us. I laugh about it now but at the time it just piled on the agony.

We just did not have enough. I was so proud of my boys in so many ways: of their effort and their desire and their slog and their spirit. But we just did not have enough.

Chelsea kept the ball better than we did in that second half and we did not do enough in front of their goal. I honestly thought, mid-way through the second half, that it would go to extra-time and then penalties. I was already imagining David James making the saves that would win us the Cup.

George Weah let us off the hook with a missed chance and we were fortunate to escape when offside ruled out a 'goal' from Wisey. But I thought that would be the kick up the backside we needed. Poyet and Di Matteo and Weah were not troubling us. The one guy causing us problems was Zola, easily Chelsea's best player, but I expected us to go on and grind out a result. It was a poor game. Not a lot was happening. I would bring on Julian Joachim because we were playing too much in front of their defenders and his pace might change that… but, yeah, this is penalties, I thought after those two escapes.

And then it happened.

Seventy-two minutes and a dubious foul, in my opinion, called against Ian Taylor gave Chelsea a free-kick from a dangerous position. Still I wasn't over-concerned. We had been dealing with them all season; I felt we could do so one more time.

Zola's delivery was, as you would expect, top quality. And despite all the traffic around him, David got his hands to the ball. He had done that 100 times in the season and will do it 100 times next year. Get his hands to the ball, pat it down, and pick up the rebound.

But not this time.

This time it bounces onto the back of Gareth Southgate. And rebounds... not to Ugo, not to Gareth Barry, or Ian Taylor or George Boateng or Mark Delaney... it rebounds straight to Di Matteo.

And that was it...

You don't panic. You concentrate on the job. You try changes. You try anything. And there were a couple of moments when we might have pulled the game out of the fire. But no. They could not have tried any harder or put more into it. And there comes a time when you simply have to give the opposition credit. Chelsea are a highly accomplished team and we did not do enough to beat them.

The sense of failure at that final whistle was suffocating. The feeling that accompanies victory is 10 times better as a manager. The other side of the coin is that defeat feels 10 times worse.

I didn't know what to do with myself. If the truth be known, I wanted to dash to the dressing-rooms, pick up my bags, hail a cab, get to Heathrow, straight to the check-in desk and grab a flight, anywhere, there and then. Oh shit, I was thinking, there is even worse to come. We've got a banquet tonight to get through and then a civic reception in front of six men, two old dears and a dog and endless people coming up in the meantime trying to cheer me up by saying, 'Never mind, John, you did so well to get there.' And that's bollocks. It would be time to get out the aerosol marked 'Spray On Smile'. There's no avoiding it. If I had known this was ahead of me, I thought, I would rather have got knocked out against bloody Darlington.

But I found myself out on the pitch knowing that the next few hours, days, weeks and months were going to be bloody awful. I was supposed to go up and get a finalist's medal. But I wasn't interested. Sorry. I've no idea where it is, whether one of the lads picked it up or not. If it ever turns up, it will go straight into the loft without my looking at it.

Our fans stayed to applaud the team and that was terrific. But back in the dressing room, it was silent. I certainly could not think of anything to say that would not be a lie. This was going to hurt a great deal. And anyway, no one would have been listening. It would all have been very hollow. I looked around at them. One by one, they had all given me everything. We had been to hell and back together in this season and none of them deserved to be feeling this now.

I don't know whether the civic reception, the homecoming, made me feel better or worse. We were honestly not looking forward to it. Had we got a call on the Sunday morning to say, 'Sorry, everyone, it's been cancelled' there would have been no complaints from anyone in our party.

I had managed to put on a brave face throughout our banquet that evening. I had drunk some champagne on the coach from Wembley and expensive pink champagne that night at our 'celebration' dinner.

But it all tasted very sour indeed.

And then we came home. And they're right when they say that's where the heart is. I don't know how many were there, thousands, bloody thousands. It was an astonishing display of loyalty. No, it was more than loyalty. It was an act of total devotion. But with that uplift came, equally forcefully, a reminder of how I had let them all down. And I went away thinking, 'Right, this is serious now. They deserve that trophy. And I will not rest until I give it to them.' You know?

There's not a lot I can do about it now.

Here I am, five, six days after the final, on a staff trip to Marbella, hoping that a few beers will blur what has happened. I have avoided all TV clips, all the newspapers, all the radio broadcasts. Everything. Cup final? What Cup final? But an hour does not pass without my thinking of the game.

No matter how much beer and how many laughs and how much banter there has been, I wake up in the morning and we have still lost 1-0.

It has been the most astonishing journey of my life and it is far from over. I sense there are more dramas ahead. And I pray that everything I hope and dream I can bring to this job materializes.

264

I am very proud to be the manager of Aston Villa. It doesn't daunt me. I thrive on it. I would much rather be put to the test than be sitting mid-table at a club content to survive. It won't be too long before we are back in the madness, getting ready to do it all over again. And if you can't handle it, then get out. There is no room for self pity.

It has been a little more than two years since this all started. And there was me, running to Steve's car parked outside that Bristol hotel thinking, 'Please don't let this be dull'.

I feel I have lived a lifetime since then. I have been praised and acclaimed and slagged off and slaughtered. I have tasted the sweetest of victories and the most bitter, painful defeats. There have been huge satisfactions and incredible frustrations. But it has been a fantastic opportunity and I have tried to give you just a little sense of it in these pages.

I know Aston Villa took a huge gamble appointing me. And I am convinced they will reap the rewards.

Because I will tell you something, I'm a much better manager than when I started.

But I'm not half as good as I will be.

Aston Villa Statistics

Aston Villa's League standings and cup results for seasons 1997/8, 1998/9 and 1999/2000 under John Gregory

1997/8 season

FA Carling Premiership final standings

	P	W	D	L	F	A	Pts	G/D
7 Aston Villa	38	17	6	15	49	48	57	1

UEFA Cup

Mar 3	Atletico Madrid	Quarter-final 1st leg	A	0-1
Mar 17	Atletico Madrid	Quarter-final 2nd leg	H	2-1

1998/9 season

FA Carling Premiership final standings

	P	W	D	L	F	A	Pts	G/D
6 Aston Villa	38	15	10	13	51	46	55	5

UEFA Cup

Sep 15	Stromsgodset	1st round 1st leg	H	3-2
Sep 29	Stromsgodset	1st round 2nd leg	A	3-0
Oct 20	RC Celta Vigo	2nd round 1st leg	A	1-0
Nov 3	RC Celta Vigo	2nd round 2nd leg	H	1-3

Worthington Cup

Oct 28	Chelsea	3rd round	A	1-4

FA Cup

Jan 2	Hull City	3rd round	H	3-0
Jan 23	Fulham	4th round	H	0-2

John Gregory

1999/2000 season

FA Carling Premiership final standings

		P	W	D	L	F	A	Pts	G/D
6	Aston Villa	38	15	13	10	46	35	58	11

Worthington Cup

Sep 14	Chester City	2nd round 1st leg	A	1-0
Sep 21	Chester City	2nd round 2nd leg	H	5-0
Oct 13	Manchester Utd	3rd round	H	3-0
Dec 1	Southampton	4th round	H	4-0
Jan 11	West Ham Utd	5th round (restaged)	A	3-1 (aet)
Jan 25	Leicester City	Semi-final 1st leg	H	0-0
Feb 2	Leicester City	Semi-final 2nd leg	A	0-1

FA Cup

Dec 11	Darlington	3rd round	H	2-1
Jan 8	Southampton	4th round	H	1-0
Jan 30	Leeds Utd	5th round	H	3-2
Feb 20	Everton	Quarter-final	A	2-1
Apr 2	Bolton W	Semi-final	W	0-0 (aet – Villa won 4-1 on penalties)
May 20	Chelsea	Final	W	0-1

Index

Campbell, Bobby 118, 119
Campbell, Kevin 17
Carbone, Benito 177–8,
   193–4, 198–9, 202, 205,
   210–12
Carlos, Roberto 113
Celta Vigo 89–90
Charles, Gary 51, 52, 76,
   85–6, 124
Charlton Athletic FC 60, 93,
   104, 129, 131
Chelsea FC 34, 38–9, 75, 86,
   97, 102, 113, 117, 118,
   120, 123, 125, 160,
   253–265
Chester City FC 160, 161
Clough, Brian 13, 127, 147
Cole, Andy 55, 60, 75, 102,
   107
Collins, John 63, 214
Collymore, Stan 23, 24, 25,
   26, 30, 31, 34–5, 36–7,
   38, 42–5, 46, 62, 66, 70,
   77–8, 89, 90, 94, 97–8,
   103, 104–5, 107–9, 114,
   120–1, 139, 147–8,
   173–6, 200–2, 205–210
Cottee, Tony 206
Coventry City FC 34, 80,
   81, 87, 88, 99, 117, 124,
   139, 140, 144, 145, 176,
   178, 180, 181
Cox, Arthur 13, 16, 20–2,
   49, 55, 80, 117–8, 169
Cruyff, Johan 84
Crystal, Jonathan 200
Crystal Palace FC 34
Curcic, Sasa 61–2, 124
Cutler, Neil 230

Dalglish, Kenny 72
Darlington FC 185–6
Davies, Robert 200
Delaney, Mark 164, 188, 233
Derby County FC 14, 21–2,
   77, 117, 120, 202–3,
   208, 215, 226, 227
Desailly 113, 259, 260
Di Canio, Paolo 190
Di Matteo 113
Don, Phillip 165
Draper, Mark 51, 52, 94
Duberry, Michael, 212
Dublin, Dion 64, 86–9, 90,
   94, 102, 103, 104, 107,
   108, 119, 123, 139, 144,
   145, 164, 177, 182, 190,
   197, 198–9, 204, 205,
   227
Dugdale, Damian 231
D'Urso, Andy 163, 187

Edwards, Martin 54
Ehiogu, Ugo 36, 37, 62, 69,
   77, 108, 110–111, 119,
   124, 145, 146, 185, 195,
   213
Elleray, David 160, 164–5,
   166
Ellis, Doug 1, 3, 5, 6–8, 19,
   22, 45, 55, 57, 58, 59,
   87, 139, 140–1, 153,
   158, 170–3, 176, 179,
   193, 201
Enckelman, Peter 124, 160
Evans, Allan 28
Evans, Chris 19
Evans, Hayden 47–8
Everton FC 34, 47, 48, 49,

Oakes, Michael 53, 81, 82, 90, 96, 120, 133
O'Leary, David 182–3
Omoyinmi, Emmanuel 192, 194
O'Neill, Martin 205, 206, 208–9
Owen, Michael, 24–5, 98

Paisley, Bob 13
Paladini, Gianni 112
Panathanikos 148, 150
Paul, Jim 28, 38, 39, 147–8
Peters, Martin 11
Poll, Graham 25, 166, 256
Portsmouth FC 14, 16–19, 20, 28, 39, 117, 119, 122, 146
Preston North End FC 28, 29, 62
PSV Eindhoven 227

QPR FC 13, 14, 21, 118
Quinn, Niall 164

Redknapp, Harry 47, 189, 190, 193, 194
Reid, Peter 164
Rennie, Uriah 155, 156
Revivo 90
Richards, John 141
Richardson, Bryan 88, 140
Roa, Carlos 134
Robson, Bobby 13, 157, 184
Robson, Bryan 67, 68, 182

Sacchi, Arrigo 112
Samuel, Lloyd 93

Saunders, Dean 58
Saunders, Ron 10, 122
Schmeichel, Peter 134
Scimeca, Riccardo 40, 51, 52, 64, 66, 104, 138
Scholes, Paul 102
Scunthorpe FC 11
Shearer, Alan 54, 72–3, 74, 88, 108, 111, 154, 155
Sheffield United 226
Sheffield Wednesday 36, 63, 177, 193, 194, 197, 198, 201
Sibley, Frank 118
Sibon, Gerald 198
Smith, Dr Barry 198
Smith Gordon 57, 58, 149
Smith, Walter 63, 225
Solskjaer, Ole Gunnar 58
Sorensen, Thomas 133–4
Southgate, Gareth 23, 30, 66, 67, 68, 77, 84–90, 91, 95, 106, 123, 145, 150, 151, 154–5, 161, 162–3, 182, 191–2
Southampton FC 34, 60, 93–5, 117, 122, 123, 129, 167, 183, 206
Spencer, John 63
Springsteen, Bruce 149–50, 151
Srnicek, Pavel 197
Standing, Michael 92
Staunton, Stan 23, 30, 35, 40–1, 47, 51, 53, 62, 63, 69, 70, 83, 124, 132–3, 135, 157
Staunton, Steve 164
Stephens, Tony 53–60